GOD, TH & JAMES BROWN

Memoirs of a Funky Diva

(Revised Second Edition)

By

Marva Whitney

with

Charles Waring

(PIZZICATO PRESS)

This book has not been created to be specific to any individual's or organizations' situation or needs. Every effort has been made to make this book as accurate as possible. This book should serve only as a general guide and not as the ultimate source of subject information. This book contains information that might be dated and is intended only to educate and entertain. The author shall have no liability or responsibility to any person or entity regarding any loss or damage incurred, or alleged to have incurred, directly or indirectly, by the information contained in this book.

CONTENTS

CO-AUTHOR'S NOTE

A Brief History of God, The Devil & James Brown

I had been an avid fan of Marva Whitney's music since the late 1980s when some of her old James Brown-produced singles dating from two decades earlier were revived by the UK's Rare Groove scene. Part of her allure for me was that she was a woman of mystery. No one seemed to know much about her except that she came from Kansas City, possessed a voice that could shatter glass and recorded two albums and a clutch of funkafied singles under the aegis of James Brown for King Records in the late '60s. Then, in the 1970s, she seemed to disappear without trace.

Some of her fans even speculated that she might have died but those rumours were dispelled when, in 2005, after 35 long years in the wilderness, she was miraculously back on the radar of soul and funk aficionados. That was due to an enterprising German promoter called DJ Pari, who ran an organisation called Soulpower, and brought her to Europe for a series of successful comeback concerts.

It was at that point that I had an opportunity to interview her for *Blues & Soul* magazine. What was originally supposed to be a 30-minute phone interview – for an investigative piece called *Whatever Happened To Marva Whitney?* – evolved into a fascinating, two-hour-long conversation where I was able to fill in many of the missing pieces to her life story.

We got on so well and had such a good rapport that at the end of the interview, Marva surprised me by asking if I would be interested in helping her to write her autobiography. I tentatively said yes but didn't think it would come to anything. We exchanged email addresses and not long afterwards, Marva again expressed her desire for me to collaborate on her life story. Now sure that she was serious, I happily agreed and we commenced work, though I had to try and squeeze the project into a life divided between a local government day job and freelance magazine work.

To begin with, she emailed me some written reminiscences but for the most part, the bulk of what eventually became *God, The Devil & James Brown* derived from myriad phone conversations that took place between 2005 and 2011.

From the outset, I believed that it was important for the book to have a singular narrative voice. I didn't want it to project the kind of bland, rather anonymous persona that inhabits most autobiographies of famous musicians. Often, you find that the ghost writer or editor has ironed out some of the things that define a person's character, like the natural rhythms of their speaking voice and its grammatical quirks. After reading Ray Charles's 1979 autobiography, *Brother Ray*, ghosted by renowned R&B historian, David Ritz, I believed I'd found a stylistic template for Marva. In that book, it sounded like you were overhearing Ray Charles talking and that's what I desired for Marva: I wanted her memoir to have a frank conversational tone so that when you read the text, it was like you were listening to her speak – complete with her unique colloquial inflections and strong Midwest American accent.

Also – and this was an important aspect for me – we wanted *God, The Devil & James Brown* to include a lot of detail about the music itself. So many biographies I had read of soul music artists (particularly female ones) seemed to relegate any discussion of the music that made them famous to a cursory afterthought. As a longtime fan of Marva's, I wanted to hear the stories behind the songs and learn what went on in recording sessions, especially when James Brown was at the helm.

Writing a book is one thing but selling it is another and I discovered after approaching a couple of UK publishers that despite Marva's (albeit short) association with James Brown – and the explosive nature of some aspects of her story – they didn't think the book was a viable proposition in terms of its sales potential. They thought its audience would be too small to justify any financial investment. But then Dave Randle came to the rescue with his small company, Bank House Media. Dave was enthusiastic about the book, wanted to publish it, and we agreed to place the manuscript with him. Sadly, for a host of reasons, it took a while to get it to the marketplace, and when it eventually appeared in May 2013, Marva had passed away.

The book received a few favourable reviews but Bank House's lack of clout in the marketplace and almost non-existent promotion meant that ultimately, *God, The Devil & James Brown* didn't get the attention I thought it deserved. The fact that it was never available electronically in Kindle form also contributed to its obscurity and hastened its early demise. To make matters worse, Bank House went out of business in 2014.

In my mind, I had laid the book to rest but then in 2019, an email from a staff writer at CNN planted the seed for this revised edition. He told me that he was doing some research on James Brown and was trying to locate a copy of Marva's book. He had seen one for sale on Amazon in the US but it was priced at an exorbitant $600. Intrigued by this, I looked at Amazon's UK site and found one available second-hand at an even more ridiculous sum: £3,000.

To circumvent unscrupulous booksellers ripping people off, I decided to resurrect *God, The Devil & James Brown* and this time make it available electronically. But it needed some tweaking and editorial pruning. In fact, there were several aspects of it that I wasn't happy with; in particular the lack of consistency in relation to Marva's narrative voice. I also hated the gaudy, cheap-looking front cover design of the original. And there were careless factual and spelling errors that needed correction and I also believed that the book would also benefit greatly from having an index. With six years having elapsed since I last leafed through the manuscript, I could now be more objective about it.

And so you hold in your hand, then, the second edition of *God, The Devil & James Brown*. In essence it's the same book that came out in 2013 though augmented by a few, mostly cosmetic, alterations, which to my mind improve it as a reading experience. It's still Marva Whitney's story and her authentic voice, with its Kansas City cadences, comes through loud and clear.

Charles Waring

January, 2020

FOREWORD

by DJ Pari

Soulsister Number One:

Marvelous Marva, The First Lady of Funk

In the spring of 2019, I got a call from a reporter from CNN, asking to speak to me about Marva Whitney for the network's ongoing investigation into James Brown's sudden death more than 12 years ago. Soul Brother Number One and most of his notable alumni, including Marva, are long gone, but their stories still inspire public fascination. And so does their music. The 2014 biopic *Get On Up*, starring Chadwick Boseman, marked the first time Hollywood produced the James Brown story for the big screen, including his now legendary June 1968 trip to Vietnam to entertain U.S. troops, with Marva at his side. In June 2017, the Ford Motor Company licensed Marva's last hit song 'I Am What I Am' for a TV spot promoting the new Ford Explorer. Never before had her music reached such a wide audience. Marva would have been filled with joy, and she would have been so proud.

Born Marva Ann Manning, Marva Whitney almost had as many names as her mentor, James Brown. Her collaboration with the Godfather of Soul was brief, but she has helped define the Funk and left us with a legacy that few female singers of this genre can claim.

I first met Marva in September 2004. My friend Martha High, James Brown's veteran background singer, suggested I book some solo dates for Soul Sister Number One in Germany. Marva had not toured since the 1990s, when she joined Martha, Lyn Collins and Vicki Anderson in the Bobby Byrd Show. I was sad – embarrassed even – that a legendary artist like Marva Whitney struggled to find work and make a living. I made it my mission to revive her career and put her back in the spotlight, where she belonged.

In the following years, Marva and I became close friends, family even. I was like a son to her. We did almost one hundred shows together, from Germany to France, England, Holland, Scandinavia, the United States and even as far away as Japan and Australia. After about a year or so, she started introducing me to others as her manager. There was no contract, no signed agreement, just the mutual understanding that we were in this together, as partners.

At the very beginning of our collaboration, I encouraged her to write a book about her life in the music business. Most knew about her two-year tenure with James Brown, but there was so much more to Marva Whitney, so many more stories that needed to be told. And trust me, Marva was a hell of a story teller. There were too many legends that did not leave behind their story, leaving it to biographers to put the pieces together. I didn't want her to be one of them.

When she teamed up with Charles Waring, a good friend, fan and skilled music writer, I knew that this project would be in good hands. We were on the road somewhere in France when she gave me a first draft to read. It was good, really good. I did not put it down until I had finished it, reading it the entire way from Paris to Marseille. It was one of those books that just draws you in.

I admit that I had concerns with the title – *God, The Devil and James Brown*. But Marva brushed off my worries. She was a woman who always told things how she saw them. James Brown may have been the personified devil to Marva, but she never failed to acknowledge his genius. And she never stopped loving him.

This book has been long in the making, and a lot has happened since Marva and Charles first started talking. As the writing progressed, she was still making history, recording an album with

Japan's mighty Osaka Monaurail, a record that would be her first in almost 40 years – and her last.

But in 2009, Marva had a brush with death when she collapsed on stage at Falls Festival in Lorne, Australia. She pulled through, but the stroke essentially ended her career because she never fully recovered.

My final encounter with Marva was on New Year's Day 2011 in New York City. She had done a show in Brooklyn the night before, which was her last. She sang beautifully, but she had to sit down during the entire show.

On December 23, 2012, Marva's brother called me and told me that she had passed away the previous night – three days shy of the sixth anniversary of her mentor's death.

Unfortunately, Marva didn't live to see the release of this book. She was very proud of it and she wanted to do a book tour. It wasn't meant to be. But she left us her music – and her story, in her own words.

DJ Pari

Richmond, Va.

November, 2019.

FLASHBACK

James Brown is holding a gun against my head. I think I'm about to die. I can feel the cold metal pressing against the side of my skull. I'm terrified. It's 1969. We're in James's suite at the Beverly Comstock Hotel in Beverly Hills, Los Angeles.

A few minutes earlier, downstairs, I'd told him I had decided to leave his show and stay with some friends in LA. James didn't want that. He turned on his charm and persuaded me not to go. He said he was going to change and I believed him. So I went with him and Charles Bobbitt, his manager, into the hotel elevator to go up to his room. As I walked into the elevator a sharp, violent kick to my backside pushed me to the floor. I lay there while James kicked me, over and over. Charles Bobbitt stepped over me but did nothing to help.

A few minutes later I'm being bundled into James's room. 'So you were goin' to leave me, Whit?' he grunts. 'I tell you what you gonna do. You're gonna shit and fall back in it. Shit and fall back in it!' He almost spat the words out as he pulled a gun on me.

So now I'm praying. *Help me, Lord,* I'm saying to myself, *help me, Lord,* and wondering how I got into this mess in the first place.

CHAPTER 1

Armourdale, Kansas

May is usually a time when most people start knowing for sure that they can start their gardens and plant greens and peas. But on the day I arrived in the world – 1 May 1944 – I was told it rained, sleeted and snowed. Thankfully my parents didn't see that as a bad omen.

I was born Marva Ann Manning at Douglas Hospital in Kansas City, Kansas. It was the only black hospital in Wyandotte County, located on Quindaro Boulevard. I was delivered there by Dr Charles W. Alexander, as were all my younger brothers.

My father was Ray Manning – who was away in the navy when I was born – and my mother is Willie Mae Manning. I'm told she was a tough girl who got into fights at school and could hold her own with the boys. I'm the oldest and the only girl. I had six brothers under me – that's a chore in itself. After having me, my mother had boy triplets: Ray, Raymond and Rayford. Then, two and a half years after that, she had twins: Melvin and Marvin. Then, much later – nine years in fact – she had Winfred, the baby boy. All of us are alive and well, except for one – Rayford passed, I think in 1991 or '92. But God has really blessed us. My mother is the rock that keeps the family together, and I'm the second rock.

My mom's sister, Aunt Thelma, named me Marva after the wife of the heavyweight champion boxer Joe Louis. In those days his wife Marva was considered a beautiful woman, and she was like a Cinderella for Joe as far as we was concerned. When I was growing up there wasn't many girls named Marva, and people often commented on how unusual it was. Family and friends usually put my first two names together and call me Marvan.

My mother and father first met in the early 1940s. This is how Mama remembers it:

I met your dad, Ray Manning, on a winter's day. Me and my girlfriend, a Mexican girl, was together shoveling snow. It has been so many years I can't think of her name. So he winked and smiled at us. My girlfriend kept saying, 'Girl, he's cute, let him come over and shovel this snow.' We were just giggling and smiling. Then he came to help me. I think if he'd not come to me my girlfriend would have taken over. She liked black men. She was always with black people. We were good friends. In fact, she stayed down the street from us.

Your father hadn't been in Kansas City too long, I guess about five or six months. He came from a big family. His brothers sent for him to live with them to get a job. He came from some little town in Oklahoma. That's the way most of the Southern people got out of the South and came to the cities: they sent for one another. Anyway, we got married before the year was up. I can't think of the year, maybe 1943. I was young. Your father came to my parents and asked for me. He said he loved me and wanted to marry me. My dad laughed at him and said, 'You don't know what you're doing.' But my mother said, 'OK, I'll sign,' and she signed and agreed for us to get married. We had a wedding at our home church.

Although Grandfather Collins laughed at my father for wanting to marry his daughter, after my parents were married they stayed in my grandparents' house. But one night my father took my mother to the movies and Grandpa Collins found out about it. They came home, I guess about ten or eleven o'clock, and Grandpa was waiting with his strap out. He was going to whip my mother because she went to a movie and that was a sin. And he didn't want to recognize my father. Mama says Dad said, 'This is my wife now and you don't put a hand on her.' And that's how my mother and father got out of the Collins's house and bought themselves a four-room house, with an outside toilet and a barn. That happened when I was about two years old.

I grew up in a small place called Armourdale, Kansas, which was a part of Kansas City, Kansas, but on the outskirts in Wyandotte County. The town was off the main road and was a place where a lot of Indians lived. Mama and Daddy had gotten all new furniture and a car.

We lived at no. 636 on South Sixth Street in a mixed neighborhood. We had four rooms. Mama was very neat. I still remember the phone number: Finlay 2271. My daddy worked for the Santa Fe railroad until he retired, and that was considered a good job. We wasn't what you'd call dirt poor, because I didn't know what poor was, but I did know that we wasn't as badly off as some in Armourdale. And Mama always gave me the best. Whereas some children had one dress for Easter I had two: a dress for Sunday morning and a dress for Sunday night. She'd either buy them or have them made for me.

Our house was close to the Kaw River, which was about four blocks away. We associated with Mexicans and Jews, and some black people worked for them. We got along, and there was very little trouble. The only thing I heard as a kid was about a man who spent ten to fifteen years in prison for murdering a black man and two Mexicans with a knife, though he said he was defending himself. But trouble was rare. In those days you could sleep on the porch and you didn't have to lock your doors; and as children we could stay out on the street and didn't nobody bother us. And you didn't worry about your child in those days. I often played with Mexicans. They always went fishing in the river. I sometimes visited other places in Kansas City too, like the zoo and the shops uptown, where there was a big Milgram grocery store on the main thoroughfare.

They said I walked early. And Mama said that when I could barely walk I went to church and took the tambourine and started to shake my head, jumping up and down and dancing, turning around in circles. People said, 'Oooh, look at her, look at her!' They said I did my first little solo at three years old. People ask me, where did you get your music from? It's always been important to me. I imagine I started singing in my mother's womb, because she was the main piano player for the church – and so when I was born all I'd do was go to church. Mama was known as the best piano player down there. When they wanted to dance and shout she had to get on that piano;

and she'd be so tired when she came home. She had a job getting away from the church, 'cause they'd tell her to stay there, stay there, stay there: the spirit was in her fingers.

My spiritual roots are grounded in the Church of God in Christ in Armourdale, Sixth & Osage. We were the kind of church that many people called fanatics, like the Jehovah's Witnesses. I remember the church elder, C.J. Jackson, and his wife, who was known as Big Ethel. She was really the pastor. My grandfather was assistant pastor at this time. When we met we always had a big crowd of singing and dancing with drums, horns, spoons and piano. We made a big noise and had a big crowd outside, consisting of Baptists, Methodists and just passers-by as well – who might have thought we were strange but enjoyed and understood the music we made. You couldn't be at a better place for music, and that included nightclubs. As soon as the church service was about to end the crowd outside would disperse. They made fun of us but they liked that music. Our church was something else. Sunday night was a great night.

CHAPTER 2

The Neighborhood

In our neighborhood it was like a village: the people shared with one another because most of us was related in some kind of way. On our street everybody knew everybody. You couldn't get in trouble in them days because hell, if you did something wrong they'd get you when you came round the corner. And when you got home your mama would whip you too.

During that time there were two local stores we went to in Armourdale. Miss Gracie's was on one side of the street and across the street was Mr Craine's. Now Mr Craine was a nice man and we went there for some things, but usually I went to Miss Gracie's because Mama had an account there.

Miss Gracie's was less than half a block from our house. Next door to Gracie's store on the left lived a lady I liked when I was little, before I went to school – aged about four or five. Every time I went to the store at this age I dressed up as a young woman with high heels and a long dress and a hat. Yeah, playing house was more than just playing house in the yard. I always got a pair of high heels when me and Grandmother went to the Goodwill store, a place where second-hand clothes and things were sold. Anyway, my grandmother used to sit on the porch and watch me go over to the grocery store. Whenever I arrived this lady used to come out. She wasn't old; I guess she was in her twenties or thirties. I can't recall her name but she's worth remembering because she was so kind. They told me she never had any kids. When she saw me she always kissed me on the jaw and bit my face, then gave me a nickel. After a while she kissed me and bit me harder on the face, which hurt, so it got to the point where I wasn't glad to see her and told Mama about it.

The people on the right of Gracie's store were the Nances. They were high-class people. I remember they had a son called Butch, with curly hair, and a daughter, Sheila. They were kin to my father's sister-in-law, Aunt Sarah, who lived across the street from us with Uncle Tot. As I said, you couldn't get too far without someone being kin to you in some kind of way.

There was a lady who I thought was so beautiful. Her name is Edwina White: she's still alive and in her eighties; but all her family's dead now. I waited for her to pass our house every day during the week. I always looked at her and thought how beautiful she was. She always spoke and smiled. I found out later she was a waitress in downtown Kansas City, Missouri.

My grandmother and grandfather were on Fifth Street behind us; their house and ours were back to back. As I've said, my grandfather, Nathaniel Collins, was a minister: he played piano and guitar. My grandmother Annie Lee Collins played too: she was a missionary for the Church of God in Christ.

In those days my grandmother was considered well off. My grandparents always kept a good house: it was big for that time: four bedrooms, a front room, a dining room, a kitchen and an L-shaped porch. She didn't have an inside toilet or inside bathtub. In them days there were outside toilets, a one- or two-seater. If you wanted a bath they boiled hot water, and there was a little room in the back where you could take your bath. You got in what we called the number two tub, which was the big tub. Mother bathed us, dried us off one by one and changed the water for each of us – the triplets, the twins and me. Hardly anyone had proper bathtubs unless they were just adding on to their property, like Grandmother did later when she came into some money.

We had a phone in my grandmother's house. I remember you turned a handle and asked the operator to call a number for you. There were party lines: if someone was on the line too long you had to ask them to get off it. Some folks listened to others gossiping. Sometimes people got mad, and they'd pick up the receiver and shout, 'How long you gonna talk? I got to use the phone!' I picked it up sometimes either because I was calling or just because I wanted to see who was on the phone and listen.

One thing my grandmother had that I particularly loved was one of those roller pianos, a pianola. She always had it play one song, 'Glory Hallelujah' – and that's the only song I ever heard her play. It was in the black keys. As it was a roller piano I'd get up there and have fun pumping those two pedals. I just loved that, sitting on the middle of that piano and pump, pump, pump, pump. I pushed them pedals and watched them dots on that roller thing and them keys playing them songs.

My grandmother married my grandfather against the will of her people: her sisters and her mother were dead set against my grandfather because he wasn't of the class they wanted her to be in. She came from really highbred stock; her brother was one of the first black doctors. They were devout Jehovah's Witnesses. The family had migrated up to Kansas.

I don't think my grandmother finished school but she had another kind of intelligence you can't learn: she had the power to see through muddy waters; she could tell you what was going to happen before it happened. She was, I suppose, what you'd call a clairvoyant. She could see and tell you things about the future. I remember one time this woman had a big growth on her throat: I guess it was a goiter, and she couldn't move it. Grandmother had prayer service at her home every day at noon, and she had a group of three or four ladies who came and prayed with her. They were praying to help this woman with the growth who was there with them. I'd be listening and they'd say, 'Satan, the Lord rebuke you! Come out of her, come out of her, come out of her!' And one day I saw it with my own eyes, that lump actually coming out through this woman's mouth. It didn't just happen instantly: it came out because they'd been fasting and praying for days on end. I remember they kept praying and praying and praying, and this thing came out of her mouth. See, my grandmother and her friends believed in the laying on of hands – and after they got that lump out they went a-praising God. You probably think they was a bunch of witches, but what they were doing was like faith healing.

My grandmother and I was very close. I was the only grandchild for a long while, until Mama had the triplets and twins. Basically every chance I got I'd be with my grandmother. She stopped me from getting every whipping but one, when I got punished for disobeying her. My family had always taught me not to talk with strangers, but one day I got sidetracked. As I said, a lot of times when I went to the grocery store my grandmother watched me go over there. She waited on the porch to make sure I came out, and watched me as I walked home with the groceries. This particular day my grandmother said – for she was a natural-born psychic – 'Don't you stop for nothing. Don't talk to no strangers.' Although she was watching me as usual she still warned me. I remember walking to the store with the tumbleweeds blowing around me; it was kind of windy that day. In fact the tumbleweeds almost knocked me down but I didn't mind. The store was half a block from the house, maybe even less. This particular day, as I came back with my garb on, a car full of Mexicans pulled alongside, and kept talking as I walked. 'Come over here. See, we have these beautiful balloons for you.' I ignored them at first, but those pretty balloons made me go to the car. They handed me a balloon and I took it.

My grandmother was looking at me, but I wasn't aware of her until I heard her hollering at me, 'Marvan, Marvan, you come here, you come here!' I quickly moved away from the car and started walking fast towards the porch. She fussed at me, and then she told Mama. That's the only time Grandmother didn't shield me from a whipping – and I realize now that it was because I didn't obey her. I knew I was going to get it, but she wasn't going to be the one giving it to me. She was going to get my mother, who was a sterner hand: she used switches wrapped together or a leather strap.

They both said, 'Get ready: you're getting a whipping.' In all my other whippings Grandmother put her skirt in the way to shield me from the licks: to think of it, she seemed a bit like a matador at a bullfight. I loved my grandma, but this time she was mad at me like I'd never seen before. I knew I was going to get it.

I went into the next room, thinking, *What am I to do?* Then I got this idea. I decided to put on lots of clothes under my dress so that I wouldn't feel the pain as much. I went and found every skirt and every towel – anything I could find that was going to stop me from feeling that paddling. I was really padded up, but they didn't seem to notice. When Mama hit me on my bottom with the belt I hollered, like those licks were getting me, but really I felt nothing 'cause I was so loaded up with clothes. My mom never suspected. I later figured out why they were so mad at me: the 'balloon' that damn carload of men gave me was a condom.

Another time I got in trouble was when I was a bit older. When I started going to school my mother often said, 'Here's a note. Tell Miss Gracie I want a loaf of bread and some milk and put it on the bill.' The school was almost across the street from Miss Gracie's: I just had to go by Miss Gracie's and walk three or four steps to be at my school. When I got in school I usually came home for lunch, so on my way back to school I often stopped at the store and got myself a peppermint stick and my teacher, Miss Jones, an apple. I'd tell them at the store to put it on the bill, just like Mama had taught me.

You know in them times you could get two Baby Ruths for a nickel or a dime. They're still around today: chocolate bars with nuts in. I was crazy about them. You could always get a big pickle for a nickel as well. And doughnuts were two for a nickel. They were good, but I liked that peppermint stick and I'd suck on it, and I'd sit that apple on Miss Jones's desk. But one day Mama found out what I'd been doing. When she went in the store to pick up her bill she had a shock. 'Miss Gracie, what my bill doing like this? This is too high,' she said. When my mother found out I'd been getting apples and goodies she scowled, but I didn't get a whipping. But I knew if I did it again there would be trouble.

CHAPTER 3

My First School

I couldn't go to school until I was between five and six because there was no kindergarten. You started school in the first grade, and if your birthday wasn't in a certain month you had to wait until you were almost six.

My first grade school was Phillips Elementary School. My mom and her sisters and brothers attended that school also. I liked it so much. My favorite teacher, whom I dearly loved, was called Miss Jones. I'd watched her when I was playing on the sidewalk before I started going to school: she used to pass my grandmother's house on the other side of the street. She always smiled and spoke to me. She usually came up to me and said, 'Hi little girl,' and I'd say, 'Miss, I'm going to school next year.' I really liked her. When I found out she had the first grade room, wow, I could hardly wait for school to start. It was like waiting for a dream to come true.

When I got in first grade I was happy to be there. I really enjoyed going. Every now and then, maybe once a month, there was a movie for the whole school. It cost 10 cents and a bag of popcorn was a nickel.

As I said, I used to walk home every day for lunch but at one time the short journey started to become a problem because this boy called Johnny Shepard a grade ahead of me was always picking on me. I was scared, and mad at him too. His sisters, Delores and Mattiebell, were my babysitters. Mama and the whole family was friends with them. I remember they used to do my hair. In those days we didn't have a hairdryer, so after Delores had washed my hair and towel-dried it as much as possible she'd turn on the oven, I'd put my head close to the heat and my hair would dry. Before school let out in first grade Johnny had stopped picking on me 'cause my mama and his sisters got on him. A few days ago while looking at our local black newspaper, *The Call*, I saw his obituary. I didn't learn until we got grown that he'd had a crush on me.

Miss Jones was a very light-skinned lady. In them days you couldn't be married and be a schoolteacher. I guess she took the bus every day to Armourdale, carrying her satchel with her. She was short and kind of wobbled when she walked because she was a little chubby. But she was a pretty woman and very nice. She truly was a good teacher because she encouraged me and made me work harder; and it was Miss Jones who instilled in me how to read and write. At first I found it hard, and although she tried to help I just couldn't get the hang of it. She thought I wasn't doing my best in reading and she told me I had to improve or I was headed for a bad grade. This is why I started bringing her apples every day, because I so wanted to please her.

I was nervous about my grade card. When I finally got it and found it said U in reading I cried and cried and cried. A U was the lowest grade you could get, a total bum-out. That's why I was so hurt. A U+ was a little higher than a U, but S was the best: it stood for Superior. S+ meant you were doing a very, very good job.

After Miss Jones gave me a U I got talked about. Miss Jones knew how hurt I was but she said I just had to work harder: 'Marva, I know you can do better, and if you apply yourself you can go far.'

I felt bad bringing a U home to my mother, but she didn't seem too concerned. She said, 'You got to work harder, Marvan. I know you can do it.'

Miss Jones put it on me in such a loving way that I was determined – with my heart and my whole spirit – to make an S. I was scared I wasn't going to pass second grade, but I worked hard and I kept on trying, and the next grade card day I got an S. I jumped up and down and Miss Jones was happy with me. She got out of me exactly what she wanted. I feel sorry for children today because they go to school and their parents for some reason have the idea they're not going to let the teachers treat them like they got treated, so there's no discipline. These kids today are half-raising theirselves.

Miss Jones, I'm sorry to say, died quite early. I think I was a sophomore in high school when she passed. They said she died on the school ground. I had a beautiful relationship with her and I shall never forget it.

CHAPTER 4

Friends and Family

As long as I'd known that I was alive, and I suppose I've been conscious of that from around the age of three, Bettyan Turner was my mud pie buddy. She is truly one of the few friends left from my early years. We hold on to each other. We're blood sisters and to this day we're still the best of friends. My mother calls her Better Ann.

Bettyan was a few years older than me, and bossed me around and took care of me like the baby sister she never had. I followed her lead for we were together every day, but we always ended up fighting. We'd stay away from each other for a few hours but then we'd get back together again.

Bettyan and I roamed the streets and the alleys, but sometimes we had to watch the triplets and twins. We loved to pretend we were cooking. We got dirt and put it in a bowl and stirred it up until it was creamy. Then we slipped in some of Mama's sugar and sometimes even an egg. Now we knew that was a no-no, and we'd sweat hoping that my mother wouldn't notice. We put the mixture in pie or cake pans and let them bake in the sun. When they were dry we pretended to serve them with something to drink. Sometimes we even tasted a little of the dirt.

We could get devilish too. I spent some days killing frogs. It sounds horrible, I know, but children do things that make your flesh crawl. We lived near the river, and it seemed there were so many of those things. I used to kill a few, especially in the morning when I first went outside. Sometimes I got tired of seeing them jump in the yard. There were just too many of them, so I'd pick up a rock and kill them to get them out of the way. We also used to pass the time chasing grasshoppers, and we'd reach up into the air and catch light bugs – they used to turn a bright yellow and glow in the dark – and put them on our fingers and pretend they were rings. When it rained lots of snails came out, and we'd go and get the salt box and sprinkle it on them to get rid of them.

One day a bird dropped an egg. We cracked it to see what it was like inside. It was just a yolk: the bird hadn't formed. As the weather was hot we put the egg on a brick in the backyard and let it cook – which it did really quickly.

Then there were times we got scared out of our wits. There was an old lady named Miss Douglass who we all thought was a witch. She had a lot of Indian in her. I never knew who her husband was or if she had one, but she was known to many of us as the neighborhood witch. Just to look at her was like looking at the bogey man. She lived in an old train in her yard and kept a fire burning there. As kids we thought she would get us and put us in her pot. She'd come through the alley, looking for woodchips or taking a short cut, and when we saw her we'd sweat and hide quietly, shaking, waiting for her to pass. The boys made faces, going, 'Here comes Miss Douglass! You'd better run!' And we'd run and hide in the barns 'cause we thought she was going to cut our heads off. When Freddie, Bettyan's brother, and his gang threw rocks at her we got really scared, because we thought she was going to cut our heads off and put a curse on Freddie, or on us if she saw us.

We'd sigh in relief as she went back to her house on Fourth Street, across from the Baptist church that Bettyan belonged to. I often saw her pass the church with her daughter, who I think was blind, strapped on her back. I don't know where they were going, but it seemed like I saw her every Sunday night. I'd say to Mama, 'How come the neighborhood boys laugh at her when she walks through the alley?'

She said, 'I don't know nothing about why they laugh at her. She's a good woman.' Miss Douglass was just different, and didn't bother nobody.

Miss Douglass wasn't the only thing that scared me when I was young. There were two other things that I was really frightened of:

motorcycles, which scared me to death, and this man called Mr Bagsby. Motorcycles scared me because they looked like heavy monsters and they made a lot of noise. This man, I think his name was Charles Bagsby, was a very dark man who made bootleg liquor. He used to sit on his porch, and it was said he had a little hole in his chair where he just reached down to get his liquor. So he was drunk most of the time. His wife gave him no trouble, and it was said he'd bring his girlfriends over and they'd all drink together. It was the talk of the town. You know, everybody knew everything in Armourdale. His wife was very tolerant, but we thought she was crazy. She was an Indian – or you might say Eskimo – from Alaska. After her husband died she found a new lease of life and dressed real nice and went to church. Everyone was so surprised.

Another thing I was afraid of was cement trucks. Cement trucks scared me because the thing that's turning, the mixer, looked like a big-headed monster to me – so when it came along I ran for my life. I was just scared. I wasn't too bad about fire trucks, as I don't remember too many of them. In them days when you got fish the fish man arrived in his truck and the husky man brought the coal in. But they didn't scare me.

Bettyan Turner and I got our butts whipped sometimes. Once, my Aunt Jerldine told us to watch a pie she wanted to cool while she went to town and left my brothers in our charge. We watched them every now and then, but mostly we were playing. When Aunt Jerldine came back and looked at her pie she started hollering at us. The triplets and twins had slipped in it, and it was practically all gone. Luckily we escaped a whipping that time.

Bettyan Turner's father had one of the best jobs that was ever known in them days and that was working at the meat packing house. I knew exactly when to leave my mother's front porch on Sixth Street and pass their house in the evening: Bettyan's mother was a good cook, and the Turners set a fine table every day. To get there, I had to go down past the church and into a place called Osage. This was where my mama said them Osage Indians used to do their dances and had a big parade every day. And it was where, when the war came and times were hard, people got their free sandwiches and soup. Mama said she didn't need no sandwiches or soup, but her girlfriends were eating sandwiches and soup 'cause that's all their families could afford – so she went down there and got hers too.

When the Turners saw me they'd say, 'Marvan, come on in, it's time for dinner.' Bettyan's mother made homemade rolls that were so light they seemed to float in the air; they tasted so heavenly. Yeah, I knew when to pass their house.

Like Bettyan, I've known Sharon Hooks since childhood, another good friend. Sharon was much quieter than Bettyan. Her mother, Sister Hooks, my grandmother and Sister Bea were those who'd pray every day at noon without fail. If any one of them was late they still got started on time. If I was in the dining room I'd hear them praying and speaking in tongues, laying up prayers for their children and everybody in sin and sickness. Sister Bea had a condition, as I remember, which was about to get serious, and the way I heard them talking it was like if their prayers didn't straighten her up she was going to die and go to heaven. For days they prayed. My grandmother really was the praying kind. Mama said if she woke up at night Grandmother would be lying flat on the floor, praying. It didn't scare me – nor Sharon, who had the same thing going on in her house. Mama let me stay the night there once in a while. I remember the potbelly stove they had. Once I got too close and burned my arm; I still have a scar.

I spent my time between the Hooks' house, my grandmother's house and Bettyan's house. Sharon and me played together most times at her house, which was next door to my Uncle Tot's place, near the back of my grandmother's house. He sold bootleg liquor, and his wife, Sarah Manning, collected his money from this. She liked to dip snuff, and spat into a spittoon on the side. As the Mannings came up from the South they all stayed with Aunt Sarah and gave her money, but she fleeced them as much as she could. My mother was a threat to her pocketbook, so she didn't take to her. In fact, my mother couldn't stand her. Compared with Aunt Sarah, who was a bit of a lowlife, Mama was a high society woman. Aunt Sarah was mostly Indian and very light-skinned – a pretty woman, but hefty too. She always wore two long braids in front of her that went almost down to her waist. She lived to a good age.

When Daddy and Mama got together Aunt Sarah caused trouble and was constantly a thorn in Mama's side. Aunt Sarah didn't like Mama 'cause my mother didn't fool with people she considered were on the wrong side of the tracks or did things that she didn't think were right, like running whisky and keeping a good-time party house. My mother didn't want to associate with her kind, so she didn't visit or go over there. Aunt Sarah used to call Mother 'the uppity woman'.

Aunt Sarah once wrote my father when he was away in the navy and told him that I was not his baby, but a Mexican baby. My mother said my father wrote her and told her, 'I heard that my baby is a Mexican baby and I want a die-vorce.' Mama laughs about that now: she says he couldn't even spell divorce. So when Daddy came home, Mama said he looked at me and I started screaming and hollering, and because of that he could tell I wasn't used to having men around me – so she never had any more problems on that score. But as I grew older you could tell from my appearance and mannerisms that I was his baby.

I really didn't know what poor was, but I heard the people saying how pitiful it was that Sister Hooks had to raise five girls by herself. As a child I noticed I never saw Sharon's daddy at her house. You saw her mother on her own working her garden to make ends meet. I used to go through the garden on my way to her house, and smelt the peppermint she grew. My father was close to them because he knew they were dirt poor and was aware of the hard times they were having. He was generous. When he brought food the poor people that we grew up with came over and congregated at our house. The Hooks and others knew when it was payday like they were part of the family, and came over to eat some fruit or whatever was scarce at their house. Everyone shared and helped each other. We had a real community spirit.

Our friends and neighbors were good to us too, and would baby-sit us when we was small. Our house was central, a place where we grew up together and people came to eat my parents' fruit and play the piano. They knew my father was kind and that they was going to eat good. He was a deacon of the church and he always did things like that. One thing I liked about Sis' Hooks was that any time you went to her house, even though she was poor, she gave you something nice to eat.

Sharon was more timid in nature than Bettyan and me but we had lots of fun together. We were church buddies and played mostly around the yard – usually hopscotch. She was the baby of five sisters and they watched us, so we couldn't venture far. Sharon's sisters sometimes invited me and Sharon to go to the zoo with them. Mama always said yes, but often when I was going someplace I really wanted to go I either had a headache or cramps in my legs. I don't know why but we sometimes called these cramps charlyhorses. The muscle in the middle of my leg started hurting. What caused it I don't know. I still get them sometimes even now: at times in bed I just have to get out of the bed 'cause it hurts so much. I stamp my feet and stretch my leg to try to get the muscle in the middle of my leg to relax, but nowadays I take potassium and that helps keep it at bay.

I used to travel with Daddy to Oklahoma to see his relatives, and sometimes we had to walk to the bus line to take us to the station. We could be just walking when my legs suddenly stiffened up and became painful. In those days a headache or charlyhorse was something you just lived with. So when I was with Daddy and had a charlyhorse he picked me up and carried me to our destination. Sometimes they gave me an aspirin but usually I just rested until it went away.

Sister Hooks, I believe, lived the straight and narrow but I didn't know why I never saw their daddy. Then after we moved to Wyandotte County a few years later I saw a man on the porch, when I was around fifteen or sixteen. Now you never saw a man sitting on their porch unless it was kinfolk, my daddy or the church pastor. The man said, 'So you are little Marvan? My, my, my.'

I said, 'Sharon, who is that man?' and she replied, 'Our daddy.' That was all.

Anyhow, when I told Mama what I'd seen she told me the story. The Hooks were hush-hush about it at the time and are pretty much the same today, but they counted Mama and Daddy like real family. It turned out that Mr Hooks served many years in Leavenworth Penitentiary. That was big time. I asked what had happened.

Mama said, 'He was a good man. He bought that house of theirs in Armourdale but the devil got in him. He started going to the wrong place, got jumped on and he killed two men.' My eyes got big. I was shocked. The Hooks had never said a mumbling word about it. My daddy said, 'He stayed in prison so long, the concrete gave him the worst arthritis there was.'

When he got out of prison Mr Hooks went back to the church, became an elder and was called to preach. I do not remember his sermons really but in the service I would hear him yell, 'OOOHHHHHHHHHHH!' It scared me. I thought it was the Holy Ghost.

Sister Hooks died first, in her eighties. Mr Hooks lived to be ninety-nine or a hundred years old. I saw him about two weeks before his death: there were no wrinkles in his face, and he'd stayed sharp and wore a suit. Through all the hard times the sisters and mother had to go through they came out all right. Two became schoolteachers. The others had good jobs too, one of them working at General Motors.

Our next-door neighbor was Miss Ressey. Miss Ressey had the first television in our street: I first saw it when I peeped through a crack in their door from my yard where I could see the light. I was in awe. She was kind of well-to-do and had the best of everything, although our house wasn't shabby either. We had a combination, good furniture, and Mother was a great housekeeper with six children.

Miss Ressey's husband was a music man, called Paul Gunther, who played the drums. He was always away: little did I know that he was playing with the pianist Jay McShann, one of the jazz greats in Kansas City. He was his drummer until he couldn't drum no more.

Mother and Miss Ressey sometimes got into a disagreement. She was uppity, although she was never mean to me, and her ways pissed Mama off. Me and the children (they were cousins to the Hooks) got along all right – her daughter, Joan, and I played together – but she and Mama had run-ins once in a while. One day Miss Ressey put her nice white clothes out on the line just before my mother felt it was time to burn the trash. And, oh boy, the smoke from our trash blew over Miss Ressey's beautiful, white, clean clothes. She got mad and called the police on mom. The police came and said, 'Mrs Manning, didn't you know that you can't burn trash at this time? You smoked up Mrs Gunther's clothes.'

Mama told me she went into her act, and played 'nut roll' with the police. She said innocently, 'Oh, I wasn't aware she had clothes on the line.' All I knew was that Mama was ticked off, but felt better for getting one over Miss Ressey who thought her kids were better than anyone else's.

On the weekend in the summer the hayride passed our street. As I saw everyone having fun on the big truck I said to myself, when I get older I'll be able to go on the hayride too. At that time we just played mud pies, ran from Miss Douglass and looked at the chickens. My grandmother had raised chickens in the back and my ma was the chicken killer. Grandmother would say, 'Tootsie, come and kill a couple of these chickens.' I watched mother wring their necks until they went limp. Sometimes they were still moving afterwards. I marveled at that.

I was scared of chickens. In fact, I'm very scared of any kind of animal that's walking. I wouldn't run from a cat, though: I'd just shout scat at it. Maybe I get it off my grandmother, who had a fear of dogs: one must have attacked her when she was young. When we went to the Goodwill shop, as we did almost every day, she always carried a large stick, and if a dog came onto our side of the street we crossed over to the other side. This went on every time we went out together.

We didn't believe in having animals in the house, although I used to have a little white bunny with pink ears and a black rabbit one of the neighbors had given me. She had lots of pretty bunnies, white and pink, white and black. I wasn't afraid to pick up an animal of that type. This lady who raised the rabbits – her daughter was plum crazy. You passed her house and you thought the gorilla from Manila was there. She was born that way. And in them days they didn't put them in the institutions. Her mother kept her on the porch where she couldn't get out. I know I never passed that house on my own.

The only problem I had at home was with my Uncle James. He was my mama's baby brother; his twin died at birth. Uncle James didn't like me, the first grandchild, getting all the attention. He was so jealous of me. We'd often squabble and fight, until the time he tried to knock me down and my mother and grandma gave him hell. Mama said she was going to give him a licking if he didn't stop. I'm so sorry to say he was mean and stingy all his life. He always had money and a new car but was mean to his first family, second family and his third wife. Mother would say, 'He just don't like children.' He had apartment houses, and he even cheated himself when it came to dressing – I think he got everything second-hand out of the Goodwill store. When he died nobody knew where he'd kept his money, not even his last wife. He died a couple of years ago after our favorite uncle, Uncle Joe, died. They were together every day. Every job Uncle Joe had Uncle James got the job first and later got Uncle Joe taken on. When Uncle James got on the fire department he tried to get Uncle Joe to follow him, but Uncle Joe said, 'No, I'll stay with the city: I ain't about fighting no fires.' Uncle James retired as a fireman and Uncle Joe retired as a city worker.

CHAPTER 5

Mama's Family

My mother's real name is Willie Mae Collins. She changed it and got it legitimized to Willa, because Willie as far as she was concerned was a man's name. Her nickname's Tootsie. Anybody that calls my mother Tootsie, she says, 'Ooh, Lord.'

When my mother steps into any room you can't help to look at her. She's eighty-four now and you're gonna say what is Miss Manning wearing today? She's known in Kansas City to this day as being one of the sharpest, cleanest-dressing women. Mother loves hats and she seldom goes anywhere without one.

Even at eighty-four she's one of the best Hammond B3 organists and piano players in Kansas City. She has a lot of history behind her. We work together when I'm not on the road, playing for the church choir. I'd put her up there with James Cleveland, one of the gospel greats that passed on, and the jazz organist Jimmy Smith. She plays like that at eighty-four years old. You can't imagine that a lady of her age could do that, but she can groove better than me – although she can't dance a lick in the road!

She was the second oldest girl in her family. There were three girls and four boys, but one died in birth. My grandmother's last two children was twins – Uncle James and his brother: one made it and one didn't. My mother was always the one who seemed to have the greatest stamina of all the girls. Grandmother saw something spiritually special in her.

In each family, there's one member that has a lot put upon them in some kind of way; they have to shoulder the responsibility. Sometimes this can work out favorably and make them stronger, but at other times it can be too much and lead them astray, making them the black sheep of the family. But my mother carried the burden of being the chosen one. My grandmother prayed, and actually anointed Mama's hands with olive oil, asking the Lord to give Mama the gift of playing piano, for they were building a church in South Park, Kansas, and needed music. Grandpa played a little piano and guitar, but that was not enough. So Mama was called upon to play the piano.

Her sister, my oldest aunt, Aunt Thelma, still lives today and is eighty-seven years old. She is one beautiful and gracious lady, my mother's oldest sister and the one who named me. After high school she went to cosmetology school and became a licensed beautician, owning and running her own beauty shop until she was ready to retire. It was a long time before she could have children and because of that she considered me her little girl. She dressed me up, buying me all kinds of outfits, dresses, coats and shoes. I was her little doll. She kept me beautiful.

She lived in a big two-storey house a little ways from Armourdale, and always had the finest of everything. She and her husband, Jim Overton, owned the house and they wasn't poor folks at all, because he had a thriving business in the chicken market, one of the biggest owned by a black man at that time, and he also kept apartment houses and ran a record shop on Tenth Street. Tenth Street in those days was very populated and it was a good-time place, like Fifth Street. Back then Fifth Street and Tenth Street was where you had the black nightclubs and the theaters. Uncle Jim was also a gambler on the side.

Mother says that at about the age of nine Aunt Thelma was earning good money pressing hair using the hot combs they had in those days; she also took customers from a woman who had a cosmetology license. The lady that was doing hair in Armourdale – the only licensed beautician – was losing her customers to my Aunt Thelma! She stood up on crate boxes and did people's hair and got her a little money – she always had a bagful. Her work spoke for her. And she was also the teacher's pet: sometimes she'd go away at the weekend and stay with the teachers. So she kind of lived the high side of life.

Aunt Thelma would say to my mother, 'You wash the dishes for me and I'll give you a nickel,' 'cause she didn't like to clean. Mama said she'd be waiting on that nickel forever and they'd end up fighting over it. She did the work but Aunt Thelma didn't pay her.

During a time when the economy was bad and money was tight, Aunt Thelma was married and doing fine, while my mother's friends had to get handouts and get in line to get sugar and butter sandwiches. But Mama didn't have to because Aunt Thelma was doing well and helped her. She helped pay for my mother's wedding. So did my dad, because my grandfather just laughed when they wanted to get married.

When Aunt Thelma finally had children she had a girl and two boys: Carol, Jimmie and Ronnie. Ronnie's now deceased: Vietnam took its toll on him. He was a tower of strength for the whole family, but Agent Orange prevailed. He had his own platoon and was a good soldier, but the stories he told would have made anyone shudder. On his last day in Vietnam he was sent on a mission with his troops. He wasn't given much chance of making it back alive, but made it with some of his troops. He paid a heavy price for his bravery, though, and was never the same afterwards.

My other auntie, Aunt Jerldine, was younger than my mother. Her being the baby, she didn't have to do too much and wasn't interested in no housework and no cooking. She had Mother and Aunt Thelma to vouch for her with her education. Mama and Aunt Thelma told Grandma and Pa that they would call the police if they didn't make sure Jerldine got the things she needed to go and finish school, and that gave her the kick she needed so she got to finish high school. She worked for many years for the Post Office, and died a few years ago. They said it was from a broken heart because her daughter treated her so bad.

Aunt Jerldine and Aunt Thelma got clean away with things. They snuck out of the house and nothing was noticed or said. But for Mama it was different. She was in straights: her parents watched her like a hawk and she couldn't get away from nothing for she was the chosen one. She had to play for the revivals, services and for other churches: they said they couldn't shout unless she played the piano, and when she played they had a high time in the Lord. That's not to say that Mama didn't want to play piano, for she did, but it became a hard chore. She was at church every time the door opened.

One of my Mom's brothers was Nathaniel Junior. They called him Ned for short. He went in the army and I remember him coming back a different person after the war. When my uncle was outside and airplanes came across he ran up under the house because he was scared. In time he got over this fear. Later he became a barber.

CHAPTER 6

The Barrys and Shaws

Let me tell you about Grandmother Collins's family. Her maiden name was Barry. We originally come out of South Carolina on my mother's side but they migrated to Texas, and through marriage there was another side of the family called the Shaws.

The Barrys slighted my grandmother because they thought that Nathaniel Collins wasn't good enough for her. They heard he was a player and a womanizer and that he had another couple of women who he had babies from. Mama says she remembers playing with these kids when they sent her to visit relatives in Texas. They told her these kids were her sisters and brothers, but they'd never tell her why or how.

The Barrys and Shaws owned all kinds of land outside a place called Longview in Texas, and on some of that land they got oil from an oil well they had. All the relatives profited from it, and it was handed down through the Barry and the Shaw families for generations. The land never went to anyone who wasn't blood kin; they don't care who you marry, but if you don't have Barry or Shaw blood you don't get it.

My great-grandmother, Matilda Barry, was a wealthy woman and expected everyone to go to college. She was the only person in her neighborhood who had a horse-drawn carriage with her own personal driver. I'm told she was a fancy dresser and you could hear her before you saw her because she wore lots of beads and bangles.

All my aunties dressed up-to-date even as they got older, so I guess that's where they got it from.

In about 1950, I think, my grandmother got a lot of money from the oil well. Sometimes it was only $30 or $40 but this particular year she got, so I heard, about $10,000. Now one of the reasons why my family wasn't poor was because of this lump sum: we got a brand new bathtub, and Grandmother put a new sink in the kitchen.

Her husband, Grandpa Collins, worked for the railroad as a porter. In Oklahoma he had a little dinette, 'cause he didn't always come straight back: sometimes he'd be gone one or two days. He said he remembered as a young man when he had to get his family out of Oklahoma 'cause the white people was talking about hanging this nigger like they was going to a picnic. Apparently a black man had looked at a white woman and all you heard from the white folks, he said, was, 'Are you going to the hanging?'

I remember my grandfather coming home from work and the first thing he wanted to do after eating was play the guitar – he played the electric guitar. But he got on Grandma's nerves. Grandma would say, 'Nathaniel, you ain't playing nothing – you don't do nothing but play the same thing!' He played sort of gospel, but it had a beat going and he played the same tune all the time. Grandma got sick of hearing it and she'd say, 'All you're playing is the same thing, the same thing!'

And then Grandpa said, 'What do you know? You ain't got no timing. Your timing is bad when you sing.'

I'd be listening and laughing. Then Grandma would say, 'You need to pray, you need to pray! Get the Bible out and read it 'cause all them scriptures you're sayin' up in that pulpit, that ain't right.' See, Grandmother knew the scripture well and had the anointing. She'd say to my grandfather, 'You ain't reading and giving the word right – all you're doing is hollering, hollering, hollering!'

As I said before, my grandfather was a preacher and the assistant pastor to our home church – which started out in Armourdale, Kansas, and then moved to South Park, Kansas. Grandpa got a good deal when he was building the church in South Park. When he got windows put in he got them for a good price. The only thing wrong was that the man who put them in was a drunk, and we could never get the windows open to let in air. So in the summer it was really, really hot.

The Church of God in Christ was the only sanctified church out there. The place was always packed. But all Grandpa would do was holler as far as Grandma was concerned. This was no lie, and anybody who knew my grandfather said they thought he had iron in his feet 'cause he stamped when he was preaching and busted the floorboards on the pulpit, and had to come back Monday morning and fix them.

We used to die laughing about this. There was lots of funny things that Grandpa did. To get to his church you had to go through a lot of turns on a dirt road, and if it was wet, you had to go around slippin' and slidin' in the mud to get to it. One night after church when we got to the bottom of the hill the lights went out on the car. What were we going to do? Well, Grandpa made Uncle Joe, his son, sit on the middle of the hood with a flashlight so he could see on the pitch-black road.

Another time, Mother said that Grandfather saw a wood rat by the dining table. They must have left the side door open and one got in. Mom said he panicked and jumped up on the table, hollering to my grandma, 'Get him, get him!' We always laughed that he seemed so scared of the rat when he, being the man, should have been the one to kill it.

My grandfather also believed in saving. He said, 'I don't care what you make, but if you make a dollar save a dime.' He was a tight-wad to the bone.

CHAPTER 7

Daddy

Now it's time to tell you about my father, Ray Manning. He lost his mother at the age of about thirteen, down there in Louisiana and Mississippi somewhere – although Manning women are long livers in general. My Aunt Maggie, Uncle James's wife, helped raise him, and he called her Mother.

His family were bootleggers for the white man. They had a still where they made moonshine and then The Man came and got it.

My father had two sisters, Ola and Ora – twins. They looked plum white and had blue eyes. Some of his family had straight hair and some of them had curly hair. When my father joined the navy and went to war his papers said he was white, but he got his ID changed to say Negro. It's interesting that some of my father's folk have to be buried within a few days, as they turn dark after they die. To look at them, though, you'd think they were white. And in my youth Spanish and Mexicans used to start talking their language to me, thinking I was one of their people. I'm proud of my roots, but in many places it's better to say you're anything but a black American. That's such a pity. This world has got to grow up some day.

Daddy was funny. If he liked you he'd come out of his room and greet you in the house. If he didn't think too much of you he'd just let you be. He could do three things at one time: he could watch the television, read his paper and listen to his ball game on the radio. It wore us out.

Daddy worked most of his life for the Santa Fe railroad. He started in the '40s and at first he couldn't take it. He said he worked there about a year and he said hell, they were working too hard, so he stopped. He was a lineman beating them tracks and laying them down to make the line. I remember him working when it was below zero. And sometimes they didn't come home at night when the weather got bad because they had to keep the line from freezing. When it was cold they'd keep that snow and ice off them tracks by beating them. In them days the Santa Fe railway company didn't give you nothing to eat. If you didn't bring enough to eat with you at that particular time you was out of luck, 'cause you was going to be cold all the time.

But my daddy stayed with the company and made it all the way up to be one of the bosses. Daddy got one of my triplet brothers, Rayford, a job but he couldn't take it: he couldn't take the work. He said he couldn't handle it and quit.

One time I had a premonition that my father was in the line of danger, and he said there were a couple of times he almost got hit by a train. He said that when trains were coming you'd think they were far away, and then before you knew it they were right upon you.

Daddy always kept a big garden, and had what we called a growing hand. He'd bring home great big sacks of apples and sweet potatoes. In them days everybody who had gardens shared with each other. His garden was an allotment about half a block from the Phillips Elementary School, no more than a mile from our house. As we were close to the river the water always settled there, so the ground was very fertile and would always yield a whole lot. He grew okra, some tomatoes, peanuts, sweet potatoes, turnip greens and collard greens – everything, I think, except rice. Daddy brought it home and shared it. It was a pretty big-sized lot.

My daddy worked hard. The Mannings were never lazy. They always worked and they always was going to have a pocket full o' money. And that was the way it was from down South.

I remember my dad owning a Buick, a '48 or '49 model. It was dark; I think it was brown or black. Right across the street was a little church where white people went. Daddy said one time this white man asked him for a ride, 'cause Daddy had a car. Like I said, we wasn't rich but we wasn't poor.

My grandfather was driving Cadillacs back then and kept a brand new car. He said one day when he was coming out of Union station he had to duck and hide because the gangster Pretty Boy Floyd had a shootout there. In those days Kansas City had one of the biggest and most beautiful train stations; now it's a museum with restaurants and things. I think it's owned by the city, which takes care of it because it's one of the great landmarks that people go to see. There's a lot of history in that place.

There were Manning men that strayed sometimes, and occasionally they left their wives, but my father never left us. I'm not saying every day was a rosy day with my mother and father but he hung in there and brought home his check whether they was getting along or not. One time before Winfred, my youngest brother, was born, I was taught how to go down to the bank, because my daddy didn't like doing those things. I think he once cleared $112 and $115 for two weeks from working eight hours plus a day on the railroad. Daddy didn't even like to dial a phone, 'cause his fingers were too big. He'd say, 'Come here, Marvan, dial this number for me.'

Daddy used to go hunting, and he put a lot of money in hunting dogs. His brother-in-law, married to one of his twin sisters, was also a hunter; they'd hunted together for years. I remember they were out hunting one night and my uncle told Daddy, 'Follow me.'

Daddy said he was getting tired; then he began to notice that the places were beginning to look familiar. Daddy checked it out and told his brother, 'Man, we been running round in circles all night. No wonder we haven't seen nothing!' Daddy was tired and they went back to the house.

Uncle told his wife what had happened and she said to us, 'I knew he was beginning to show old age, but I didn't know he was getting that bad in the head.' My dad was pissed. He came home and told us. But coming home empty-handed really got him, and he was tired. He never went hunting with Uncle no more.

CHAPTER 8

The Mannings

My father's family, the Mannings, have an interesting history, from running whisky to being highly educated folks. One by one they migrated north, up into Muskogee, Oklahoma and then places like Tulsa, Okmulgee and finally Kansas City.

My cousin, John H. Manning, wrote and researched a history of the Manning family. He's my favorite of the male Mannings. We attended high school together and were in the same homeroom. He was a whiz at trigonometry and anything that had to do with mathematics. He was an A student in all of his classes and was on the honor roll every grade card. I guess he's my favorite because when I look at him he looks just like my father. My daddy, Ray, and his father, James, were brothers. John went on to be an FBI agent and also worked as an investigator for an insurance company; he's now retired. I'm so proud of him.

My grandparents on my father's side were Noah Manning Jr and Alice Spinks Manning. Apparently the Manning name comes from Ireland. Through our ancestry we're related to our former slave owners. The records go back to Caroline Manning, whose maiden name is unknown. She was born into slavery in Kentucky in 1810 and died in 1912 at the age of 102. My Uncle James remembered her and said she was so old that she had gone blind. Caroline and my great-great-grandfather had five sons.

Noah Manning Sr, my great-grandfather, was born in Mississippi in 1851. He was the youngest, and the only son who was allowed to remain with Caroline and my great-great-grandfather. The other four sons were sold to new slave owners.

There was another child out of slavery. I think they sold him and he went to another area but he never could be found. We had another uncle like that and we didn't find him either: we didn't know if he was dead or living.

My grandfather Noah Manning Jr, and Alice Spinks Manning had fifteen children. My father was the baby, the youngest. The eldest was Noah III (also known as Tot), who died at the age of sixteen. He was followed by David (1900-72), Mary (1903-93), Mattie (1906-93), James (1907-80), Quincy (1910-75), John Quincy (1912-48), Jessie (1913-42), Ola (1915-99), Ora (1915-2003), Mamie (1916-97), Mabel (1920-83) and Willie, known as Sonny (1924-68). There was also another daughter, Bessie, who died at the age of eleven months.

Most of the Mannings are workers and proud people. They've never been dirt poor. They had money because they had property in Mississippi and a big nightclub on the land, I'm told. It was supposed to be a big fine nightclub down there and they profited greatly from it. Maybe that's where I got my singing itch from – because all the Mannings were talented singers. Not only that, but they had a talent for running whisky, getting college degrees and even giving someone a good kicking if they had to. They loved to have a good time, eat good food and didn't seek to hurt no one if they could help it. If they couldn't help you at least they wouldn't try to make trouble for the hell of it.

I remember my grandfather, Noah Jr, my father's father, as being a reddish man with good hair. He was mixed: you could see that deep Indian in him. He was kind of thin and of medium build, around 5ft 7in. I remember this man picking me up saying, 'Do you know who I am?' I would hesitate, and he'd say, 'I'm your Grandfather Manning.' He'd always stop by and see us on the way to St Louis, where Alice Spinks – his wife and my grandmother – lived, because he had folks up there too. Alice Spinks was a very light woman; she looked white if you didn't know her.

Going back to the Mannings, it was true that for a long time no Manning male had ever lived to be over seventy-four. That was until two years ago when my first cousin, Doughbelly, reached seventy-five. The cycle is broken now and it means a lot to the Mannings. I can't even tell you his real name: we just call him Doughbelly. He smoked and he drank and he lived his life but now he's a deacon in the church. And the reason why I point him out is because he made it over seventy-four and he still lives. He's in the church now: just as much as he liked to drink and fish back then he likes to pray for people now, and say what he missed. He's taking care of his family and, like I said, there was no lazy Mannings. That's one thing we can say.

A lot of people have heard of Grandmother Manning's side of the family, the Spinks. Leon Spinks, the heavyweight boxer who fought Muhammad Ali, that's my grandmother's nephew – but we've never met.

On the Manning side of the family there's a lady who made fame as a track runner, Madeline Manning. She was an athlete in the '70s and '80s, who we believe is related to us. There's also Danny Manning and his father, the coach, who plays professional basketball. We believe that they're related to the four Mannings who were sold into slavery. You might say that all Manning males have some things in common: big ears and the way they hold their heads.

I have a nephew who played pro football named Brian Manning. He played for the Miami Dolphins and the Greenbay Packers. His brother Loren got a scholarship to play basketball and went to Florida. He then decided he didn't want to do that and now owns his own gospel label, AFINIA, based here in Kansas City. Both of my nephews are the sons of my oldest triplet brother, Ray Manning Jr.

Now, my father's side of the family were not back-downers. As I mentioned earlier, in the South the Mannings were doing some bootlegging for The Man down there. They had so much ground and land that they could do it and get away with it, so they worked with The Man. Down south in Mississippi a white man picked a fight with one of the Mannings. That was a no-no, 'cause Mannings don't back down. I guess they were what you call a gang, but they're Christian people and they're upright people but don't you mess with 'em. They stand up for themselves and stick together. So one day one of my uncles got into a fight with one of the white men – who got too smart, and my uncle killed him. He had to get out of town, so he got in his car and started going north. He changed his name to Smith, and although he made it he later died in a car wreck, his car turning over while coming from Oklahoma. His children, my first and second cousins, still go by the name of Smith. They live in Omaha, Nebraska.

I mentioned Aunt Sarah and Uncle Tot earlier. Uncle Tot was something else. He had a stutter. During the time of prohibition, when they was down in Mississippi, they was making and running whisky from them stills. So finally all of them had to run up north. He just did what he had to do to make some money and he worked hard too. He was like all the Mannings – he wasn't one to back down. When prohibition was over Uncle Tot was still making homebrew and selling it in bottles and making money. He didn't have to – he could have gone to the liquor store like everyone else but he was still at it. When the police caught him he'd go up to Leavenworth Prison, but always came back looking fat and fine. He'd say, 'I... I... I... I ain't gonna do that no more,' but 'fore you knew it he was back at it again. He just couldn't help himself. So we just used to laugh at him. He was a nice man and not mean in any way. We loved Uncle Tot, but it was funny that he didn't know nothing but bootlegging whisky and giving his money to Aunt Sarah.

I remember on public holidays the bums and down-and-outs always came by my Uncle Sonny's house. He was Daddy's brother. Aunt Lester, his wife, fixed plenty of food; enough, in fact, for two days. At his house there was always enough food for a giant. Uncle Sonny weighed at least 400 pounds, if not more. He'd eat whole pies and cakes – and his wife used to sell what was left over. He went to work every day too, big as he was. Uncle Sonny always had a big smile on his face. My daddy used to say he was crazy, but he was the sweetest man. Aunt Lester used to say, 'Sonny, why don't you go join the circus?' My Uncle Sonny was dear to me.

It tickled me when Daddy said that as kids they teased him a lot. He told us about one day when they got on Uncle Sonny's nerves: they messed with him and made him mad. Uncle Sonny chased them in and out of the house with a double-barreled shotgun, laughing. My dad said Sonny was going to shoot them, and they had to make him tired until he let them go. When he said that Uncle Sonny was mad but laughing a bell struck with me, and I'd never known I was like him. If I got super angry I started laughing and a little after laughing I was getting ready to hit you. So when Daddy told me that I realized I did the same thing.

Uncle Sonny eventually got on a diet because of his health. One time I think he lost 50 pounds in one week, staying off the pies and cakes. And he said to me, 'Marva, it's just hard, it's just hard.'

I remember one time I looked at his bed and said to his daughter Annette, 'Sister' – the Mannings always called each other sister or brother – 'why are all those bricks under Sonny's bed?'

She said, 'If he don't have them he'll go through the floor: we have to make sure that bed's strong.'

Boy, I remember it being a real big bed. I also remember everyone had to get in the front of the car when Uncle Sonny got in the back – because he weighed so much they had to stop the car from dragging. He also had to come sideways through the door to his house.

When Uncle Sonny died we were so sad but we had a big laugh at his funeral. He being so big he had to have a big, heavy casket. They had to have a lot of men to carry him. I remember it was muddy and there was snow on the ground and we had to go up the hill to the cemetery. The hearse looked like it wasn't going to make it. It struggled with Uncle Sonny's heavy casket. We got tickled and wondered how it was going to make it up the hill. It was going up that hill almost like a snake, writhing from side to side. It was slippin' and a slidin' and in the end everybody was trying to push the car up the hill. Then, when they got ready to take Uncle Sonny out, all the pallbearers looked at each other nervously. It was awful. You're talking about big men breathing hard. Although there were a lot of them the hill was slippery. They was very careful and you could see that they were thinking, *Please don't let him fall out of the casket and Lord, let us make it up this hill.* That was really funny. And then, when the pallbearers tried to get him out again they were so scared. That was a slow walk because they were afraid of dropping him.

I have some other kinfolk that are Creoles, and they talk Creole amongst themselves. I met some of them at a recent family reunion down in New Orleans where the Mannings and the Spinks got together. I heard them talking amongst each other and asked what the hell they were saying. This was just the year before last. They said, 'We're Creoles. We'll talk in English now so you can understand us.'

We Mannings have skeletons in the closet. It's said that an untimely death in the Manning family was caused by voodoo from in-laws. There are also some Mannings who've got into trouble with the law.

The Manning men wasn't perfect but some of them could be slick playboys. My mom was just one of several strong women married into the Manning family who knew how to stand her ground.

CHAPTER 9

Twins and Triplets

It is sometimes said that if one generation of a family has multiple births it usually skips a generation. In our family that's not so. Grandmother Annie Lee Collins (Mama's mother) had twins; my mother had twins and triplets and her granddaughter had twins. And on my father's side of the family there were his twin sisters, Ola and Ora Manning.

Mama's triplets followed about two and a half years after I was born. They were the first triplets to be born at Douglass Hospital. Mother had almost died giving birth to the triplets. Daddy had to come home from the navy and they had to give Mother a blood transfusion from my father. They were both lying on separate tables with the tubes going into each other. She needed more blood, and I guess that's the way they did it in those days. I remember Mama said, 'Hell, it got so bad that Daddy fainted.'

The twins came two and a half years later. All the triplets and the twins were breach babies. I think one of the twins, Melvin, came out with a broken arm, so it's a blessing that my mother's alive.

I was the only one of my mother's family that was breast-fed. The rest of them was too many for Mama to cope with at once. Our doctor, Dr Alexander, tried to get us help because at that particular time the authorities were taking care of triplets.

My mother broke a record for triplets as she had three boys: the first mother to have all boy triplets in America. Dr Alexander did all he could to see if she could get help because we wasn't dirt poor but hell, we wasn't rich either and mother wasn't ready for triplets. The only thing he could come up with that would do anything for her was to get the Pet Milk Company to send her free milk. Pet Milk and Carnation was the two most famous milk products that you could buy in America. We all used milk on the cereal and stuff like that, of course, and my brothers were all on Pet Milk. And so Pet Milk arranged a picture session for us. They took photos of me – I was about five at the time – on the piano, and there was another one with my mum and dad and a train. In those days when you went into a store sometimes they had a string that reached the ceiling with different pictures of their products hung on it. Our pictures as Pet Milk babies appeared in some of these stores, and even appeared in magazines (we were in the February 1951 issue of *Ebony*). Later on, when I got with James Brown, *Jet* magazine did a feature on me and printed one of the Pet Milk pictures.

The only other help my mother got from outside business sources was diaper service for a year. By rights the government was supposed to take care of the triplets, but it ended suddenly and wasn't done any more.

The triplets were often in trouble. They were really mischievous and always ended up killing my mother's goldfish. I often had to be the mama and watch all of them. I'd change the diapers and help with the clothes and keep an eye on them. See, I think because there was three of them Mama didn't take them out into the world as soon as she should have. I remember one time in particular when she was gettin' 'em ready for church for the first time. She said, 'Well it's time for them to go.' She dressed them all just alike after their bath, but she hadn't gotten the number two bathtub empty. And Raymond, the third one, fell back into the water fully clothed. Boy, there was some goings on that day! Mama said a few curse words, she was so mad – and they didn't go to church.

When they finally went to our church for the first time, and heard the noise of all these drums and all that singing, they started running and hollering. When they got to the church steps Daddy said they was like a bunch of wild horses and he had to bring them home. He couldn't take them in the church. They was too scared.

CHAPTER 10

The Flood

School was out. It was 1951 and I was almost seven years old. Little did I know what was to come that year, though my grandmother had a premonition. One day as I came into her house and went into the dining room she said, 'Marvan, we're all going to have to move away from here, and after we move I'm going to get sick and die, and I'm going to heaven.' I remember her words just like it was yesterday.

I said, 'Grandma, please don't talk like that.' I knew what death was from going to wakes for my father's people. In those days they had wakes in the house and then the service at the church.

She went on, 'And when I die I want you to be a missionary and be a good girl. Do you understand?' I'll never forget it as long as I live.

My grandmother called it right. Not long afterwards it began to rain, rain and rain some more. It started in April and didn't end until July. I'm telling you it was raining all day and all night during that time. People began to talk about a flood. Going to church we learned about a man of God called Noah, and how people laughed at him for building a boat when the morning dew was the only source of water. With everybody in Armourdale being so close and sharing their faith in God, we began to say that it was raining like forty days and forty nights in the Bible.

I remember going to sleep very scared because I thought the water would come in the house and drown me or I'd wake up in water. We lived just a short walk from the Kaw River, and I had nightmares about it.

And it kept on raining and raining. In those days people listened to their radios and heard people like Gabriel Heatter, the newsman, who made you think a bomb was to going to destroy the world any minute. There were also programs like *Gangbusters* and ghost stories. Now that I think about it, it was good, 'cause we learned to use our imaginations. Imagination is a key in the key of life.

During these rainy times my brother Raymond, one of the triplets, got sick and we thought at one time he wasn't going to make it.

And it kept raining. So when the flood came, what my grandmother said seemed to have taken form. We was scared. And still it rained. People began to talk about putting sandbags at the river, but I was too young to go to there to look. They began to say we might have to get out, and then we were told the government would tell us when to start packing and when to move out of Armourdale. Mama and Daddy had only just got all new furniture, including a new bedroom suite, a divan and a combination, although they didn't have a TV like Miss Ressey.

Some of the older boys and grown folk kept going to the river to see how the levees, which were really built-up sandbags, were holding up. Then one day – on Friday 13 July of all days – they started hollering from house to house, 'Get out! The water's coming up over the bags. Get out!'

It's documented as one of the worst floods in Kansas City. Like Hurricane Katrina in New Orleans we wasn't warned; the government told us nothing: they were supposed to tell us when the levees broke, but it was our neighbors who made the SOS calls. As the word was passed we all tried frantically to work out how we were going to leave. Not everyone had cars. There was no time to pack furniture. There was no room for my mother's wedding gown that she was saving for me. Miss Ressey had to leave all her finery behind, even her new TV. All of Armourdale was scampering. But some refused to go. That is why I can relate to Katrina.

The first load was the children and what we could get in besides. All we could really do was leave with the clothes on our backs. Our car was full of the family, all eight of us: Mom and Dad, me, the twins – who were still babies – and the triplets. Eventually I found out we were going to our cousin Miss Lena Parker's house in Wyandotte County, about 7 miles from home. In Grandpa's car were my grandparents and two of my uncles, who were still living with Grandma and Grandpa.

After they'd taken us to safety my father and mother doubled back and collected a few more clothes; Mama said they tried to get as many clothes for the kids as they could. And then they drove like hell to the Seventh Street bridge. They knew they were taking a chance, and when they got halfway up onto the bridge – that's about a third of a block past Kansas Avenue – they looked back and could see the water coming; and they drove like crazy. Thank God they made it, but some of the old folk wouldn't leave. I'm told that some of them were sitting on their roofs. It was just like that in New Orleans. When old folk are stubborn they can really be that to a fault. Some of them drowned. It is said that over forty people died in the flood and about fifty thousand had to evacuate. There were even cattle floating around, for we wasn't far from the place where they kept cows for market.

We moved in with our cousin and her husband; we used to call her Aunt Lena. They took all of our family, as her own children were grown and married. Now with all these people going to Cousin Lena's house you can imagine how packed we were – but we made it. They had a big house east of Fifth Street: it was two storeys like my grandfather's home, with four bedrooms plus the dining room, front room, kitchen and back. For black people that was a lot in them days. Even though they wasn't what you'd call poor they wasn't rich either.

Cousin Lena was my grandfather's brother's kinfolk. She was so nice and we had a ball. I remember we had to take a lot of shots to immunize us against diseases like typhoid. I cried and cried 'cause them doggone shots was hurtin'. I hate needles even today.

Everyone was glad we were safe but we wondered what the next step would be, and in the end we stayed with the Parkers a few months. Those among us that worked went back to work after the water subsided, but because there were so many of us it wasn't easy for Mama and Daddy to see where we could go. The authorities informed us that the Red Cross was gonna help, but they didn't do nothing: I remember my mother talking about it. There were still bills to pay: my mother had to pay for the new furniture they had to leave behind, as well as find a new shelter and buy more furniture and stuff for a home. That put my parents in a hell of a bind, and it caused them hardship for years, but they stood together. The loss of our new furniture, clothes and house came under an act of God by the insurance people. But the Collins and the Mannings have never been a lazy people: my folk knew what had to be done to survive.

So when we left our cousin Lena and her husband, my grandfather's first cousin, we went to live in a church. It belonged to our old pastor, Reverend C.J. Jackson, who had moved to Wyandotte County to build a church not very far from where Cousin Lena lived, just a matter of a few blocks in fact, at Fourth and Stewart; it's still there today. Reverend Jackson had started a new church using people who could build and who really knew their craft. They built a beautiful church. We stayed there for a few months, getting more shots and hand-me-downs from the Red Cross. I remember Mom and Dad saying, 'This is a crying shame: the white folk get way better and more.'

Reverend Jackson's wife we called Big Ethel. In times past she'd worked at an army base, and she ran the church even though her husband was the pastor. She loved children and believed in letting young people exercise their gifts. There was a group called the Sunshine Band, which I started singing in when I was about three. For some reason, when it was time for someone to take the lead in a song I always ended up doing it. This has happened to me almost all of my life.

Mother Jackson was the First Lady in Armourdale, and from time to time she kept me over, for she had no children. She was so good to me. She made these oatmeal cookies but boy, they were so nasty. I smiled like I really enjoyed them, but I couldn't wait to tell her I was full. She sent me home with a lot of them, which I threw away. I loved her but those cookies was like taking bad medicine.

Me and the triplets slept in cots in front of the offering table and the twins were in the balcony part of the church with Mama. Everything should have been OK, but Melvin hollered all night long because Mom was training him to sleep without her in his own bed. He just made up his mind that he was going to sleep with Mama and Dad. So Mama let him holler it out over a week. Lord, I couldn't sleep, and besides it was kind of creepy sleeping in the church.

Living in the church was so-so. I say so-so because downstairs where the kitchen was, where we ate, there was a coal bin with lots and lots of black coal. I was often left in the basement all by myself, and the coal bin area became a torture room to me: it was where I had to wash the dishes, pots and pans while the holy rollers were upstairs dancing and praising God. It seemed as though the more I washed the more there was to wash. To this day I've never liked to wash dishes and wherever I've lived one of the first things I ask is if there's a dishwasher.

Little Sis and her husband stayed in the church too. I can't recall her real name but Little Sis – who was a small woman – was married to Claude L. Jackson, the brother of the church pastor, C.J. Jackson. For a long time they lived in a section of the church balcony and it's said that one day she woke up and found Claude, her husband, lying next to her dead. I think Little Sis is still alive today.

There was another family that moved in, the Cruises I think they were. They must have had about eight kids. The coal bin was cleared out for them and it was so clean you'd never have thought coal had ever been in that room. There was an old man called Mr Thornton who lived in the basement too. Brother Thornton lived just a few feet from the coal bin. He made a room for himself by sectioning off part of the basement with draped curtains to give him some privacy. He said he'd rather be down there than be with his wife 'cause he couldn't stand her. He said she was the meanest woman. She died just a few years ago.

The only real good times we had was when the church had a weenie roast on the weekends. We put our hotdogs on a stick and cooked them, and we had plenty of Kool-Aid.

My second year in school was not a happy one. After the flood I went to a school called Keiling Elementary for one year, which was across the street from the church. I didn't like Keiling, the teachers or the children. I don't even remember my teacher's name. It felt bad, and I was miserable. It wasn't that they did anything to me and there wasn't a bad element, but I was used to Armourdale, where we were all kinfolk and people left their doors open. When I got to Keiling that wasn't the way and they wasn't the same.

It was like this until we moved from the Church of God in Christ to stay with Dr Alexander and his family, who lived about two or three blocks from the church. The Alexanders had a big three-storey house. Even at that place we were still given shots. I helped to watch over my younger brothers, which is why my mother tells them to this day, 'Marvan is your second mother: don't you ever forsake her.' I knew that was right. I was always washing and ironing for them. I ironed jeans for six boys: can you imagine that? Back in those days the iron was really heavy, and I used to just straighten the clothes out and let the iron sit on a spot for a minute. I'd almost cry. In fact, I'd rather get a whipping than iron all those jeans.

Dr Alexander and his wife picked us up from time to time and bought us things we needed. Mrs Alexander, who was a nice, beautiful lady, and looked almost white, would fetch me sometimes and take me to get shots, and sometimes she'd take me to one of her friends' restaurants. Dr Alexander, who delivered all of us, looked like he was from India. They had two children of their own – a boy and a girl. Their son was named Clyde: he was so handsome that I dreamed about him. Little did I know he was sick; I think he had seizures. His sister was Idora, who was in California. We stayed with them at their house for a few months until Idora came home to get married to this big-time doctor. After that Mama and Daddy started looking for a new place. Idora was a nice person, and she only died last year. They found her sitting in a chair in her home.

Living with the good doctor was beautiful. They had so much class and everyone knew them. They were big shots, and Dr Alexander was so proud to have delivered our triplets and twins.

My parents found a house in North Allis, and we moved there in 1953, when I was nine. After what my parents suffered during the flood, they got a house that sat upon a hill. Mother said, 'The water will get me no more.' It's our homestead to this day. It started as a shotgun house but has been added to over the years. Daddy bought the property from the street corner to where the house is located, so we have like two vacant lots that lead to the house. He grew beautiful flowers and bushes and everything in the garden. One year we even had a Christmas tree which we'd bought, and for some reason my daddy planted it on the lot near where you come onto the driveway, which we call the alley. See, in them days, kids didn't play in the front and tear up things like they do today. You played in the alley or in the backyard, to keep the front of the house looking nice.

So many times he said to Mama, 'Let's move out on a farm and have plenty of fresh air and space,' but he might as well have been talking to hisself because Mama just wouldn't leave the house, even when they were in good enough shape to buy a swanky place and even though many other people began to leave the neighborhood and it started to get run down. She's still there today. I try to get her to stay with me, but she says, 'Aw-naw.' She needs her space and she's very happy there; besides, memories of Daddy are in the house.

Mom kept a clean house, and you better believe we had chores on the weekends. But we also had fun too. Our Uncle Joe stayed with us. He worked for the city and on his payday he brought us a big bag of popcorn and vanilla wafers too. Ooh wee! On some Saturdays we watched the scary movies on TV. The next-door neighbors came too. You never had to worry that we were going to mess up your house. We were well-groomed children and respected people's houses and their possessions, like we did our own house. People used to visit and say to Mama, 'Ms Manning, how do you keep such a nice house with all these kids?'

They were good times – but although we enjoyed living in Allis, I think our best years were in Armourdale, because that's where I was very close to my grandmother. My mother was strict with us: she wasn't the kind of woman who didn't look after her children. Every fifteen or twenty minutes she used to say, 'All right, what you all doing out there?' She kept a watch on us all the time. But I was kind of rebellious, you know, and sometimes I'd sneak off. Two of my brothers would sneak out of the windows at night when Mom and Daddy was asleep. They told us that when they got grown.

After we fled the flood Grandmother Collins got sick, and on her sickbed she called each grandchild and talked to us individually. My grandmother wasn't a dumb woman but she was different from her high-flitting, educated sisters. She knew of Grandpa's weaknesses and would get on him in her own way. One time he wanted to save money for the church and wanted to cut back on house things. Food was one. Mother said she gave Grandpa potatoes and water with no seasonings. No meat, no cornbread – just potatoes and water. Oh, he rose up and fussed and she said, 'You said we had to cut back.'

Like I said, Grandmother was not a dumb woman. She knew her husband was tight and she had to look out for her children. On her sick bed she had a lawyer to come in and put the property in her children's names, for she said, 'Nathaniel will disown all of you and you'll get nothing.' She also said that because of his hard-headedness his church wouldn't grow. I'd often heard her fussing with Grandpa.

Grandmother loved to dress like her mother. She'd buy things and hide them for a few months. Then she'd wear them and Grandpa would ask, 'Is that new?'

She'd say, 'No, this is an old dress.' Mama said she liked to comb her hair and make sure everything was in place.

One day, in January 1954 when I was nine, I was coming from school and my triplet brothers and the twins hollered out, 'Grandma is dead, Grandma is dead!' They didn't know what death was all about, but I fell down dazed next to the curb of the street. I realized what she said had come true, even though I never wanted to believe it. We found out she'd lived with a tumor in her head for a long time.

After my grandmother died my grandfather married again. My step-grandmother's name was Rosie. We didn't like her at first but she proved herself to be a beautiful woman. She wasn't very educated but she loved the Lord.

This was around the time my baby brother, Winfred, was born. He came nine years after the rest of us; I was a teenager by then. All my life when my mother was pregnant I knew what it was but not exactly, because they didn't talk about those things freely. When I was small and she was pregnant I'd say, 'I want a baby tutter.' I couldn't say sister, I said 'tutter'. And so when mother got this baby up to nine years after all of us was born, she swore up and down that she had too many kids and that she couldn't afford to take care of another one. She decided that she would give it – whether it was a boy or a girl – to her oldest brother, Nathaniel, who stayed in Topeka. He worked for Firestone and was the one that ran from airplanes after the war; his wife wasn't able to conceive. So when my step-grandmother called and said, 'Tootsie's had a 9-pound boy,' I was angry. That's all I heard: '*boy*'.

I said, 'You tell her, don't she bring that baby in this house. I don't want it. I don't like it.' I was mad because that was my last chance for a baby sister.

I don't know why we called Winfred 'Calteaky'. We called him that first but ended up calling him Gee Gee. I really don't know where either name came from. Right now he's a fireman and it pisses me off because they call him Winnie. I got onto him about it two or three weeks ago. I said, 'Why the hell you let them call you Winnie? How come they don't call you Gee Gee or Winfred?' It makes me mad. It brings something up in me, you know what I'm saying. It brings some negative feelings about times past of things that white people have called black people. But they love him, there's no doubt about it. He drives the fire truck. He's well thought of and everybody knows him. They've made him one of the union men and he goes all across the country representing the firemen. He's been sent to functions for the Federal government as their representative. He's also musically inclined. If anybody here in Kansas City needs a bass player in the gospel field they'll turn his name in. He's like my mother: he's a fanatic. He knows every song that comes up and can play it. He played drums first and then he went on the electric bass.

CHAPTER 11

The Manning Singers

Before she died, Grandma prophesied that we children were going to sing. After the flood she told Mama, 'Tootsie, you keep hollering about these kids. The Lord gave them to you for a purpose and they are going to sing.'

Mama said, 'Ah, you're just talking.'

Grandmother replied, 'Oh yeah, you just wait and see.' She was right. Every word came true.

Not long after Grandma died, Mama called us in one day. She'd seen a lady called Louise Nolan who had two girls: they were known as the Nolan Singers. They could really sing, and they were so popular. Louise was considered the best piano player in town. Something happened to Mama when she saw and heard them, and that's what led her to believe that what Grandma had said a few years before was true. So we started to perform with our mother as the Manning Singers, a gospel group.

I liked to sing, but Mom drilled and drilled us to a point that I wanted to hide. She'd even threaten us if we seemed like we wasn't interested enough. Sometimes she'd almost give up and we'd stop for a while. I'd be kind of glad but before you knew it there we was again. 'Yah come on in here,' she'd say, and get on the piano and start drilling us again. She drilled us in harmony for about a year. We came into the knowledge of how to keep our parts in harmony, learn the words and perfect our timing. Sometimes she'd bribe us: 'If you learn this song I'll give you a nickel.' That usually worked and we'd get down to it.

We began to venture out to the churches to perform. We were good, very good in fact, and the triplets and twins were an added attraction. People often said that I sounded like a grown woman singing. From Friday to Sunday we sometimes did four or five selections. Later, as we grew in confidence and experience, we began to sing for longer and do full programs – and when you did that you got half of the church collection.

We helped to make ends meet, because although Daddy never missed a day's work the railroad did not pay very much and Mama and Daddy still had to pay the bills from the flood.

Sometimes Daddy was the narrator, saying what the next song was and what it meant. He knew the scriptures. We sang a lot of songs by The Caravans, Dorothy Love-Coates and the Gospel Harmonettes, the Davis Singers, the Blind Boys of Alabama and the Clara Ward Singers. Mama kept us up to date. Our reputation spread and we began opening for different singers when they came to Kansas City. We also traveled to places like Chicago, Minneapolis, Memphis, Texas, California, Oklahoma and Iowa. Sometimes we went on the train because Daddy worked on the railroad and we could get passes. We were a disciplined bunch of children. We didn't dare be unruly – as Mama had only to give us a look that meant we were headed for a whipping. People gave us money and porters on the train gave us food and candy, 'cause they didn't know that children could be well behaved like that.

We were on the road for quite a while. I remember one time Daddy went with us. When we were driving from Texas to Oklahoma we came through a flood. We thought we were going to die as the water was deep when we waded from the car. Daddy could hardly see, but they'd put sticks in the road to help guide the way. Most of the boys were asleep but not me. Even I thought our time might be over: the only ones who could swim was me and Daddy. Thank the Lord we made it.

Sometimes it was real rough. It was stipulated in our contract that people were to feed us, and they'd come up with hot dogs. Mama didn't go for that – she'd go and buy groceries and show the people what a real dinner was like. They'd be ashamed, and sometimes she ended up feeding them as well.

We did this for six years or more, but when we went to California it started to get too much for Mama, who did everything for us and had never thought of employing a nanny. She developed Bell's Palsy – which was like a stroke – at the age of thirty-six, and she lost the zest to go on. I was about sixteen when we stopped.

CHAPTER 12

School Days

After a few months at Keiling, during the time we lived with the Reverend Jackson, I went to a school called Dunbar North Elementary School, which went to the sixth grade. It was on Seventh Street but it's gone now – they tore it down. I started there the last half of the second grade and I liked it a lot better. There was also a Dunbar South, about a block south of our school, which all six of my brothers attended.

The principal at Dunbar North was Miss Superior Miller. She was friends with Dr and Mrs Alexander so of course she gave me some special attention. Miss Miller was a beautiful person, but in those days teachers took no mess and sometimes they could be too mean. She took a liking to me and sometimes she'd call for me out of the class to hand-deliver a note to other teachers. There wasn't no pigeonholes, or what we called squawk boxes.

Miss Nicolas was my second grade teacher and I liked her very much. When it was time for reading she'd brag on me to the other students: 'Girls and boys, do you see how Marva gets compounds and words together? She picks out the root and she comes up with her words.' I was so proud. It made me think about my Miss Jones from my first school.

In the third grade Miss Wilson was the meanest woman I've ever been around in my life. She was mean to everybody and acted like she didn't like children. I got tired of her. I'd been telling my mother about her and how I didn't know how much I could stand, then one day she went too far. We usually took our lunch to school, but that day I went home and told Mama I wasn't going back because of how she was treating everyone. My mother wrote her a letter, telling her to have a heart and not a gizzard. After that Miss Wilson didn't bother me any more: it straightened her up. Even so, I was glad to get out of that third grade class.

Miss Martin in the fourth grade was a good teacher, very pleasant. Even though she was teaching all classes she was the school's music teacher and could play the piano pretty good. When it was time for our music lesson my voice must have stood out above the rest, except for my friend Louise Hollinshed. She had a beautiful voice. Every time there was a play or a song to be performed I was first in line for the lead part, and if another was needed it was Louise. You could bank on that. This happened all the way to the tenth grade.

In the fourth grade both me and Louise sang in a play called *In The Land Of Dreams Come True*; I was the star. I had to remember lots of lines and sing different songs. We performed it at Sumner High School, where I would eventually graduate. Mrs Alexander got me the most beautiful blue and white dress for the show.

By this time I was used to singing in public, but it was in school, I suppose, where the performing bug really got me. Everybody at school thought I did very well; they were crazy about my voice. So from the fourth grade all the way up to the ninth any time something came up they wanted me to be in it.

The same happened at North East Junior High School on Fourth and Troup, which I attended from the seventh to the ninth grade. I walked there, because by then we were on Allis Street. The music teacher was Miss Thelma Hamilton. She's deceased now. That lady was very good at her craft, and Louise and I continued to get lead parts.

Now they had a girl group at that school, called The Rayons. One of them played the piano and later on they made a record. The Rayons and I worked in the same classes. Years later they recorded for Forte, my husband Ellis's label. But they didn't do too much in school as I remember.

When integration eventually came they closed up North East Junior High School and bussed the black kids to the white schools.

In my opinion that was the worst thing they could ever do. Bussing the black kids to white schools was supposed to help promote integration, give the children a better education and teach them how to know and accept other races, but I believe the authorities didn't think it through properly. They thought that by forcing blacks and whites together and creating integrated schools it would get rid of prejudice. But, believe it or not, all races have their prejudices, including American blacks. If some of us are really honest, we don't necessarily want to mingle with whites no more than they want to mingle with us. When integration in schools happened, lots of the children and teachers held on to their prejudice even though they tried to hide it. Looking back, what makes me angry is that the government took perfectly good black schools and closed them up: many newly built black schools were torn down in the name of integration. I felt it made out our teachers wasn't good enough to teach our own children. All the black schools needed was the same equipment and the same resources that the white schools had, so they could keep up. But at that time it was like the rich (the whites) got it all and the poor (the blacks) got nothing.

So they bussed our children to schools in white areas. Because of that, black children was on the street corner standing in the rain, sleet and snow at six o'clock in the morning waiting for a bus. Not only were they vulnerable to child molesters lurking about but also their playtime was shortened.

Once integration started in education some black children got out of hand and started behaving badly. This was because they went out of the area where people knew them and kept them in line. When I was a kid every parent in the neighborhood knew every child and where they should be. If they saw the children doing wrong they'd reprimand them and then tell their parents. Often my mama knew how we'd acted up before we got home. But when the children went to school outside the local neighborhood there was no way to keep an eye on them. When we had separate black schools most of the kids went to church and neighborhood gatherings. They went swimming together and did arts and craft. Once they started going to out-of-neighborhood schools the sense of community got broken up. Gangs started, and became riddled with outsiders who brought dope and bad habits to the community.

To my mind integration hasn't really worked. Things have got better in some ways, but there's still a deep-seated prejudice in many white Americans. One thing I discovered on my travels is that the American white person thinks differently from white Europeans.

After North East Junior High School I went to Sumner High School on Eighth Avenue. It was 1961; I was seventeen and in the tenth grade. By then I was a person who preferred my own company rather than being around other girls. There was a teacher there by the name of Oyama Tate. We used to laugh at him because when he got in his car to drive to school it looked like it was going sideways as it was so old and badly in need of repair. One of the teachers who really impacted my life at Sumner High School was Mr Edward Beesley. He knew his black history and everybody feared him. He was also the football coach. When we had assemblies the boys would actually boo him on the stage; he'd be speaking and they'd chant his name, 'Beese, Beese, Beese, Beese!' And we'd think oh my God, worried about what he'd do when he got hold of them. When you went to his room you were afraid. He got me one time. The way our school marks were graded in those days was one, two, three, four, five – one being the top, of course. So the first semester, I think, I got a four minus, and he kept me after school. He ran with me until I came up to a two, which was a very good mark to get out of his room. I liked his class because he made black history so interesting and he was so intricate about things; like he'd tell us about the slaves being used as belly warmers and things like that. He went into a lot of detail, and it was like he was acting when he talked.

There was also Mr Thatcher, who owned one of the first black funeral homes in Kansas City, and Miss Jo Ann Featherson, who I really liked. She was an English teacher, and used to tell us poems. I think she lives in New York now and does some acting. I made 2s in her room in the eleventh grade. One of my favorite subjects was English, and I always liked to read. Miss Bloodworth was the senior English teacher. When I got to the twelfth grade she taught me. She'd taught everybody in my family who had been through the school. She was elderly, and I remember she wore her hair up in a pompadour and had glasses. You could tell she was a high-class woman. She had never gotten married: the story was that her husband-to-be was in a car crash on the way to the wedding ceremony and died. But not everybody wanted to be in her class 'cause she was known as Miss

Tough Bird. You had to know *Macbeth* and all that stuff, and I'd get mad because I said how the hell's *Macbeth* going to help me to make it in the world? But she was a really good teacher. Let me tell you, the smartest of the smart was blessed if they got a 3 out of her class. When she realized that we wasn't catching on and saw a whole class full of dummies she started crying. That kind of tickled me a little bit, but then I felt sorry for her. She said, 'I don't know what I'm doing, for I can't teach you all well. You all don't seem to catch on.' I think I finally squeaked out with a 3- . Bless her heart; she's gone on to glory now.

We had another teacher called Mr Van Trese who didn't take no messing from us. He had what he called the Board of Education. We girls knew better, but some of the fellas acted up in his class and then he'd say, 'Come here,' and he'd get his Board of Education – a board like you'd roll dough on with a handle, with 'Board of Education' written on it. He'd take 'em out the door and that Board of Education would be on their butts. Bam! I mean, you could hear that bitch hitting someone from a long way away.

I had another very good teacher by the name of Mr Lyons; I think he taught math, like Miss Hannon. She and my grandmother was friends: they belonged to the same church. When you got out of her room you knew the basics of math and you knew other things about life too. Those are just some of the teachers I had who had an impact on me.

At Sumner High I was pretty quiet and laid-back: I didn't have too much to say. I remember Mr Boon walking down the hall one day and he saw me standing outside. I wasn't a person that kept up trouble in a class, so I think I'd probably been talking in class or was a minute late or something; you only had a certain amount of time to go to the next class. He said, 'Marva, what are you doing standing out here?'

I said, 'Miss Nicholls told me to come outside.'

He said, 'Uh-huh. Well, for that you're going to sing a song in the assembly.' That was my punishment.

They had gym classes at school but I didn't do much sport, though I was a pretty good runner. I sure can't run now.

I got expelled for fighting at Sumner when I was in the tenth grade, about fourteen or fifteen. We didn't have gangs for girls when I was in Junior High, but we did have what we used to call groupies. Our group was a group of peace most of the time, but for me this trend ended in my junior year when I was bullied by one of my groupies. I don't know why – perhaps it was my looks or something that was upsetting this particular girl, Myrtle Givens, who started gunning for me. She was short and a bully – and a fast girl too. I don't think she was more than 5ft high. My parents had trained me to stay away from trouble, so I kept away from her: I ate my lunch in the English classroom. I did this for about two months, but then one day I heard she'd brought a knife for me and was going to let me have it. I made up my mind I was tired of avoiding her, I'd had enough, so I decided to go to the lunch room and be ready for whatever happened. So I went down to the cafeteria and sat at the table where they were and started eating my lunch. They really had good food there: I'd usually have something hot or sometimes I'd bring a sandwich from home. So I sat at the long table, about 8ft in length, while Myrtle talked loud and gave wolf calls to degrade me. I was sitting quietly, holding my cool, minding my own business and not saying nothing, when Myrtle got up from her seat and came over. This hen peeled an orange and threw the peel in my food. What did she do that for? Before I knew it I'd picked up my glass of water, doused her, leapt out of my chair and tried to kill her, whipping her and socking her all over the floor. I was in a blind rage. We was near the entrance door, and before I knew it I'd accidentally kicked my teacher and knocked off her glasses when she was trying to break us up. I think I had the best of it, though. Myrtle was bleeding, and I'd torn off her blouse. I even shouted to my other so-called friends at the table, 'Come on! Do ya want some too?' They never opened their mouths.

The principal of Sumner High School, Mr Thompson, came in. He was so mad, and said this kind of thing had never happened in his school before. Fortunately my fourth grade teacher spoke up for me, telling him how I'd tried to avoid a confrontation with the girl. They found out that Myrtle really had brought a big dagger that she said was for me.

In the end we both got expelled. Mr Thompson called our parents and I told them what happened and why. He sent us home one at a time, for he didn't want us to fight any more: Myrtle lived only half a block from me. I remember him telling my mother that I just tore the girl up with no mercy. Mama looked innocent, but when we got home she said, 'I'm glad you whooped her ass. It was long overdue, and she's supposed to be your friend.' She didn't get mad because I told her what had happened. A lot of times Mama said that if we got in a fight and we got beat that we'd get beaten again when we came home. She knew her kids: we wasn't the kind to start nothing, but she didn't want us to cow down either. I was kind of tomboyish. I had to fight many a battle when my brothers were in school, and had to look out for them because they was kind of scared until they got to Junior High, when they could handle it. But until then I was the one that fought all their battles.

So I was expelled, but it was only for a couple of days because my teacher had stood up for me. She said, 'It wasn't entirely Marva's fault – she was provoked.'

When I got back to school I thought I was going to be embarrassed, but everybody said, 'Hello, Joe Louis.'

Even my art teacher, Mr Redding, smiled and said, 'Hi, Joe Louis.' I think this went on for a couple of weeks. All of a sudden people looked at me differently and they were glad I'd done what I'd done because Myrtle was a bully. Before, see, they'd known me as a quiet person. They knew I could sing and play the piano because I was on the talent shows and things like that, but I wasn't a fast girl because my mother was strict. When girls were going out at fifteen and sixteen I had to stay home – and that kind of made me an outsider to the happenings that was going on during the weekend. When the kids were going to the shows and wearing stockings I couldn't go: it was because of the way I was raised and the churches that I came under. But the main thing was that Mama wanted to be sure I didn't mess up. And because of that people at the school thought she was a good mother.

So I stood up for myself, and Myrtle didn't say nothing to me for a while afterwards. Her boyfriend warned me that she was still out to get me, and I had to get protection from teachers at ballgames in school. But at the end, when she began to mature, everything was all right between us again. We didn't run and do stuff together, but she was very nice and Myrtle's family was nice too. I used to go to their house sometimes and have a good time. She was just a young teenage girl going on twenty-five or thirty.

When she got grown and left school she got married. Her first husband she shot with a double-barreled shotgun, but she pleaded self-defense and they let her off that time. She got married again and did the same thing to her second husband. So then they sent her on up to serve time in Lansing State Penitentiary. She did some time there, and one time my mother went up there visiting. Myrtle remembered my mother but Mama didn't recognize her. Myrtle was glad to see her and said, 'How's Marva? Is she with James Brown? Oh, I'm so happy!' And years afterwards, when she got out of prison and was with her friends, she'd see me and say, 'This is my friend Marva that used to sing with James Brown.' I heard years later that she'd passed away. I don't know if she was sick but I do know she was on narcotics.

My girlfriend who used to help her said, 'One thing about Myrtle, when she was that way, she stayed away from the children. She didn't let the children see her.'

Later, when I got with James, Sumner High School presented me with a picture in the school yearbook. They invited me back and I gave a talk about working with James Brown and how children should be prepared for life after school.

It was while I was at Sumner that I went out with my first boyfriend, a young boy called George Bagsby who really liked me. He was able to go and come as he pleased on the weekend because his father, Charles, was a drunk and a bootlegger. As I mentioned earlier, he was the one who sat on his porch and scared me. George partied with one of my so-called friends: he wasn't faithful to me or her, and he had a drinking problem too. The Bagsbys also had a daughter, Annie Lee, a very pretty girl. She accidentally shot and killed her husband's mother, and his family vowed to kill her – although she was trying to protect herself from her husband. The word was they were all hot tempered and nobody could understand how she could stay with him. The husband played like he had forgiven her, but one day she was found in the park dead. I guess you'll ask what has this to do with George. Well, George being her brother and my first love gave me my first taste of betrayal from a man. And that experience to some degree carried over as I grew up. I tell you this story because all the men who came into my life, educated or not, have caused me pain.

CHAPTER 13

Out in the World

I graduated from Sumner High School in 1962. After school I got my first full-time job at a clothing factory: I was eighteen years old. I worked at Fashion Built Garments in Kansas City, sewing fox fur collars to some of the best coats in the world. When you got a coat from Fashion Built you got one of the best-made coats there was at that time: they were top of the line coats for well-off people. I did this for a couple of years. My hours were from eight till four and I made $1.40 an hour. I was lucky I didn't have to travel far from home: I had to walk about two blocks to the Quindaro bus line, which still runs today, and I didn't even have to change buses because it went to Missouri and Fashion Built was down the street from Folgers's Coffee. I'd smell that coffee every morning; the aroma was just beautiful. I think Folgers's is still there today.

I was a green little girl and I worked with women who could sew double and triple the number of furs to silk collars. They worked like machines. The quota was seventeen to nineteen a day, and after that you were on piecework: your hourly wage went up for each collar over what was required. The other women doubled and tripled their quota, but I fell behind and struggled even trying to make the initial number. Some of them felt sorry for me and did a few for me, so at least I made the minimum required. I remember one day I lost my count and thought I'd lost a collar. I got so anxious I kind of hollered, because I knew they cost a lot of money. Of course, this being my first job it scared me. The other women just laughed, and told me in so many words that they were going to make a woman out of me, this so-called 'greeny'.

We worked at a lighted table in two rows facing one another. I remember a few of the other girls: Mattie, Shirley, Elizabeth, and a Jewish lady from Europe who'd been in one of Hitler's concentration camps. She showed me the number that was still tattooed on her arm and talked sometimes about how she'd lost most of her family. She had a habit she couldn't break: if just a teaspoon of food was left after she'd cooked a meal she'd put it in a TV dinner tray and freeze it. This was because she remembered times when there was nothing to eat during the war.

There's always someone in your life who tries to show you the ropes and shares their experience with you. Usually it's someone who's not from your own family. The person that helped me at this time was Eugenia Whorton Weatherby, a fantastic lady from New Orleans: I call her Gene. She'd not lived in Kansas City long and we became good friends; we're still good friends to this day, and she's been like a second mother to me. Her speech is a mixture of Creole and English, and she's proud of her New Orleans roots. Her brother, Mr Whorton, was a big shot. She's eighty now. We always keep in touch, and even though it may be several years since we last saw each other, when we get back together it's like we've never been apart.

Gene had been married to a professional army man and they'd decided to part, but she took good care of her children and they turned out to be beautiful. Andrea, her eldest daughter, had the knack of using guns like it was nothing. Of course, her father had taught her how to handle weapons. She'd march with a rifle and do those hand turns like soldiers do. She was also an A student and was ahead of her time. Eventually, as she grew older, she became a lawyer and went on to greater heights. She now works for the government in a very important post and her duties take her all over the world. Margo, Gene's second daughter, was an A student as well. She became a postwoman and now has her own tax business.

Gene knew of my struggles. One of the things she taught me was how to tell other people at Fashion Built to get off my back. In other words, she taught me to be assertive. She told me what to say to some of the silly women at the factory, and when I followed her words it surprised the hell out of them and we all ended up laughing. After my initial fears it became a joy to go to work there. It was a seasonal job, though, and I was laid off for about three months of the year.

Then in 1962 I went to key-punch school. Key-punchers had just come in back then. We used special cards with holes punched into them, which they used on early computers like the first IBM machines. It was as boring as hell.

After I came out of there I worked at City Hall for a while. But I just couldn't stand being in an office, and I began to ask God to lead me 'cause I wanted to be a full-time singer. By now I'd stopped performing with my family as the Manning Singers and had joined the Whitney Singers, which was run by a lady called Miss Alma Whitney. She had several gospel groups where young people came together, had a good time and did something positive. She was studying to be a nurse and when she finally got through her exams she was one of the top administrators at the Kansas City Western Missouri mental hospital. Alma had the Whitney Tones, which were all boys, then the Whitney-ettes and the Whitney Specials, which were all girls; finally there was the Whitney Singers. We all rehearsed on a Saturday and she'd feed us with Floppy Joes, potato chips, soda pop and stuff like that. We'd be playing out in the yard having fun until it was our time to rehearse.

My brother Melvin was in the original Whitney Tones. They're still going strong today, but it's not the same group: members have changed over the years.

As a girl you worked yourself up from the Whitney-ettes. First you were a Whitney-ette, then a Whitney Special and then a Whitney Singer. I wasn't a Whitney-ette for long, and became a Whitney Special because Alma saw I could catch on: what she taught me I learnt quickly. By this time I was a Whitney Singer. There were five of us, all of us except one able to play the piano. We also had a drummer called Melvyn: I can't think of his last name – he's grown now and got kids. We also had a bass player. One time Alma had a woman bass player, which was rare in those days.

During rehearsals I met Harry Olander Whitney, Alma's brother-in-law, who became my first husband. I guess I was about eighteen; Harry was two or three years older. He played the piano but only in one key, F sharp – although he played the hell out of it. After a while we got married, but music was the only thing we had in common. We were together from about 1962 to about '65, and during that time I gave birth to my first child, a beautiful little girl, Sherrie LaYvonne Whitney.

Around that time I was asked to play piano for a female group called the Patterson Girl Group. They could really sing. Although they were younger than me and still in high school, we were doing pretty good together.

One day, though, Harry told me to quit singing. He just said, 'It's either me or the group.'

So I said, 'OK, it's the group. Bye!' I didn't hesitate.

Harry wasn't a bad husband, but he was the kind of man that if he gave you $20 to go to the store and the food came to $21, then he'd get you to take $1 of groceries back. He used to love to play cards and went out every Thursday. I decided, OK you got Thursday, so Friday or Saturday is my night out and he had no problem with that. The only qualm he had was about me singing in the clubs because he was into gospel music. It's a funny thing, though: after I got with James Brown both of his brothers quit the gospel world and followed me into show business, playing bass and piano.

After about two years together I divorced Harry and took Sherrie with me. I don't think she ever liked me. If she fell over or got a shot she'd be mad at me all day. But I loved her and did the best I could. After the divorce times wasn't always good for us. The court awarded me a dollar a day for Sherrie, and sometimes Harry fell behind. If he bought her any clothes he didn't send them home: everything she wore when she stayed with me I bought for her. She, of course, was a daddy's baby and still is today.

We still don't get along, and sometimes I wonder why. Maybe she got this negative talk from her father because I was in show business. When singing took me away from home, I didn't leave her with just anybody: I left her with my parents. She was my parents' first grandchild and we all love her dearly. She never had to want for nothing.

So I stuck with the girl group, but one by one the girls started falling in love and having babies and we just kind of dispersed. I decided I was going to go on, and things rolled over pretty good for me in the music field. My favorite singers back then were Dionne

Warwick, Martha and The Vandellas, Etta James and Bettye Everett. I could always find something in listening to what was hip in those days. And I also liked singing standards.

I was still working in an office nine to five to pay the bills and wasn't making much money. To help make ends meet I started singing in clubs at weekends. There was a popular nightclub I used to sing at regularly which was owned by Ollie Gates: I think he's still alive today. Every Thursday was talent night. I started off there making $7 a night and worked my way up to become one of the highest-paid – I think it was $14 a night. So I was really making more from singing than I was working in an office full-time. In those days $60 paid the rent. I think when I left there I was making $20 and I was packing the house, though I was too young to be upstairs where they had a bar. Mr Gates kept us younger performers downstairs, where he got us Coca-Colas and called us one by one to do our thing.

I did some gospel things and I combined preaching with singing. Boy, I tell you, they were eating it up. The crowd wasn't used to hearing a young woman preach and sing. I also did hits of the day by people like Bettye Everett, Gladys Knight, Etta James and Dionne Warwick, a wide range of songs though not too much blues. I really didn't learn to sing the blues until much later.

During this time I was still close to Gene. When I was looking for a place to stay after I divorced Harry, she told me that the woman who owned the place she lived in had two upstairs vacancies: three rooms and a shared bath, and a single room with a shared bath. First I lived in the three-room apartment and then later, when things got tougher financially, in the single room. It had gotten that bad but it wasn't so bad, 'cause I was like Gene's daughter or one of the family. Me and Sherrie was mostly downstairs. It was a home from home.

One time Gene pierced Sherrie's ears. She had done it many times for people and she knew how to work with the ear so it wouldn't hurt. Even so, I thought Sherrie should have a little bit of vodka to give her courage and numb the pain. We gave her a little sip, and I think I was more scared than she was. I went to the back porch and put my hands over my ears because she screamed anyway. I almost died, but in a few minutes it was over. Looking back, I think the vodka made Sherrie feel funny, and that's why she screamed. Sherrie had single piercings on each ear, but in later years we both got two pierced on each side as that was the style.

The ladies I worked with at Fashion Built used to talk about cleaning their houses on Saturday while drinking a half pint of vodka, and how nice and clean their houses looked. I decided to try it myself: in them days you could get it with the orange juice in it. I cleaned my house all right – it was spotless – but I drank too much vodka and threw up during the evening. I ended up on my knees I was so drunk, hanging my head over a stool. When I opened my eyes the room was spinning. When I closed my eyes my head was still spinning. Hell, I didn't know whether to open or close them. I promised the Lord that if He let me get out of that I'd never drink like that anymore. I have kept my promise.

In 1963, when I was nineteen, I joined a local group called Tommy & The Derbys, who I'd met from singing and going in the clubs. I became the only female singer the group had. Other girls sang on the show but I was part of the band. I stayed with them for about four years. A black hearse was our means of transportation many times. One time, though, we rode it to a gig in Oklahoma and lost a wheel – boy, we jumped out in a hurry. That was the end of the hearse.

Tommy Gadson was the bandleader, nicknamed Tuttie. He had a pet monkey, I remember. Even though we had packed houses, he made sure he had plenty of bootleg whisky to sell: his suits were full of bottles. He was a very outgoing character, and is now in California doing well. Tuttie's wife at the time was Ann. He had four children and his oldest, his son, Tommy Junior, is a minister here in Kansas City.

Tuttie was a man of his word, and if he said he was going to pay you a certain amount then that's what you got paid. You didn't have to worry about your money.

Harry was the Derbys' bass player – he died about two years ago. Junior Chisholm, who we used to call Chiz, played sax and died playing it. He was doing a gig one time; he walked off the stage and fell down dead. I think I was in California at the time so this was after '77. Roy was a very good drummer; his real name was Namon Thompson. We were engaged at one time. I don't know why they called him Roy. He was the Derbys' second drummer, and then he got a break with Hank Ballard. They said Hank had handpicked him to play in Vegas. Chopsticks played trumpet. I can't recall what his real name was. His brother was a famous piano player. I haven't seen him since about '64 or '65 and we don't know where he is; I don't even know if he's dead or alive.

Tuttie sang and played guitar – he could even play it with his toes. He was very popular with the ladies and fathered many children. I met one recently, who Tuttie had only just found out he'd had.

Tuttie's father, Harry Gadson, was a top drummer in Kansas City, and Tuttie's brother James was the Derbys' first drummer. He was the opposite of Tuttie, the quiet one, but still popular with the girls. He got married to a girl called Barbara and in the mid-'60s left Kansas City for California where he still lives today. He went on to play drums with Dyke & The Blazers and then Charles Wright & The Watts 103rd Street Rhythm Band. He wrote and sang on the group's hit 'Loveland'. James and Barbara are still married. I'm still in contact with him and visited him after my last tour in Japan. He has a studio in the back of his house and is still heavily in demand as a session drummer.

The Derbys were one of the top bands in Kansas City at the time and had shows at party houses. When performers came into town Tommy & The Derbys was always the band that would play the backup music. They kept abreast of all the hit songs and could play the blues too. Tuttie got offered all the best jobs there was, backing up people like Dionne Warwick. They'd usually use The Derbys to back them up but would bring their own guitar man or band director. Dionne Warwick, for example, used to come with her husband who played guitar. And that's how I got a chance to be the opening act for a lot of performers, like Ike and Tina Turner, who were living in St Louis then. We were the opening act. We also played with Bettye Everett, Bobby 'Blue' Bland, The Drifters, Etta James and Johnny 'Guitar' Watson. I remember Johnny was living in St Louis at the time. He was a cousin of our drummer Roy Thompson and he'd just gotten out of prison. I remember he had his two children with him. We played at a place called Rosemary's in Kansas City, Missouri, and I remember Johnny said to me, 'While I'm on the stage can you watch my children for me?' So I did. Rosemary's was a hot, top-notch place. When you went there you knew you were going somewhere.

Gene Weatherby and her children took care of Sherrie when I had to work with the band. The Weatherbys understood my singing career; they knew Tuttie Gadson too. All of them could sew and they helped me make my stage gowns when I performed with The Derbys. Even when I was home Sherrie was downstairs with the Weatherbys. There was a piano in the downstairs hallway and Gene, who could read by notes, played hymns. I played too, and we sang and had a good time. Gene was a good cook, of course, coming as she did from New Orleans: she could make good gumbo and she had a special touch when she made pork roast and Mac & Cheese. We were just like family. Living there was one of the most pleasant experiences in my life, and I'll always love the Weatherbys: they're my extended family and helped me when I needed it most, especially with me coming out of a divorce and being a single mom. I love the fact that my mother and father appreciated them too, for they knew I was in a safe place.

When I started getting billed up and making a name for myself in Kansas City, there was a gentleman named Dancing Bobby, a dice player who wanted to be a pimp but didn't quite have what it took. There was a place called the Peppermint Lounge on Troost (until the Catholic Church finally shut it down), which was one of the places I used to sing. Every Wednesday or Thursday night they had singing contests, and Dancing Bobby encouraged me. He said, 'Come on, Marva, come on! You gon' sing, you gon' sing.' You know, we were kind of tight. And sure enough I took part and won it fair and square. That's when I paired up for a minute with a gentleman called Little Joe. He was a very nice-looking young man and we did duets together as a couple for a while. He jumped over five or six chairs and did the splits. There was also a man who could eat glass. There were a lot of unusual acts back in those days.

The Derbys and Tuttie were loved and followed by all kinds of people: rogues, pimps and other ruffians. I didn't like it: they scared the hell out of me. I used to ask Tuttie why he let those kind of people come around as soon as we started rehearsing; I just didn't need it. One of the local gangsters always seemed to be hanging around Tuttie's house. One day I'd had enough of them all, and I said something to Bobby Lowe, one of the MCs of the Derbys' show at that time – he's dead and gone now – about the company we kept. I told him I was tired of trash hanging around because it wasn't good for the business: where Tuttie went you knew a bunch of trash was coming. I was always taught that if you dig in trash and hang around

71

with trash you get your hands dirty. And there's another saying we have: how can you walk with a chimneysweeper without getting a little smutty? Bobby, though, was a man who could walk on the dirty side of the street and still come out clean. He was able to get along with the gangsters because he had the ability to become one himself – but he chose to be the better man in outward appearance. But this didn't fool me: a few things went down and I knew he knew something about it. He had connections. Bobby took me aside, as he was afraid the gangsters was going to hear us, and he actually shook me. He whispered, 'Get your head back in there. Don't you know they'll beat the shit out of you for what you said?'

I knew that for him to do that he had to care about me, and that he was afraid for me. It made me even more nervous about them. I ran back to the house and hollered, 'Gene, get me a gun!' I was nervous and excited. So I got a gun and I think for about a week or two I carried that little .22 pistol with me for protection until things cooled off. I was right to be wary. Some of them got caught for stealing and even for rape. You name it, they done it.

I've always been the type of person that if I have something to say I say it and I stand up on it. Just because you're older or younger or even if I don't know you, I'll still express my opinions. That's the way I was raised. I've always been outspoken and I was taught at an early age to stand up for myself. My mother was just so particular. When we were children our friends didn't come over to our house until my mother had vetted them. My mother wanted to know who their parents were; she could look at them and read them, even as a child or a teenager, and she'd either tell us to stay away from them or tell them come over here. That's the way it was. Truly, that's the reason why I'm a loner today.

One day in the early '60s I happened to be on a show with Bobby 'Blue' Bland that Willie Cyrus, a top black promoter, brought to Kansas City. He still books people today, I believe. Bobby Bland came to town – his drummer was Jabo Starks; he later joined James Brown – and he evidently liked what he heard. I think Ivy Campbell was his regular singer back then, and she could really sing too. Bobby's manager, a Mr Green, was so impressed with me that he asked me if I wanted to go on the show with Mr Bland. I was very excited and said yes. That night Mr Bland talked with me and told me what he expected of me. He was very kind. Afterwards, though, doubts crept in and I started having second thoughts. Mr Green called me the next morning and told me what time we were to leave, but I made some excuses and chickened out. I was very young and felt insecure without the Derbys. So that was the end of that.

Tommy & The Derbys eventually moved to California, and I went out with there with them for a time. They moved because the work got slim when the two unions in Kansas City merged, and they hoped there'd be more going on out west. We used to have a white musicians' union and a black one, and the black union got jobs in the white nightclubs because people wanted to hear some blues and soul. That's the reason why musicians like Count Basie came through Kansas City at one time and could make good money, during the days when they were selling whisky and stuff to make a living. We resisted a merger and held on to the black union until somewhere in the mid-'60s, but when the unions joined up something got lost in the mix and black musicians wasn't getting the gigs anymore.

We stayed in Los Angeles. It was tough and we nearly starved to death as work was so scarce. As I'd learnt key-punching I did that, because music wasn't paying the bills. I remember we lived in a rough apartment where a lot of riff-raff was.

A man called Jimmy Lewis who wrote many of Ray Charles's tunes helped me to move into a better spot. That was around the time I first met Little Richard; we lived a few doors from one of his apartment houses in LA. He proved to be a man of his word. He fell for me and my talent and I remember him saying, 'I'm going to make you a star, Marva.' He took me to meet his producer, Bumps Blackwell, and some of his other friends. They all were so nice. When he saw I played piano we really had fun: he was such a sweetheart. Then he told me that he had to go to Detroit on some business and when he returned he'd start getting me ready. Well, he got to Detroit but was held up a little longer than expected: I found out in *Jet* magazine that the police stopped him for something. Eventually, when he returned to LA he got back to me and we started meeting people again. I don't know why but I just assumed that the Derbys were going to be involved too, but this wasn't the case: they were going on to Las Vegas. As long as the Derbys were with me I felt safe, but without them I got scared. I explained to Little Richard that

I'd thought the Derbys were going to be with us and I wouldn't feel right without them. He was OK with this, and so I left with the Derbys to go to Las Vegas. We did good there at first but somebody goofed up on an audition on the strip, and after we didn't get the gig things went downhill again. We soon went home. Tuttie seemed to lose interest, so we split up. I was at a loss what to do until Clarence Cooper asked if he could be my manager.

Mr Cooper had known me as a teenager. He belonged to one of the big-time Baptist churches, Eighth Street Baptist. When I was with the Whitney Singers we sang there many times, and that was where he first heard me. He seemed to appreciate my style of singing. Later on he saw me at clubs, and eventually he asked if I had a manager. When I said no he asked if he could manage me. He was a producer as well as a manager, and he was a Godsend, a nice man. We went through a lot together. Mr Cooper, who never married, had asthma, and sometimes had a hard time breathing, but this didn't stop him singing. He'd been one of the top singers at college and could write music. He sent me to Willie Rice, one of the jazz greats in Kansas City and now sadly deceased.

Willie gave me voice lessons and worked with me on a regular basis. He was short, stocky and about my height (5ft 4in), and he loved his booze. He had a beautiful big band, one of the best of its kind. Willie was a beautiful person and taught many young people who aspired to become musicians. He cared deeply about the young folk and was very serious about his work. Not only did he teach songs but he also taught some to play piano, like Donald Cox, who's now in charge of the Music Federation in Kansas City. When Willie got hold of you, you came out knowing something. The local Musicians' Union Hall where he taught was like a home away from home. We were all like family. Downstairs we jammed with the old timers, who gave us pointers. There was beer and boiled eggs served by Ernie Williams at the bar. When you first entered there was a booth, like a little cage, where we paid out union dues. In those days if you didn't have a union card you couldn't get on the stage to perform, and believe you me, they often came around to your gig and asked to see your card. If it wasn't up to date, whatever you got paid for the night was taken to pay the union dues. Lots of us practised there in the Union building, usually once a week, one on one. Willie said there were certain jazz standards I should know because it would be good for me. Back in those days you had to be versatile, and I wanted to be a singer who sang everything. He was always saying I had a long-range voice that could go several octaves. He was right about that, because one time when I sang gospel with the Whitney Singers I hit a high note and a glass broke. Everyone looked at me so funny.

When Mr Cooper asked if he could be my manager I said yes, but on one condition. 'Don't ever try to hit on me, 'cause that's something I won't tolerate. It'll make me mad and leave.' In my experience it seemed that every female singer got too close for comfort to the so-called boss. It complicated things and I didn't want that. He agreed – but I know sometimes he was jealous when I dated and sometimes even blocked people from seeing me.

With Mr Cooper on my side I felt I had a good chance of making a name for myself in the music business.

CHAPTER 14

The Hardest-Working Man in Show Business

In 1966 I got married again. It was a big mistake. My second husband was called Phil Waddell and he worked as a DJ in a casino. He was white but owned a black newspaper. He thought I was a fantastic singer, but after we were married he told me he didn't want me to talk to black folk. I didn't understand this, so I annulled the marriage after thirty days. He was furious and he came over to whup my ass, but I whupped his ass instead, hitting him with one of them aluminum pitchers. He had blood spouting out of his head. And the next day when I saw him he had two blondes on each arm. It made me feel like a fool. I guess he was an undercover racist; either that or he was jealous of me. I've always had a problem with jealous men who felt threatened by the attention I received.

I was still working in an office in the daytime and singing in clubs at night. Mr Cooper had friends on the James Brown show, and heard they needed a singer because Vicki Anderson – then the female vocalist on James's revue – was going to work for the singer Joe Tex for a while. I knew of James Brown from his big hit 'It's A Man's Man's Man's World', which I loved, but I didn't know much about him as a person. Mr Cooper set up for me to meet Ben Bart of Universal Attractions, James's booking agency. It turned out that Mr. Brown was coming to play a concert in Kansas City and Mr Bart would be coming with him, but sadly our meeting had to be postponed because a riot broke out during the performance.

I thought I'd missed my chance but a few months later, in 1967,

James Brown returned to Kansas City to play two dates at Memorial Hall. Mr Bart, though, didn't come. I think it was in April, a few weeks before my twenty-fourth birthday, and I remember I was working in an office and thinking how I just couldn't stand being there. So I began to ask God to help me, 'cause I wanted to be a full-time singer. My prayers were answered when Mr Cooper finally got me an audition with James Brown. It was Easter Sunday when he called and told me what he'd set up. To tell you the truth, I wasn't thrilled or excited; in fact, my first instinct was to say that I wasn't going to go. I told myself I wasn't interested. But this was because I was in one of my moods – I'm a Taurus and Taurus people can be prone to mood swings. Besides, I had no stockings and didn't have a clue about what I was going to wear. Being a typical Taurus, though, as fast as the negative mood came over me a normal, happy frame of mind returned very quickly.

I was told to go along to the James Brown show at Memorial Hall for my chance to audition. He was doing two shows that day and I assumed I'd only have to stay for one; that the audition would be in between shows. I was wrong. It was so darn boring waiting for the second show to end. James Brown was undoubtedly a great entertainer – maybe the best I'd ever seen – but I was a little pissed when I found out I had to stay for both shows. Thankfully two friendly guys, Bobby Bennett and James Crawford, who were part of Mr Brown's entourage, kept messing with me, had me giggling and helped ease me into a calmer state of mind.

After the second show had finished and the hall had cleared, James – who I hadn't met up to that point – told his musical director, Alfred 'Pee Wee' Ellis, to come out front on stage and put me through an audition. Before I could get to James Brown, Pee Wee had to say I was qualified. Well, as I'd studied under the great Willie Rice I knew I was ready. Pee Wee – who I thought was a genius and a gentleman – came in carrying a little tape recorder and sat at the Hammond B3 organ. He took me from one type of song to another to find out my ability and range. I believe he was impressed, especially when I started calling out key signatures and changes. Even though I played by ear, things like that were old hat to me, as my mother made me play piano for church choirs when I was twelve years of age.

This is what Pee Wee remembers: 'I first met Marva when she showed up for an audition. She sang a couple of songs for me while I played the organ. I think she did a blues and gospel song. She impressed me – she had a good strong voice, could sing in tune and had a good personality. So I recommended her to Mr Brown, who trusted my judgement, and hired her on the spot.'

Of course, I didn't know what Pee Wee's thoughts were at the time. When we'd finished the audition and Pee Wee got what he wanted he excused himself and went back into Mr Brown's dressing room with the tape. I'll admit I was a little nervous as I waited. Even though I thought the audition had gone well I was rolling over in my mind what might happen next. I wasn't kept waiting for very long. Pee Wee came back to me and said, 'Mr Brown wants to see you. Follow me to his dressing room.'

I must say I was a little scared at this point. *Oh hell,* I said to myself, *what's gonna happen?* So much came into my head as I followed Pee Wee to James Brown's room. It's amazing how much talking can go through your mind in so short a time. *What will James Brown say to me and how will I respond? Lordy, have mercy on me. Marva, you've turned down two offers already, and it looks like there ain't nothing happening here either.*

Time has blurred some of my memories and I can't really remember who was in the room, I think maybe there was Gertrude Sanders, Bobby Bennett, Danny Ray and a few others I didn't know, maybe even my manager, because my mind was focused on meeting James Brown and wondering what kind of man he was. I reminisced about how sexy he was on stage: there was always something sexy about him when he performed. I thought also about his singer, Vicki Anderson, wondering if I could I stand up to her – because she was beautiful and could sing her butt off.

I walked in and Mr Brown was in his robe looking in the mirror tidying hisself up. Pee Wee announced me and Mr Brown turned to me and said, 'Young lady, you can really sing.'

'Thank you,' I replied. I could definitely feel who was in charge. Nobody said or added nothing to his conversation. It felt like it was a professional organization and he was the boss.

'If you sound like that on this little tape you're going to be dynamite in the studio. Miss Anderson is leaving in a little while.

How would you like to work for me?'

'That would be wonderful,' I gushed.

'How soon can you leave?'

'Whenever you're ready, sir,' I replied, with a wide smile.

I was over the moon. I rushed home and threw a few things together to go to Cincinnati where they were going the next day. I was amazed I'd got the job. I know I certainly looked different from James Brown's previous female singers, as I was a blonde when I auditioned for the show. I'd been coloring my hair for several years. In my day black people were thought to be limited in their hair color and styles – but I come from a family that doesn't care what other people say. We've always been stylish, from generations back. They said my great-grandmother Barry had a servant-driven carriage and you could hear her jewelry rattle when she moved. She loved fine clothes, beads and bangles and different hairstyles. I remember my aunt had auburn hair, and some women had a streak of much lighter color than their natural hair. As for me, I never worried about being too far out. I looked at white women's fashion books showing them with blonde, brown and any colored hair they wanted, and I knew that when summer came they'd lie in the sun for a tan that was my color. I remember James Brown was crazy about my freckles when I got to know him better because he'd never seen a black woman with freckles before. I come from a mixed background – my folks are white Irish, Indian and black – so we have curly hair, straight hair and in-between hair. Some of us have green, blue, grey and dark brown eyes. My father's eyes were grey-blue and as I said before, on his Navy card it said he was white, although he was put in a black group. After seeing the blues singer Etta James who had light-colored hair I decided I wanted to be a blonde: I never gave it a second thought. Aunt Thelma, who'd owned a beauty shop for almost all her life, thought I looked gorgeous as a blonde and my parents never said nothing against it, only that the color matched my skin. That's why when I went to work at my office job before I joined James Brown some of the people there looked at me strangely – yet nothing was said about my hair.

James Brown accepted me as a blonde when I auditioned, but later when I went on TV with blonde hair instead of a darker wig he was surprised. In fact, he got mad, but then when he was told I was the first black artist to wear a blonde Afro on TV he started bragging about it. I think he thought it made me more glamorous.

That's what I was always looking for: ways to look sexy, glamorous and different from the average lady. You see, I believe that people in show business should be as showy as possible and wear beautiful outfits. I hate to see a lady artist with plain jeans and a plain top; I prefer glittery pants and a sexy blouse. It's part of the business. I was taught that if you look fabulous that's half of the job of getting over. When people love your outfit and hear that you don't sound too bad either, they see you as classy.

But let's get back to my getting on the James Brown show. When Mom and Dad found out Mr Brown had offered me a job they wasn't overjoyed, but by that time they realized they couldn't change me from my calling: they knew I had a stubborn, willful streak and didn't try to stop me, and they agreed to take care of Sherrie while I was away. God bless Mom and Dad for that: I always knew she was in a safe place with them. Although they wasn't happy, they felt more at ease with the situation because they knew my manager – but I don't think they thought I would go national. When Mom saw me on *The Mike Douglas Show* on TV and he introduced me as Marva Whitney, she said, 'You're not a Whitney, you're a Manning.' She was annoyed I'd used my married name. I reminded her about all the arguments we'd had in the first place about me not being able to use my maiden name, because of the Mannings' strict religious beliefs. My mama and my daddy – who's been in heaven almost ten years now – said, 'Forgive us daughter, you know Church of God in Christ is so strict. We didn't know any better.' But I did get a formal blessing from them eventually.

I think my mom hoped I'd be a missionary like her mother, my grandmother, had wanted. In those days they didn't understand – and didn't want to understand – that you could sing in the nightclubs and not be a sinner. In their eyes you had to be bad to sing in joints that sold alcohol, and would end up suffering hellfire and brimstone. As I became a singer this was always in my head, and when I saw people who was in show business do bad things, to themselves and others, I always heard in my head my grandmother's words, 'Marvan, I want you to be a good girl and a missionary.' I think this helped me to keep as straight as possible, but perhaps hurt me too in some ways.

I've always dated only one man at a time and not indulged in certain things like drink and drugs, and sometimes that made me an outsider. I was Miss Goodie Two Shoes. Heck, my mother didn't let me wear silk stockings until I was seventeen, and I used to slip out and put on lipstick. One day I forgot to take it off and my mother saw me. Boy, did I get a scolding.

Although I was on the James Brown show my contract wasn't actually with him: I signed with Ben Bart of Universal Attractions. It was through Mr Bart I got to sign with King Records, a company owned by Syd Nathan and based at 1540 Brewster Avenue in Cincinnati. When I got to Cincinnati the first thing I did was go to the King office and sign the paperwork that made me their artist. After that I went over to the headquarters of James Brown Productions. There I met Gene Redd, a nice man who was a horn arranger, and the production manager, Walter Whisenhunt. He was a handsome man and nice too. His skin looked so smooth. Charles Spurling was also there: he was a songwriter, a recording artist at King and later an A&R man. I'd met him before, as he recalls:

I met Marva in 1967 in Kansas City. I was performing there at some nightclub. It was pretty large and held, I guess, about two thousand people. But it wasn't a big-name place as far as I can remember. The security guards had come backstage to my dressing room and I told them that I didn't want to receive any company. But she just started singing *a cappella* outside my dressing room. After I heard her voice I told the guard to let her in and that's how we met. Marva has a great voice and a beautiful personality. I wanted to bring her here to Cincinnati from Kansas City to the King recording company in '67 but James Brown got to her first. There was a guy named Bud Hobgood and he was James's right-hand man. I heard him telling James, 'Charles Spurling has found another lady.' I heard him say, 'Well, she looks good, she sings good, she's got everything.' The next thing I know, Bud Hobgood says James wanted Marva on his productions, so that's how she got started with him.

When I first arrived at King I also met a nice gentleman, whose name escapes me, who kept the place clean and did whatever was needed. A couple of years later he and his wife saved my life after I od poisoning from eating spaghetti in some hotel. I got so sick ght I was going to die, and I ended up in a Jewish hospital for a couple of days. I'll never forget their kindness.

Although I'd only just joined the organization Walter Whisenhunt wanted to record me straight away. James Brown wasn't even there: he'd already moved on to the next town on his tour schedule. I was so surprised at how it went down. I'd always thought that maybe there'd be some grooming and artist development, but there wasn't. I got thrown in the deep end.

The studio at King Records wasn't a cold studio: studios have their own vibes and character. I didn't sing with a live band: I added my vocals to a couple of songs they had in the can. The first was 'Your Love Was Good For Me,' a slow ballad, the second a faster number called 'Saving My Love For My Baby', which is now popular in England with Northern Soul fans. They were both written and produced by J.J. Barnes and Walter Whisenhunt. J.J. Barnes was a Detroit-based singer/songwriter and had a hit around the same time with 'Baby Please Come Back Home'. I don't remember him being at the sessions. Apparently he came up from Detroit to do a few tracks with James. Anyway, I was put in a vocal booth and listened to the first song for just a few minutes. The next thing I knew they were saying, 'Let's roll!' and wanted a take. I said to myself, *Doggone, this isn't even my key, it's too high*. This was true of both the tunes: as the tape rolled I seemed to be screaming and straining to reach the right notes. In fact 80 per cent of the songs I recorded while I was with James Brown were in keys that were wrong for me.

Both the songs I recorded that first day came out on a 45 for King's Federal label with 'Your Love Was Good To Me' on the A-side. As the record didn't get much promotion it didn't make a lot of noise. But hell, at least I'd got my foot on the ladder.

After the session ended I went back home to Kansas to wait for the call to go on the road. Soon I called Whisenhunt, who'd taken a liking to me right away. I remember he bought me a beautiful watch before I left, and I knew he was trying to get next to me – but I kept him in his place. He told me to sit tight and wait.

It was about a month before I got the call. I cannot recall where me and Mr Cooper met them – maybe it was Cincinnati – but I remember that the people on the show were doing so much gossiping it was ridiculous. Nobody really spoke to me except Bobby Bennett, James Crawford and Pee Wee Ellis.

When I arrived James Brown gave me the opportunity to see how the show worked: I think I might have had a week and a half to two weeks just watching how it went. I'd thought Mr Bart played a big role in the James Brown revue, but I found out very quickly James ran his show without any outside interference. He often bragged, 'Mr Bart used to be my manager but now he works for me.' Although I was happy and excited to have joined the revue I quickly discovered that working for James Brown was like working in the army: strict and everything to the letter. After singing just weekend shows in Kansas City clubs, when I got with James my first run was thirty-one shows in thirty days. I was well and truly thrown into the deep end: it was a baptism of fire. James Brown was hotter than hot back then, and we'd fly one day on a plane for an afternoon job and go somewhere else for an evening show. It was tough, hellishly tough. I thought I was going to die, we worked so hard. I felt like a trapped animal sometimes.

We wasn't allowed to call other people on the show by their first names. It was either Miss this or Mr that. If somebody called me by my first name and James Brown heard it, he would correct them and say, 'That's Miss Whitney.' He'd straighten them out right there. It was like being put into a straitjacket, and it always put a bad taste in my mouth – because I was raised that if somebody was older than me they could call me Marva. I can understand that James wanted black people to be treated with respect, but he took it too far. Sometimes people who knew me well called me Marva undercover, but other than that it was always Miss Whitney. Having said that, after I'd been on the show a few months James gave me a pet name – he called me 'Whit'.

Another thing I soon discovered was that James Brown was a perfectionist, and moody to a fault. You could never tell what he'd be like from one moment to the next. Everyone was scared to death of him. You could be just minding your own business and that would be an issue. If the band didn't play something right during a show he'd call a rehearsal immediately after the gig. He'd say change your clothes and get back out here. And man, he'd go for another three hours directing the band: sometimes he just did it for the hell of it, to prove who was boss. It was like on stage: his female singers wasn't allowed to dance too much. That was law: only he could move about. He needed to be in charge and the center of attention.

After I got with the revue I became reacquainted with Bobby Bennett and James Crawford. They were two of the Famous Flames, the group that was still with James Brown at that time. They were friendly and real up-front people who said they'd take care of me. They promised Mr Cooper this, so I felt pretty secure and felt everything would be all right. And they were true to their word: they did look after me, they really did. It was because of them that I felt I was in a safety zone during those first few months. James Crawford had a song called 'Miniskirt – Watch It Work'. Just like Marvin Gaye, you had to push him on stage because he suffered from stage fright and was scared of the crowd. Bobby Bennett, besides playing his role in the Flames, was James's hairdresser. He was also his flunky and did things like carry his bags. Everyone was scared of James Brown except Bobby: he wasn't scared at all. I heard that one time before I joined the revue he kicked James's ass in Paris or somewhere: Bobby stood up against him and he ended up groveling. He'd met his match.

I really liked Bobby; he and I started dating not long after I joined the revue. I heard through the grapevine that James asked Bennett to finish with me. He's supposed to have said, 'I want Marva. Give her up, she's mine.' That's what I heard.

Apparently Bobby replied, 'Hey man, I can't tell Marva nothing like that. You've got your own women anyway.' But, as I was to find out shortly afterwards, whatever James Brown wanted he took.

When I first joined the revue – and I think it was the first time I had been on the tour bus – he had a beautiful woman with him called Miss Florence Brown. She was the most gorgeous doll I ever saw in my life. Her hair was so beautiful, naturally straight, and with her beautiful light skin you could tell she was mixed. And she was so poised. I could tell she was older than me, possibly James's age. One day James invited me for lunch. She was sitting there at the table, wearing a Japanese-style kimono with long braids down her back; I was on her left and James was sitting opposite her. James was talking excitedly, saying, 'Miss Whitney, we're going to do this and do that.' Miss Brown didn't say a thing; she was just smiling serenely.

When James left the room we were alone together, and she said,

'You're going to be where I am one day.'

I didn't understand. 'What do you mean?'

'You're going to be where I am one day,' she repeated. I said I didn't know what she was talking about. Her mood changed and the smile disappeared. She looked serious. 'I'm so scared, Miss Whitney. I just got my nose fixed, but I'm scared he's gonna hit me again. Then I don't know if he's gonna help me again.'

I said to myself, *Oh hell – this woman's telling me somethin'*. I believed what she said about her nose but didn't believe that I'd be the one to take her place. Why would this woman tell me she's just had a nose job and she's scared he's going to hit her again? She's trying to tell me something – maybe warn me – but at that point and with me being new to the show I wasn't sure what it was, and I didn't want to get involved in other people's business. Only later on would her words make sense.

When I did my first show with James Brown I was nervous like anybody else. Lyn Collins later told me that she didn't know how to get off the stage properly, and kept backing up and hesitating. Fred Wesley had to show her how to leave in a dignified, professional way. I almost did that hesitating and backing up one time when they had a revolving stage in New York at Madison Square Garden.

I'd only been with James Brown a few weeks when we played the legendary Apollo Theater in Harlem, New York. Apollo shows usually started at noon and went on all day, climaxing with a midnight show. By that time I knew why people called him the hardest-working man in show business – I think I did thirty one-nighters with him in thirty days. It was exhausting, but exhilarating too.

By then I'd got used to the format. A typical James Brown show began with the band playing a few instrumental tunes, the sax player, Maceo Parker, doing his thing and working up the audience. He's crazy anyway, just the way he plays his horn and walks around trying to get the audience on its feet. Then James Brown came on and did a couple of numbers. After that the MC, Danny Ray, said, 'He'll be right back!' And that was the time for me. I'd go out and do two or three songs – maybe four if I was lucky – while James changed his outfit, and because of that I never felt like a proper artist. I always called myself a time consumer. As far as I was concerned I was a support act, just filling in while James Brown got ready for the next part of the show. That's what I always felt. And when he said, 'I need you, Miss Whitney,' I thought that was poppycock. He didn't really need me. He could pack out the place by hisself. What he was doing was getting two prices for both of us and making extra money. I only found that out years later, after I left. He was a smart businessman.

So I'd go out and do my two or three numbers and after that Clay Tyson, the comedian with the revue, might come on. I think he was there at that point. And then James Brown came back for the finale, the part of the show they called 'Star Time', where he pulled out all the stops and did his cape routine on 'Please Please Please'. While this was happening me, Bobby Byrd and whoever was there – sometimes even Danny Ray – were behind the stage doing the background voices. This was our job after the Flames left.

If you didn't have what it took at the Apollo the audience let you know. They were a tough crowd and didn't take no prisoners. There was a lot of distractions for performers, like drag queens who would start walking up and down in their beautiful gear just as you was going into your song. To me it was a duel, because they wanted to see if they could make me stop singing, start crying and run off stage. They was dressed so immaculate it was difficult not to look at them – hell, even I had to look at them! They were wearing better clothes than me. They were all over the place in the theater. Some were on the front row seats, so when they walked they had to walk from the front to the back of the theater. Then you had 'em sitting on the side of the balcony. All you had to do was look to your right as you was singing and you saw them right there. They tried to distract me but I never stopped singing. Although I kept going, I was saying to myself, *What are these damned fools doing?*

My first recording with James Brown was at the Apollo at the end of June 1967. He recorded the whole show for his LP *Live At The Apollo Volume II*, and I performed a duet with him called 'Think', the opening number, which was a revamp of an old Five Royales tune. I think I'd sung at the Apollo with James a couple of times before that recording. I remember after the first time he complained that I was not doing something right and told my manager to get me in gear. Mr Cooper came and explained what I wasn't doing and what James was looking for, and by the time of the recording I was doing it right.

I got applauded that night. It wasn't lengthy applause because you went on and off really fast, but at least the crowd got a chance to give me a look over. But there were times after that when I got a standing ovation. I remember one time I got one when those drag queens tried to compete with me and failed. In the end they gave up and walked out, 'cause the more they did to distract the audience the harder I sang: I knew I had to make people look back my way. I wasn't going to give in: it was war. I'd heard that if the audience didn't like you they threw tomatoes and things, so I always had that in the back of my mind, but fortunately this never happened to me.

I was always nervous before I went on. Always. Right now, even to this day. I think there is something wrong with an artist if they don't have a little bit of nervousness in them, because on stage you can't be too relaxed. But you can't be too gung-ho either. There has to be a kind of happy medium. When I'm singing on stage I try to feel the vibes of the people, because no two shows are alike; even if I do the same songs they're never alike. Sometimes there are technical problems and the monitors don't work properly, which can throw you, but the main thing is finding the pulse of the audience. I have to look into their faces and see where they're coming from: you have to try to please the masses. But you can never please everyone. You've got to feel within yourself that you've got the majority with you, and feel what they want and what they need from your performance. And that's the way a song comes out. The crowd can even be affected by your movements, your gyrations. 'Cause, see, you can make 'em move and if they holler or give a smile you know that particular thing right there worked and you know to do it again somewhere. So it's like maneuvering. That's the reason why I tell the band that no matter what I do they should play the song as we did it in rehearsal, because my mood swings can change. If the music's right I feel I have the freedom and flexibility to do something else and go in any direction I want. When I perform live no two songs are done alike: if you were to write down all the notes from one show and another they wouldn't be the same.

CHAPTER 15

Life on the Road with James Brown

When I got with James Brown I was under a grand illusion. I'd always heard that Motown groomed their people for stardom, but I got none of that with him. But I tell you one thing: when you came out of the James Brown camp you could hold your own *anywhere*. James never had a bad singer or a bad musician. He had top-notch people who had to be strong, and their talents and their gifts were always first class. You learned to have a high tolerance level because sometimes things were crazy. I mean really *crazy*. A lot of the things I saw and heard shocked me at first, because of the strict way I was raised.

When I was introduced to the show in the ladies' dressing room, Ann Norman was the only one who gave me a real smile. She was a beautiful young lady of Jamaican origin who'd been raised up in London schools, and was smart and really on the ball for someone so young. Ann loved James and saw no wrong in him. She was a minor when her parents let her go out with him, so she could never see what we saw. She was so deeply in love with James and we knew why: the first person you ever have you'll love to the day they die. Ann never complained if anything happened to her with James, and she'd talk back to him too – which was a real no-no for the rest of us. I think he tolerated it because her parents (who were supposed to have connections to powerful people) had warned him that if he laid a finger on her he'd have hell to pay. So James was good to her.

Although Ann was the best dancer in the show by a long way - I believe she was the finest dancer James ever had - the other ladies were good too. Another I particularly liked was Joann Houston, who was originally from Philly. Cookie was their boss, who taught everybody the steps to the songs, and her personality was good. Every dancer had her own personality, and like most of the attractive young women who worked on the show, at some time or other they'd all find themselves sitting on what I called the hot seat. By that I mean that James Brown had his eye on them and expected them to respond to his advances: he was like a master with his concubines. If he tapped them they were expected to oblige him. The trouble is this led to a lot of jealousy, especially if somebody was getting too much attention from him. I remember that when this happened to me I'd get back to my room and find that a pair of new shoes, which I'd never worn, had been ruined; at other times I'd find things of mine went missing.

But Ann Norman and Joann were really good company. Ann was my roommate when I first got there, and we got along most of the time, although we both got aggravated with each other from time to time. When I left James she was the first to call me. She went on to be one of the top models for a highly respectable firm, danced for Al Green and is now a nurse in New York City. We still talk.

Cookie married Bernard Odum, the bass player when I first got there, and when James found out they were married he gave them hell and he either fired them or they left – but I think Mr Odum came back for a while after I left. Although Bobby Byrd and Vicki Anderson was also a married couple, James really didn't want married people together on his show.

When I joined James Brown he was so hot we were working damn near all week, and if we wasn't working all week we was riding his tour bus and crisscrossing the country to go to the next show. We called his bus 'The Stick'. It was a Golden Eagle and very plush, but hell, that didn't matter if you couldn't get a seat to yourself. You had to have some kind of seniority to do that. The only people who could really have a special seat was Gertrude Sanders and Danny Ray, if he wasn't on the plane with James. (James *never* went on the bus: his Lear jet was piloted by Doug Bell.) Bobby and Vicki usually sat together. But the bus was always packed with band members, and it was difficult to sleep and get some rest if you were sitting next to someone.

After I was considered James's woman, nine times out of ten I was riding in his plane, though I didn't like it. I was so glad when he told me to ride in the bus, for that was the only time I could get a little rest. I remember some of them said I slept with my eyes open. When Marilyn Jones, a violin player, sat next to me I was asleep, and said to her, 'Please let me sleep, let me sleep.' She found another seat so I could lean over and rest.

Sometimes James told me to ride the bus as a punishment because he got upset with me. When I heard him say, 'Miss Whitney, you ride the bus tonight,' that was like telling me the day was Christmas, especially towards the end of my time with him. Given his hot temper he was often angry with me, and sometimes it was hard to figure just what I'd done to upset him. He was unpredictable like that. There were occasions when he bought me a gift, but because I said or did something he didn't like he got angry and it ended up as a gift to one of the other girls to spite me. Maybe they knew it or maybe they didn't. They'd say, 'Look what James gave me!' – knowing that I was on the bus. But I didn't mind. You had to develop a thick skin to work on the James Brown show.

Thankfully James very seldom came to the bus. If he did it was a real downer, because he'd heard something that he didn't like and he'd check the bus to see if everything was neat and in order. It was like the general was coming, and we all had to be at attention. It was just like being in the army sometimes. It's a wonder that most of us who worked on the show still have our minds intact.

Although I preferred the bus to the plane any day, the people on the bus often gave me a hard time because I carried my Bible everywhere with me. They also thought I was strange because I used to collect small rocks and stones from different parts of the country we visited, which I'd take back to Kansas when I visited home. These little rocks were beautiful, and about the size of a large marble. If you go to certain parts of the country you can find rocks veined with different colors. One time I kept a small collection of these rocks on the shelf above my seat on the bus, but someone took them and threw them away.

I'm a devout Christian and I always tried to find time to read the Bible on the bus, because the word of the Lord girded me and protected me wherever I went as far as I was concerned. But this didn't go down well with most of the folks: they was suspicious of me. They was wary because they thought I was the boss's woman – which I wasn't when I first came on board – and thought I might snitch on them. But they distrusted *everybody*. James, like all ruthless rulers, had successfully divided and conquered them. That was his MO.

When I joined James I was making about $250 a week, and I had to live on the road off that. Not only, though, did I have to send home money to keep for my daughter but I also had to keep money in my pocket in order to pay hotel bills when I wasn't with James. And if you got sick you knew you had to look after yourself: nobody else would take care of you.

Now, I'm going to tell you how dominant James was. As the boss he knew how much I was making and he'd tell his business manager, 'She don't need this money. Put it in an account for her and give her $100 a week.' It was my money, which I earned, but he still wanted to control it. He had me in a vice: I could never win. You knew that if you said anything you'd be in trouble. You see, he'd be nice one minute but at the flip of a dime he'd change and be really mean. He'd make you feel like a queen one moment and garbage the next. So you always knew how to act so you didn't flip him off. Sometimes if he didn't feel good about something else, he'd flip off on whoever was closest: you never really knew how he was going to act. That made us all nervous. The first thing you'd hear the people on the show say was, 'What kind of mood is he in? What are we going to have to put up with tonight?' That was always the question, 'cause people were shuddering on the inside. And his spies were everywhere. I remember I went to the drugstore one day, and when James got back from being gone a couple of days, he said, 'What did you go to the drugstore for?' It was like being in prison.

I think James Brown liked my voice and my looks, but I firmly believe that he was a man who couldn't love and was jealous of everything and everybody. He felt he had to have control of every situation; I don't think he was a happy man.

The control he had over me even included my weight. Funnily enough, he thought I was too skinny when I joined his show. He bought me chocolates 'cause he wanted me to put on more weight. Now I don't know if that was for the audience or for him, but I think he had it in his mind to make every woman singer on his show a female version of hisself. It's the opposite with today's female performers, of course: there's pressure on them to look thin. A lot of them are really skinny, some even look anorexic, and I think they only look like that because someone else – the manager, the record company or whoever – wants them to. It seems that's the only way you can sell records. In the past there were singers like Bessie Smith, Dinah Washington and Sarah Vaughan. They wasn't thin: they had meat on their bones, and that's where they got their vocal strength from.

James had an explosive temper: no wonder they called him Mr Dynamite. Every artist has got his or her own temperament but his personality changed in a second. We were scared, and a lot of times the people who were important to the music system – like promoters, journalists and DJs – he'd purposely keep away from us. If they came backstage he'd put me in another room out of the way: he didn't want me talking to them. He was like that too with Lyn Collins, who came after me in the revue. We never got an opportunity to put our side of things. When we were permitted to do interviews he was always there, and we'd end up saying what a wonderful man he was and how grateful we were for his help. So these music biz people never really got to know us; they never knew our personalities. Consequently, when I decided to leave the James Brown camp, I knew no one. There was no one in the business I could go to for help and advice. I didn't know how to get in touch with DJs and they didn't know how to get in touch with me. More of that later.

When James wasn't around Gertrude Sanders kept us in check and made sure his orders were carried out. She was in her early forties when I joined the revue: in times past she'd been Etta James's wardrobe mistress. You could see she had been a beautiful woman, but she had a little ankle problem and sometimes limped. I think this tormented her, because I think she thought she could have been with James if it hadn't been for that. She loved him, and it was even rumored that she'd dated him at one time. Gertrude was his wardrobe person, who pressed his clothes and knew what was what, his housekeeper on the road and head of the bus, and she was also the whippin' lady: she said how high we had to jump for him. In my eyes she was the second in command, because whatever she said was law. She was the one who gave you permission to see James. She did a lot of things for James that wasn't kosher at all: she'd done everything but kill for him as far as I knew. She worked like a dog.

Whatever he said she followed through. And if she didn't like you she put a vice on you and got you in trouble. It's not surprising that she scared us: we were all afraid of her because she could make life really tough; she kept us all in line. She was the one who cracked the whip and kept everything moving. I was always chaperoned and hardly had a minute's peace. One time James told her that I was to share a room with her, which was so uncomfortable for us both. It was the last thing that we wanted, but at least no one could snitch on me when I was with her.

I remember the time Gertrude's mother died, and James told her that she shouldn't go to the funeral. I hope she didn't listen to him. I heard she was paid very well, and could have bought many houses and been well off if she'd used her head.

One day she said we were going to leave at ten o'clock. For some reason me and Pee Wee Ellis was late. We had our bags on the bus but we hadn't finished getting ready and it was like 10.01am. We were right at the door fixing to get on the bus, but the door shut and they drove off and left us. I couldn't drive at that time and we didn't have much money between us, but we knew we'd better rent a car and get to the gig before James got there or we'd be in deep trouble. So Pee Wee and I put our little pennies together. There was Pee Wee, me, and someone else – I forgot who it was – who said, 'I can drive.' So we went on to the next town, getting there while the rest of the revue was loading up: we always had to be there two hours before the show hit – that was law. We got fined anyway because Gertrude snitched. James always docked your pay if you did something he didn't like, whether it was a wrong note or whatever: I once got a $75 fine for a wrinkle on the back of my dress. I'm not saying that James wouldn't have known, but we knew what was going to happen and that we'd be punished for not being there.

I vividly remember an incident with Gertrude that made us all laugh. It was her job – together with Danny Ray – to get James's things together for the show. One night as they dressed him – they had to put on his socks, even take out his false teeth and put them in a jar until they were needed – they put two different shoes on James's feet. See, he bought his shoes and clothes in close colors. Although they put his shoes in a neat stack, that night someone put on a black and a navy blue shoe together. They only realized it when he was on the stage and performing. We were all three in his dressing room: most of the time, if I was dressed, I'd stay in James's room until it was time for me to go on. I knew James couldn't accuse me of nothing because I was with Gertrude. They began having a fit and started to blame each other, saying 'I didn't do it, you did it!' That went on for a few minutes. I was just sitting there laughing to myself.

Anyhow, James came back into the dressing room wearing one black shoe and one blue and with a face like thunder. He was furious, and demanded to know who'd put the wrong shoe on him. Gertrude and Danny passed and passed the buck. I don't know if James fined them or not.

Other than being James's hatchet lady, Gertrude loved young men, and she wasted most of her money on them. There was a fellow named Levi Rasbury she went with. James always kept intelligent young black men on the show. He hired men that were very, very smart and able to handle his business, from his book work to whatever. He knew how to pick the best. But some of them thought they knew how to outsmart James when he wasn't around by doing what they wanted or taking whatever they wanted – money or whatever – which they'd probably earned because they were unpaid. James thought the experience of working for him was enough – but he was wrong. Anyway, one night during the end part of the show Gertrude caught her boyfriend with this young lady who was also dating James. She had her suspicions about Levi but hadn't caught him in the act until that point. He was a horn player – a trombonist – and also took care of some of James's business things as one of his road managers. I clearly remember that we were all packed up and ready to go when a commotion happened. Just as the bus was getting ready to pull off Levi came running for his life out of the hotel, with Gertrude following close behind him. She was a stout woman and he was shorter than her. What was so funny was that she had taken off her shoes and ran down the street with them in her hand, trying to beat him with her high heels. They had pointed toes too, and if they'd connected he'd have been in serious trouble.

Just before I left the show Gertrude began to treat me civil, for she could see I was high on the list of the boss's favorites. Years later when I lived in LA I saw her in the bus line. I was shocked and said, 'Gertrude, what you doing here?'

94

She said, 'Well, he fired me, and I couldn't stand it anymore. I'm going anyway, I'm tired of it.'

Maybe she stayed away about six months, but like so many before her she always went back. I guess in the end – and I can understand this – she got tired of handling James's women. There were so many of them. I was so sorry to hear that she died penniless in 1995; I think she was in her early seventies by then. Apparently they put her things on the sidewalk when she died: she lived in New York, which can be a cold, uncaring place. Her bills wasn't paid and I don't think any family was around. I'm told James was fussing all the way and didn't want to get involved. During her last days when she was sick Gertrude came down, when she knew she was withering, to see him. But he wouldn't receive her. He didn't even want to go to her funeral.

Another of James's enforcers was Kenny Hull. He was a roadie but he was also in charge of security. I kept – or at least tried to keep – my distance from him. To me he was trouble: nothing more than a muscle-bound tyrant. He always got on my nerves. He was a thorn in my side, and used to throw his weight around with some of the fellers to aggravate the hell out of me. It was like he was trying to put me in a bad position where somebody would see so I'd get into trouble. There were times when he'd be at my door, making it look as if I had somebody in my room. James was paranoid and made everyone else feel the same way.

One day Kenny pushed me too far and I said, 'If you don't leave me alone when you come up on this stage you might have an accident and fall off, or something bad might happen to you.'

After that he kept chanting, 'Hoodoo woman, hoodoo woman,' when he saw me, trying to provoke me. But eventually he left me alone. Others heard him calling me a hoodoo woman and I surmised they all thought it was true. There were many times when some of James's henchmen tried to set me up, but luckily someone always warned me about what was being concocted. You had to watch what you were saying. Everybody who worked on the James Brown show had to have a strong constitution to survive.

After Ann Norman, Sylvia Medford became my roommate. She was a violinist and a lady that James put with me as my traveling companion. Sylvia was an older woman but she was well-groomed; she went on to marry our black bus driver. She taught me how to bow and get off the stage. But James's snitches sabotaged my relationship with her. She knew some people were out to get me, and she'd say, 'Marva, be careful. I heard them talking about you.' So I was wary.

When I joined the revue there were three string players – Sylvia, Marilyn Jones and a gentleman called Richard Jones. When James's music took a funkier direction he decided to get rid of one of the violin players. Sylvia came to me and said, 'Marva, would you ask Mr Brown if I can stay on? I need my job. There's not much work at the Philharmonic. Can you ask him?' I said sure. So I went in to see James and begged for her job. Afterwards somebody – probably one of James's henchmen – went and told her the opposite. They said I'd insisted that Sylvia had to leave. When Sylvia left, she went with a bad taste in her mouth and a hatred for me. I don't know if she's living today. I didn't do what she was told I did: I liked her and I certainly wasn't a backstabber.

Sylvia was with James when he was still doing ballads and sweet music, like when you hear the violins on 'It's A Man's Man's Man's World' and Frank Sinatra-style songs like 'A Cottage For Sale'. James didn't like it that he had all those R&B hits but was never as big or popular as Sinatra. And he always had a thing that he thought he was just as good as Sammy Davis Jr. He'd speak of that sometimes, and you could see that it hurt him that he wasn't accepted like they was.

James saw every other performer as a rival. When you were around him you couldn't say you enjoyed listening to another group or performer. We were traveling in a car once with the radio on; James was driving. I was listening to a record Marvin Gaye had out, and I liked it and was tapping my feet. I said, 'Oooh, I like that.'

James said angrily, 'Oh you like that, huh?' and gave me an evil look.

Later I was told by a gentleman who was sitting in the back seat, 'James was fixing to push you out the door like he did Tammi Terrell.'

I said, 'What?'

He said, 'Did you see me put my hands on James? I had to stop him.'

I thought about Tammi Terrell, who had been with James's revue in the early '60s before she made it big at Motown. There were rumors that they'd had a volatile relationship.

Talking of Tammi, there was one time we was in Philly when she came by. She made it very well known that she didn't like me and thought I couldn't sing. It kind of pissed me off, but I'd been forewarned not to pay her any attention because I'd been told her mind wasn't there. James was very polite to her, as he usually was to anybody who went to see him. He was always nice in public. And he told me, 'Poor thing, she's not going to make it.' She was near the end then; she was very fragile. She was still able to walk around but she wasn't really herself.

Going back to James's not liking to hear other people's songs, later up in years, when I was gone, I heard that Deirdre, James's second wife, gave a birthday party for one of her children. James discovered a record that wasn't his in the house and all hell broke loose. He didn't want anybody's music in his house but his own.

Don't get me wrong. It wasn't always hell in the James Brown camp. There were times when we laughed and had fun. I remember one night as James was on stage he did one of his slick moves – a split I think – as part of his usual dance routine, but then quickly ran off the stage. It turned out that he had a large tear in his pants, and panicked because he didn't want anybody to see it. Of course we laughed about it, but not openly to his face.

There was a dancer who always gave us a laugh or two. She was given to drinking, which James didn't allow: he'd warned her when she first joined the show and we played a big auditorium in New York. I think it was Madison Square Garden, which had a revolving stage. The stage went round and round, and when it was her turn to come off she missed it, and continued to go round until somebody snatched her off. That girl was a loony. She looked as if she was drunk all the time. Later, when we played a nightclub Lloyd Price owned, she went one better. We were all waiting backstage because the dancers had to queue. She'd gotten tired of standing and wanted to sit down; she might have been tipsy then too. Anyhow there was a big barrel next to where they were all standing. She jumped up on it, intending to sit down, not knowing there was hot water in it. She was wearing a feather costume, and when she jumped up her backside fell in and she started hollering. Her feathers went limp. She knew she'd messed up, and she hollered and cussed, but afterwards she was scared because she knew James was going to get her. That lady was always giving us a big laugh.

James, too, could do things that would make us laugh. It wasn't unusual to find him having a fist fight after a show with someone or other. It might be over money, women or an argument with a fellow artist or his manager. He always had an advantage, though, because he made sure his henchmen were hanging on the sidelines in case the man he was fighting got the better of him.

James had a real hatred for the singer Joe Tex, and they had a big fight when they appeared together at the Atlanta auditorium. It was a real Clash of the Titans. Although we supported James to his face, behind the scenes and out of sight of the boss most of us were having fun, laughing at them fools. They couldn't see the funny side, though; they were dead serious. Their rivalry consumed them, burned them up. James's tour bus had 'Soul Brother Number One' painted on the side. Not to be outdone, Joe Tex's bus said 'The Soul Brother That Needs No Number'. Sometimes the two buses met on the highway. If we spotted Joe's bus, ours would screech to a halt and some of James's henchmen would jump off the bus to go and fight Joe's people, who'd also stop for a fight and to hurl insults at us. It gave us some fun, excitement and light relief from the boredom of the road. Oh boy, they were certainly good ol' days.

Most of the people who worked on the James Brown show had other duties after they came off stage. I was James's road secretary and made $50 a week. I'll tell you how that came about. He always had a ritual that after the show had ended and he'd come off the stage he took time to talk to all of the DJs and promotional people. You could sometimes be hanging around for an hour or two. One night I decided I wouldn't stay. I'm the sort of person that likes to get my rest and feel that night rest is the best rest, so I wanted to go and be in my room, maybe get something to eat and then go to sleep. So I left early. James couldn't find me and asked where I was, and someone said I'd gone.

When I went back the next night James came over to me and said, 'Miss Whitney, where were you last night?'

I said, 'Well, I went through with the job and the show was over. I went and got me some breakfast and I went to my room and went to sleep.'

Then he said, 'I know you worked in an office one time so you'll be the road secretary from now on. Every night you'll have to stay behind after the show and type up a report of what money was taken in, and then you'll have the report sent to the home office at King Records in Cincinnati so they'll know the figures of what was done each night.' So after that I became one of the last ones to leave and get home. That was my punishment for leaving early.

In the fall of 1967 we traveled overseas to Europe, where we played in England, Germany, Denmark and France. I was excited about going to Europe as I'd never been overseas before. I remember thinking how beautiful it was and how friendly the people were. There was a different feel over there to America and it was interesting being in a place that existed long before America was born. It was also exciting to be there because I have grandparents on both sides of the family who have Irish roots. Daddy always liked to brag about having Irish blood.

When I was in England I thought about Queen Elizabeth, who to me is one of the most beautiful women in the world. She seems so majestic. My visit there also made me think about The Beatles, who were hitting it big as I was getting out of high school. The trip to Europe was also the time that James began to get closer to me, for I knew I had no friends on the show and I felt a coldness from my fellow musicians and dancers. The details of that first trip abroad are hazy now but I distinctly remember being in Paris and doing some shopping with James. That was the place I got my first bottle of Joy perfume. It cost a lot and James got me a big bottle: I made it last as long as I could. But it was the first of many gifts I had from him that I paid for with a heavy price.

I think my performances abroad were decent, and I don't remember any negative criticism – though I know I was still in the learning mode big time. It took a year before I began to feel I was on steady ground with my part of the show, though by that time I had to worry more about who was setting a trap for me and trying to get me in trouble with the boss.

Around the same time as our European trip my second single for King – and the first to be produced by James Brown – came out. It was a ballad called 'If You Love Me'; but it didn't make much of an impact.

When I first joined the show James kept talking about someone called Charles Bobbitt who worked on the railroad. I think he was a porter or something like that. James said he was coming and was going to be with him to the end as his business manager: Bobbitt had the brains and James liked him. Mr Bobbitt eventually arrived sometime in 1968 and truly he kept a lot of us sane. He was a softly spoken man and he knew what was going on, but he had to keep his job so he tried to pacify James or forewarn us in some kind of way. Sometimes he'd just give us a meaningful look to let us know something was up. He was a shield. I felt a little safer with him around. He had compassion, if there was any to be gotten. I felt a little safer, too, around Danny Ray, who started off as a singer with James but later became his MC – and the man who put the cape on James when he performed 'Please Please Please'. Danny was for real, a small man with a big, melodious voice who looked a bit like Sammy Davis Jr. He told you what to look out for.

And even the production manager at King Records, Bud Hobgood, warned you if he knew something was up. Sometimes one of James's henchmen would come in, set down a briefcase and walk out. After he'd left Bud would put his hands over his mouth, like 'shhhh', and point to the briefcase. In the briefcase was a tape recorder.

CHAPTER 16

Stranded in Detroit

Even though I was dating Bobby Bennett I knew James had his eye on me. He tried to break us up by telling tales on Bobby behind his back. 'He's got other girlfriends, Miss Whitney, when he leaves you,' he told me one evening.

I still had my opinions and expressed them: I didn't want him interfering so I just told him straight. 'Look, Mr Brown, he can do what he pleases. How he treats me and what he does and who he sees when he's away from me, that's mine and his business.' I could see his expression changing but I continued: 'Mr Brown, I feel that after I've done your job, been here on time and done your set then whatever I do after that is my business. As long as I meet the requirements of my job and do what I'm supposed to do, I don't think you should interfere with my private life. You don't rule my life after I leave here.' James glared at me, then stormed off. *What did I have to go and say that for?* I thought. Being naïve, I really didn't know I was in deep trouble because I didn't feel any fear. I went about my business as usual, and after that he totally ignored me, didn't even look at me.

I remember shortly afterwards we was going to do a show in Las Vegas with the comedian Flip Wilson. Flip was strange too. You could be walking past him and he didn't have a damn thing to say. He'd do his show and he'd speak to nobody. Often he'd stay cooped up in his dressing room until it was time to be on stage; then he'd do his show, go back to his room and shut the door. I heard he didn't like James.

Although James was giving me the cold shoulder, with Vegas coming up I decided to approach him about what he'd said a few weeks before, when he'd seemed really excited: 'Whit, we're going to Vegas soon and I'm gonna buy you two or three gowns. You'll be out of sight.' See, that's the way he got you – he be doing the good things for you; making you feel special and trying to reel you in. I hadn't forgotten what he'd said and approached him even though he'd been doing his best to avoid me. 'Mr Brown, we're getting close to Vegas. When are you going to let me go shopping to get these gowns that you want me to have?' He just looked at me like I was shit and said that he wasn't going to get me a fucking thing. I was very surprised, but I still had fight in me and decided to get the joker. I saved my money and when we got into Vegas a few days before the show started I went out and bought me three of the baddest gowns that ever was. Afterwards James treated me as cold as ice but I knew he was mad as hell.

We were supposed to be in Vegas for about two weeks but he only let me do about three or four dates. It all came to a head one night as he came off stage. I said, 'Hello, Mr Brown.' He was real ornery and gave me a cold damn-it-to-hell look. I felt icicles. This happened every day for the next few days.

Then he came up to me and said in a matter-of-fact kind of way, 'Miss Whitney, I'm sending you to Cincinnati to record some new tunes and I'll send for you to come back here within a couple of weeks.' Little did I know that he'd sent for Vicki Anderson to replace me.

I was disappointed to be leaving Vegas, but he was the boss and I had to do what he said. I also believed him. So I went to Cincinnati and recorded some tracks and did a couple of shows with Rufus Thomas, the gentleman who did 'Walking The Dog'. He was Carla Thomas's father and a DJ in Memphis. So me and Rufus, we did a couple of jobs that Walter Whisenhunt got us there. Whisenhunt was still the producer when James wasn't there. We had fun working together just over the county line in Kentucky: I think you could buy liquor there on a Sunday when Cincinnati laws didn't allow it.

After that I went back to Kansas City for a short visit. Or so I thought. I was still waiting on James to contact me, but he didn't call and he didn't send no money. No nothing – although I'd understood I'd still be paid even though I was away from the show. Two weeks went by, then four weeks. Nothing. I started getting edgy. I called James's office for a draw because my money was getting short. I got no reply. Then I felt I had to get out of town, because Kansas is only little and I didn't want the people to think I'd bombed out. I was embarrassed because 'local girl makes good' had been spread all over the papers.

I decided to call my friend Daisy Stubbs. She was in her sixties. I'd met her a year or so before when I went out with her son Joe, who'd been the lead singer with the Motown group The Contours, and I'd also met his brothers Charles and Levi. Levi was with the Four Tops, who used to come to Kansas City quite often to play club dates. Their brother Charles, who's deceased now, lived in Kansas City, and we got to be friends. One of the group's members, Lawrence Payton, married a girl from here and took her back to Detroit. She was a young girl, a beautiful model, and they were so in love, but it turned out to be a battle of hell. Lawrence had had children with his first wife, and she just wouldn't let go until she'd driven this girl to an early grave.

When I went out with Joe I thought he was unattached. Any time I date a man the first thing I ask is if he's married or hooked up. That's thanks to my mother, who when I became of age, say about seventeen or eighteen, put me in front of a mirror. 'Look at yourself, Marva,' she said.

'Yes, ma'am.'

'Look at yourself real good,' she said.

'Uh-huh.'

'Let me tell you something. You're pretty. You've got nice features, you're shaped, you're small and you have beautiful legs. Don't you ever let a man put you down and don't you ever play second fiddle to nobody, 'cause I'm your mother and I'm telling you that you got it, girl.'

So I don't care if the man is single and he has a girlfriend he's been fooling with for over a year; I'm not going to be the chick on the side. It's a losing game. OK, so I knew that, but I also foolishly believed Joe when he told me that he was single. We quickly grew very fond of each other, had fun together and were having a real good time.

Joe Stubbs promised me a lot of things. He wanted me to go back to Detroit with him to try to get me in with Berry Gordy. 'Come on, I'm going to take you to Motown.' I agreed to go, and my father got wind of it. Lo and behold he came over to my place one Saturday morning – I was still living in the three rooms in the same building as the Weatherbys – and told me I was crazy.

He said, 'I'm going to take you to Osawatomie.' That was one of the infamous nuthouses in the state of Kansas. One of my aunties had promised me that she'd come round to back me up, but she never showed and I had to tackle him by myself. I respected him, but I went to Detroit just like I said I would. As I said, I'm a Taurus and I was a young bull head: I was strong-willed and stubborn.

So I went with Joe intending to go to Detroit, but on the way he decided to stop off in Youngstown, Ohio, for a few days, and that was where I found out he was a married man. Little did I know that he was going home to see his wife. I was staying in a hotel. One day he brought a young woman over to the hotel named Eleanor to keep me company. She told me what Joe was doing: he had plans to leave me in Youngstown and turn me out. By that I mean turn me into a trick baby, a whore. Thankfully God always has a ram in the bush, and thanks to Eleanor I managed to get away from Joe and get out of Youngstown. Eleanor was AC/DC and really liked girls. She was a beautiful lady, but she told me straight up she was gay, which was unusual as back in them days people preferred to keep those sorts of things in the closet. She was my good Samaritan. We snuck out of the hotel, went to Joe's mother, Ms Stubbs, in Detroit, and we told her what happened. She didn't like it. She said, 'He's been married to this woman for years. Marva, you're too good for him. Forget that man. I say that even though he's my own son.' So me and her, we became very close. I was like a daughter to her. She'd walk with me to the grocery store every day and we talked a lot. She took me under her wing and I'll never forget that. I called her Mama Stubbs or Ms Stubbs. She was always trying to find me a husband: she said I was pretty and I deserved someone to treat me right. I heard she passed about five years ago. Ms Daisy Stubbs was an angel.

Anyway, when James didn't call me after I stayed a while in Cincinnati and then Kansas, I called Ms Stubbs. She was pleased to hear from me, so I went up there to stay for what I thought would be a few weeks, because I was still thinking I was going back to work any day now. It turned out to be a few months. I was frantic by that time.

In Detroit I became friendly with Levi Stubbs. I got on well with him. He was a beautiful person. His father was deceased by that time and Levi had become what you would call a father figure, keeping the family unit together. He took care of his mother and made sure she had what she needed. I have the utmost respect for that family. While I was there I asked Levi to look at my contract with James. I asked him if I could get out of it, and he said he'd take it to his attorney. So he got me an appointment, and his attorney said, 'Yeah, this contract ain't worth nothing but James Brown is so big and powerful it's not worth getting involved. You'd better let it alone.' People were really scared of him back then.

So Levi said, 'I'm going to see if I can't get an interview for you with Mr Gordy at Motown. I'm gonna call him.' And he did exactly that.

It was late in the evening, maybe about ten or eleven o'clock at night. Levi called Mr Gordy who said, 'Bring Marva to the house.' We went to his apartment, where, if I remember right, everything – the decor and furnishings – was all white. It was beautiful. I played the piano and sang some church songs and a few standards. He seemed pleased by my performance and said, 'I'll tell you what, Marva, why don't you come down to the Twenty Grand club? I want you to sing there.' He needed to hear me with a band. I said OK. I was elated. In fact, I was so happy I didn't know what to do with myself.

Unfortunately, as I didn't have a car and I didn't know my way round Detroit, I relied on Levi's brother, Joe, to get me to the club. I know it sounds foolish but I was still messing with Joe a little bit at that time, even after he tried to turn me out. So he said he'd make sure he'd get me to the Twenty Grand, but he let me down and never showed up. I guess I should have known better. Even so, I'm grateful that Mr Gordy and Levi looked my way.

I hadn't heard from the James Brown camp for so long that I decided to start a group with Thelma, Ms Stubbs's daughter, and Joyce Wilson – who was Jackie Wilson's sister and could sing her butt off. We were nearly the same age. We began rehearsing once or twice a week and we made a great sound together, but we wasn't really serious about it. I often saw her brother, Jackie. He was crazy but in a good way, outgoing and very lovable. Once, when I performed at Detroit's Cobo Hall, he dropped by to say hi and brought with him two big German Shepherd dogs.

As I spent more and more time in Detroit at the end of 1967, it seemed my career in show business had ground to a halt. I began to get desperate. Although Ms Stubbs was looking after me and treating me like a member of her family, I was out of money. So I called my manager. I worried the heck out of him and he sent a little money. Then I told him to ask James Brown why he'd abandoned me: I felt it was time for me to go back. I even asked him to beg for me. Finally Mr Cooper – I always called him Mr Cooper – went to St Louis and had a face-to-face talk with James. He said, 'Marva's in Detroit and wants to come back.'

James said, 'OK, tell her that when I come to Cleveland you and she are to come and see me.'

So the Sunday night of that week, in December 1967, Mr Cooper landed in Detroit to meet up with me. The weather was bad: it was freezing and there was a lot of snow. That was the fateful weekend we heard that Otis Redding had died in a plane crash. I remember we were watching the TV and they said his plane had gone down in the water. As I watched the news I remembered what James had said a few months before about the state of Otis's plane, which was an old-fashioned propeller airplane, a rickety old thing. He told me he'd said to Otis that he needed to change it, but he wouldn't listen. James used to make fun of Otis and Ray Charles, laughing at what he called their 'old-ass planes'. See, he had a Learjet. When he heard that Otis's plane had crashed and he'd been killed, he said, 'I tried to tell him that plane was too old.'

Although Otis Redding's death made me think about the dangers of flying, and despite the bad weather, I got on a plane with Mr Cooper and went to Cleveland to meet James. This time I was determined not to put a foot wrong and do whatever it took to stay on the James Brown show.

CHAPTER 17

The Prodigal Returns

When we got to Cleveland Mr Cooper went in to see James alone. Not long afterwards James called me in. Oh my, I was nervous – but he'd done what he wanted: broken my spirit to the point where I said yes, yes, yes. I'd do anything to be back on the show. Now, there were whispers going around that Vicki Anderson – who had been my predecessor in the revue and had come back to cover for me when I was in Detroit – was getting ready to do *The Dick Clark Show* on national TV. I had mixed emotions about this and didn't have a clue how much James would do for me in the circumstances. After all, he'd virtually kicked me off the show. Then – and it came completely out of the blue – he surprised me by saying, 'Miss Whitney, I'm sending you to do *American Bandstand, The Dick Clark Show.*'

I gushed, 'Oh, that's fantastic! Thank you, Mr Brown.' It was more than I could hope for, but I felt sorry for Vicki. She must have felt bad that I got to do the TV show instead of her, especially when James had said she could do it. But I was glad of the opportunity.

Hallelujah! I was back in favor. And how! This was to be my first national TV show. Dick Clark's show was watched by millions of people and could turn you into a household name overnight. James said, 'Miss Whitney, you get ready. You go back and get your stuff and I want you to meet me out there, OK?' OK, yes sir! Hell, I didn't damn near starve for several months for nothing.

But this came with a cost, and at what price was soon to be seen.

All I knew was I could put food on the table for my little girl, and send money home to Mom and Dad to make life a little easier for them all.

Although I was thankful to James Brown for putting me in the limelight, I was also more than a little worried about my position in the revue. I felt vulnerable, because when I returned in early '68 I discovered that Bobby Bennett and James Crawford of the Famous Flames had left. Bobby, my protector and my friend, was gone. I felt like a chicken in a cage with James Brown, the fox, licking his chops outside. I was angry at Bobby when he left because I was close enough to him to think that he and I could try and make it without James. But he didn't call, and it was a shock when I returned to find he'd left. I never saw him again after that, but I've talked to him once or twice since on the phone. These days he's in a wheelchair and not well at all; he's had many strokes.

Indirectly I had something to do with Bobby Bennett's leaving. James had decided to get rid of the Flames – which was never his group anyway – because I'd gotten smart, and he was pissed at Bobby for protecting me from him. By this time James was so damn big he didn't need them anymore. He wanted me back, and the only way I was really going to be under his thumb was if they were gone – so he got rid of them.

James saw me as fair game. He'd been stalking me for about a year, ever since I joined the revue back in May '67. I was the rabbit and he was the hunter. It was only a matter of time before he cornered me.

I was happy to be back in the organization, but everybody was looking at me. I didn't know if some were happy or some were sad but I knew some were going Oooh Lord! There was always tension between me and Vicki Anderson from day one. She thought she was Queen Bee. Every time somebody left or went missing James called for her, and sometimes we even did a show together. Even so, he treated her bad. When she was with us on the way to her home town he'd say, 'Vicki, only Marva is going to sing tonight.' That would hurt her so bad. Who wouldn't want to sing in their own home town? But she always managed to get him to give in, even though she was never able to have her whole spot: he'd cut it short. I felt sorry – not just for myself – but for all of us: all of the women who had to be with him and put on a false face. Eventually Vicki left to go and have a baby.

Before the TV show I cut a new record called 'Unwind Yourself'.

I think the song might have originally been intended for Vicki Anderson. The wild horn riff that opens the song always seemed ugly to me, but I didn't complain: James had decided I needed a change of musical direction, and 'Unwind Yourself' followed the new funk style that he'd started with 'Cold Sweat' only a few months earlier. Funk to me is when your heart and mind come together in a place that makes you feel good. And most of the time this saying comes into play: he who sits on a hot stove will soon rise. With funk music you just can't keep still; it makes you go through many healing emotions that the body needs. It's a type of doctor, and makes you feel so good naturally. Although the song didn't chart when it came out in early 1968, it helped establish my own unique style, and twenty years or so later was sampled by many DJs and hip-hop artists. A hit song in 1989 called 'The 900 Number' sampled the horn and drum sections, though I've never gotten a penny from it, and a year later someone called Chad Jackson had an even bigger hit when he sampled it on a record called 'Hear The Drummer (Get Wicked)'. Amazingly the song was even covered by a Japanese funk group called Mieko Hirota featuring Singers Three. The song's title in Japanese was 'Anata Ga Inakutemo'.

Charles Spurling, a songwriter and A&R man at King Records, was responsible for 'Unwind Yourself'. This is what he remembers:

I wrote that with Hank Ballard in '65. He was bigger than James then; he was the one that started James. Together with his band The Midnighters he had several million-selling records in a row. Hank used to use James to open up his shows: they were very good friends. I didn't know the business well then. After I wrote 'Unwind Yourself' Hank let James hear it, and the next thing I know this song came out, and it was a big seller for Hank. After James got Marva he turned round and put it out again with her. I liked both versions of it, but on Marva's version James's horn section was much better. I mostly had rhythm guys on Hank's version because I hadn't really improved myself (as an arranger) all the way yet.

Over the years I've learned to like 'Unwind Yourself' and get used to that darn horn. Some of the other songs I cut I didn't care too much for either but they sound better to my ears now since they've been remastered for CD. The mixing process is different and I can now hear notes that wasn't up in the mix before. Sound-wise, much of the music was hazy to me, like 'Things Got To Get Better', which I cut a few months later. The saxophonist, St Clair Pinckney, was dynamic on there. I'd often been ashamed of my music. I couldn't stand to hear myself sing. A lot of artists are like that. But now, with modern technology and remastering, I don't mind listening to my own music.

When I look back, I realize my recording sessions were always too hurried for me. I like to rehearse until I can become a part of the song, but back then I hardly had any time to rehearse before a recording. James, on the other hand, used to work his songs on the road with the band for a good length of time until he got them the way he wanted. I've always tried to do my best, though. James picked all of my songs, of course, as well as what I wore.

After I cut 'Unwind Yourself' I got my things together and went out to the West Coast to perform the song on *The Dick Clark Show*. I was scared but got a good reaction: I was elated. I've got a picture somewhere showing me and Dick in someone's dressing room. I wore tight dresses back then, and I think it was a black and white number that night. After the show James said he had to go to Portland, Oregon: 'You go back home and I'll call you in a few days, so you can catch up with us. OK, Miss Whitney? Now you go back to the hotel and get yourself packed up.'

'OK, Mr Brown!' I'd learned my lesson by now and I knew what to say and what not to say.

So I went back to my hotel room and was praising God for his goodness to me. I was packing when someone knocked on the door, then knocked again. 'Who is it?' I shouted.

'Mr Brown,' was the gruff reply.

Oh Lord, I thought. I opened the door and let him in. Why was he still here? I was scared.

'How are you, Miss Whitney?'

'I'm fine, Mr Brown. How are you?'

'I'm good, Miss Whitney, good.' So we made small talk. He said he'd really enjoyed the TV show. I sat down, and he sat down on the couch beside me. We made more small talk and he edged closer to me. I said to myself, *Uh-oh, he wants something. Lord, help me.* Then we started playing musical chairs: he'd get close and I'd nervously move somewhere else in the room. When I sat down he'd move close again. Eventually he got tired of this game, and I could tell by his expression that I wasn't to move any more. He wanted to talk about something serious.

'Miss Whitney.' I could feel a strong sense of authority in his voice.

'Yes, Mr Brown?'

'I don't fatten frogs for snakes.' I'd never heard that term before. What did it mean? I didn't really understand. 'I don't fatten frogs for snakes,' he repeated.

I said, 'Oh?' Then he told me point blank what his intentions were.

'Miss Whitney. You will be my woman and do what I tell you. I have the power to make or break you. You will never work again if you don't do as I tell you. Do you understand? You'll come and go as I tell you.' I will never ever forget these words. They burned into my soul. In later years, when I talked to Lyn Collins, my successor in the James Brown revue, about our experiences, she told me he'd said the same thing to her after he'd managed to break up her and her husband.

My mind began to spin, and on the inside I kept asking myself what I was going to do. I thought about what he'd done previously, when he sent me home and didn't recall me. I thought about my contract, which the lawyer had said wasn't worth the paper it was written on. I told myself I had a child to take care of. I couldn't let down Mom and Dad and be the laughing stock of the whole community. I'd heard things about how James Brown treated people, but up to that point I'd never experienced it myself. What the hell was I going to do? I mean, this joker had me in a vice. *Help me, Lord Jesus,* I pleaded. My mind raced for an answer. But then I thought, this man has so many women he probably won't have that much time for me, and surely I'll be able to put up with him once in a while. I could stand being tapped every now and then. That's the truth. I was in shock initially but then everything became clear: I had to submit. So I said, 'Yes sir, Mr Brown, I understand.'

He said, 'When I tell you to come, I don't want no damn static, and you come and you do what I tell you. You understand?'

'Yes sir, Mr Brown.'

He got up and said, 'OK, now I got to go.' He said he was going to some place where one of the Black Panthers was to meet him.

I was so damn glad when he got out of my room. I had to get my mind together, and I didn't know what to do. I said, *Jesus Christ, help me please.* So I got packed and was waiting to leave that morning. I lay down on the bed and was still thinking about my situation when the phone rang. It was only about an hour after James left, and I wondered who in the hell was calling me. I picked up the phone. 'Hello?'

'This is Mr Brown.'

Oh Lord, I thought. 'Yes, Mr Brown?' I tried not to sound shocked or surprised.

'I want you to pack your bags, make a reservation and come to me right now. There's an eleven o'clock flight leaving from Burbank. Make sure you're on that flight. You're coming to the hotel where I'm staying. When you get to the desk you'll say that you're Miss Brown, and they'll contact me and you'll be with me. Is that understood?'

'Yes sir.'

So I did it. Oh my God, I understood the rules now. His ultimatum had made it crystal clear. I had no choice but to get on that plane and follow him. I realized, too, that the conversation I'd had with that beautiful lady called – strangely enough – Miss Brown many months previously made sense at last. I was indeed going to be where she once was. Her prediction had come true.

On the flight out to Oregon I was wondering what kind of shit I was going through and what the hell I'd gotten into. I was caught in a trap: damned if I did, damned if I didn't. So when I got off the plane I went to the hotel and went up to the desk, to say what I was instructed to say. 'Hello, I'm Miss Brown,' I said, feeling awkward. 'I have a reservation here.'

The hotel clerk's face lit up. 'Oh yes, ma'am!' To my utter amazement they rolled out the red carpet for me. Well, I don't have to say no more. You'd have thought I was the Queen of England.

But I was sadly mistaken when I thought that James wouldn't have time for me: he had plenty of time. In his autobiography, *The Godfather Of Soul,* James said I was his girlfriend. It's true: for a time I was. There was a time I really loved him, and we went on a few dates. But our relationship, for the most part, was a sham. James always liked light-skinned women, and there were maybe only two brown-skinned women on his show. So that's why he made a bee-line towards me when I first arrived on the show. But it wasn't popular for a black man to have white women out in the open, so most of the time when I was supposed to be with him as his 'girlfriend' I was actually next door while his white women secretly came to see him. Then when they left, James and me would be together when we walked out, so everyone assumed we were a couple. Like I said, it was a sham really. I knew what the real situation was: every night James was going to have a different woman. I might be with him in the evening, but tomorrow there'd be another one, someone else he'd go off with. He loved nobody but himself.

I was the first person in James's revue that he truly tried to push, so maybe he looked favorably on me. It was said that he did more for me than any other singer on his show, and I believe he did. I even believe he cared for me, and I certainly cared for him, but I left a little space in my heart to protect myself because I discovered he couldn't be true to anyone. He certainly kept up the appearance that I was his woman, but when I found out who the real James Brown was and saw the real man too often any love and affection on my part withered. I wasn't raised to behave like he did. I pleaded with him not to have me travel with him on the plane when he had another woman with him. 'Please don't do that to me,' I'd say, but he didn't care.

So for a time after I got back on the show we got very close, and I think we began to have a special relationship but much of the time it made me sick. Although he could be good to me, in a blink of an eye he could turn nasty: that's why my face often wore a sad look in those days. The same was true of Lyn Collins. Not so much Vicki, though, for she was Bobby Byrd's wife. But even she didn't escape from Brown's mind games, as I've mentioned. It took a toll on all of us. The emotional rollercoaster – with all its ups and downs – was draining both physically and emotionally.

When I returned with James everyone knew the deal. If looks could kill then I'd have been dead as soon as I set foot back in the organization. There was no doubt that to everyone else on the show I was his woman, and there was a lot of jealousy from the dancers and my roommates. I had to suffer smart and cutting remarks, because they all wanted to be with James. They'd say, 'Girl, you don't know how lucky you are,' and then give me that look that says, *I don't like you because you're with James.*

I tried to learn how to enjoy the good moments and ignore the rest, but often there was no relief. It was awful, so demeaning. I tell you, here was a grown man who wouldn't even bother to put his own socks on. He'd put his false teeth in my hands and I'd have to put them in water for him. Everything was done for him. We were like servants. And then there was always the threat of violence. One time I walked into a dressing room and James was in there beating a pregnant girl. I don't know who she was – one of his many girlfriends probably. She was cowering on a concrete floor. When I went in and saw what was going on I said in a reproachful voice, 'Oh, Mr Brown!' When he saw that I'd witnessed what he was doing to her he stopped, looked sheepish and walked away. This kind of thing happened often.

Even if I went home back to Kansas James called me at odd times to let me know that I was being watched. My dad saw the change in me, and in the end when I couldn't hide it any more he became furious. It was the same for Lyn Collins. Her Uncle Shortie, I think, asked her if James had been hitting on her and she told him yes. He wanted to kill James after that. He and my father both said, 'If he hits you one more time let me know and I'll take care of it.' Lyn and me just tried to hide our emotions, often with some success.

So that evening when the red carpet was rolled out in the hotel, that's when my place was made as one of his women. It was easier for me to get labeled the worst kind of woman because I was single. All the rest of them that was there had husbands or boyfriends, but for me it was wide open and I soon found out what it meant. No peace followed, even when he was in the next town. Traps were laid for me. There was no one to trust or talk freely to, not even my roommates. No doubt about it – I was in jail.

In March 1968 Syd Nathan, the owner of King Records – who I never met as he was sick and didn't come to his office when I went there – died from a heart attack. Many people assume that James regarded Mr Nathan as a kind of father figure; after all, he'd played a big part in James's success. The truth, I've been told, is that Mr

Nathan hated James, and the feeling was mutual. They were a bad thorn in each other's side.

Later the same month James took the revue to Africa for the first time. We flew 7,000 miles to Abidjan on the Ivory Coast in West Africa at the invitation of the Ivory Coast's Ministry of Radio and Television, which was celebrating its first anniversary. We were only out there a couple of days – I think it was over the weekend – but it was a memorable experience. We did two live shows plus an hour-long TV special and were put up in the country's top hotel. They'd built a bandstand in the hotel grounds where we performed. I think 3,000 people paid $12 a head to see us.

The prospect of going to Africa was exciting to me for I was going to set foot on the land where my roots are. James was excited too, I believe, because he said, 'Whit, we're going to have African clothes made for you.' I think I had two dresses.

When we landed in Africa I could tell the difference right away: the smell of the country combined with the heat and look of the place was so different. Every place in the world has a smell of its own, and Africa has a strong smell of heat, vegetation and animals. As we got off the plane I remember thinking that I'd be in my spiritual homeland, and they'd see that I was dressed like them and respected them. Ah heck, as I looked down at all these African people hollering and screaming at us they were wearing mini-skirts and long wigs. Doggone it, how silly I felt. I almost felt out of place – but James said nothing. He didn't admit it, but I think he was surprised too: it had been his idea to dress me in traditional African robes.

I remember James saying, 'Stay close, Whit, the men over here are something else and they're going to look you over.' He was right. I remember seeing a big, powerful-looking man when we were walking somewhere. Just by looking at him I felt he had some kind of supernatural power. I couldn't tell if it was a good or bad power, but it scared the hell out of me. I remember saying, 'Lordy, I sure wouldn't want to be left alone in his presence.'

As we rode in the car to the hotel we passed a village. There were big black pots in the yards of mud huts, just like I'd seen on TV. The people were dirt poor. I felt sorry seeing my roots, my people, looking like this.

When we rolled up at our hotel we waited to be told to get out of the car. The Africans close to us stared at me in the same way I looked at them.

We went in through a side door, and I heard someone say in the background of the kitchen, 'Move, nigger, move!' I couldn't believe it, and my blood began to boil. The white person who said it shut the hell up when he saw us. That, I shall never forget. Although I really didn't know anything personally about racial prejudice my soul knew. I heard James and others talking, saying that Africans made only about $200 a year – and that was good money for them. My heart cried out, especially when I saw wealthy white children with their black nannies.

The Africans treated us like royalty. If I needed something brought to me they'd be bowing and scraping. I said, 'No, no, no, don't do that,' and tried to tell them that it wasn't necessary. And when I tipped, I tipped big. The life we were living was a real contrast with the life outside.

So we did our two shows – by which time I'd gotten out of my African garb and was wearing my mini-dresses – and then went home back to America. Although it was a whirlwind trip, it really made me aware of how other people in the world lived. God bless America, I said: maybe it ain't so good, but it ain't as bad as some places I'd been to.

We'd only been back a few days when the Reverend Martin Luther King Jr was assassinated in Memphis. It was Thursday 4 April 1968. I'll never forget that fateful day. I was staying in New York City at the Great Northern Hotel. I heard the news on the TV. I recall I was in a real little room, for I was only going to be there a day.

I didn't really care for Martin Luther King at first, because I thought he was a little bit too milk toast. You know, he was taking all them beatings and going on all those damn marches but it didn't seem to be changing much. I sometimes wondered why he was pussyfooting around, and believed he should be taking care of business by any means possible. But as I grew older I found out that he was doing it the only way you can do it in the United States. And still it cost him his life.

On the day he was killed white folk was scared because they didn't know what we black folk was going to do. They were humble as lambs, and my service at the hotel was never so prompt. Back home, in Kansas City, I heard folks were rioting and tearing up things, while in New York I kept hearing that the powers that be were afraid of what was going to happen in places like Philadelphia and Washington DC. I believe the president, Lyndon Johnson, asked James to go to DC and quiet the city down. They felt they needed him urgently, because James had power back then and was seen as a spokesman for black people. He went to DC, and around that time recorded the song 'Say it Loud – I'm Black & I'm Proud'. Don't burn but learn was his motto. As egotistical as he was, he really wanted to help and do something positive.

The day after Dr King's death we had a concert at The Garden in Boston. James was insistent that we do it. He said, 'We're going to do that show like nothing is going on: we got to help keep this mess down.' We started the show – which was broadcast live on local TV with the hope that it would help ease racial tension – and the mood and atmosphere there was charged and edgy. I sang four songs that night, starting off with Etta James's 'Tell Mama' and following it with a version of the dramatic Debbie Taylor ballad, 'Check Yourself'. Then I did Aretha Franklin's 'Chain Of Fools', finishing off with the Gladys Knight & The Pips' hit 'I Heard It Through The Grapevine' (Marvin Gaye's version didn't come out until later). I remember I sang so strong and hit a high note that was so loud and deafening that the sound man had to run back to the board to adjust the mix. That's because I was taught by a man named Pico Payne – who became my play father – how to sing from the stomach, which is the proper way to sing unless you're singing falsetto.

Midway through James's set folks jumped up on the stage and the cops wanted to beat them back, but James managed to calm the situation down in a dignified manner.

We all knew America was in a mess but we didn't want a bloody revolution. At least I didn't. Trouble was breaking out in towns and cities across the country. We'd had a taste of it ourselves that year in Memphis – where Dr King died – after we did a show there. Instead of taking a car as planned, James was forced to take the bus with the rest of us. The reason he did was that Jimmy Smith, one of the men who took care of the high-level dollar jobs on the show, went to the car and found it smelling strongly of gasoline. 'This don't smell right,' he said. He checked, and discovered that somebody had messed with the fuel tank. If we'd got into that car and someone had lit up a cigarette we'd all have been blown to kingdom come. It was frightening that somebody meant to get us. We were also angered, and like most black folks were even more determined to seek equality and justice. I was proud that James was taking a stand on civil rights, but sometimes I was scared because I felt something else nasty might happen.

Later on, in 1969, James went to Washington DC to see the new president, Richard Nixon. James's advisors had told him to stay away, but he thought he knew better and had to have his way. From that point onwards James gradually began to lose power. The authorities saw to that: they saw a black man with too much power over black people, and they didn't want that. When he went on TV shows James talked about racial issues: he was right to but being bold and saying what was true didn't help him. It was a real no-no – and it wasn't long afterwards that I think he was hounded by the IRS over unpaid taxes.

CHAPTER 18

Going To Vietnam

In May 1968 James announced that we would be traveling to Korea, Japan and Vietnam to perform for the US servicemen out there. Senator Hubert Humphrey and Mr Johnson, the owner of *Jet* magazine, played a big part in organizing the trip. On 5 June we took off from JFK airport in New York, over twenty of us all on one plane – the band, the dancers and most of the usual entourage. We had to have lots of shots for all the diseases you can pick up over there. We flew to Los Angeles and then to Hawaii, where we stayed over.

Then it was Seoul, South Korea. We didn't stay in a hotel but in somebody's house, as far as I can recall. The thing that struck me was that you had to walk into the kitchen from the front door. I remember thinking, *Hmm, this is different: the bedrooms are downstairs.* Then it dawned on me: it was in case bombs came from the North – you'd be protected, already underground.

I remember looking out the window and seeing an old woman pulling a large two-wheel wagon. I don't know how she did it. And I was amazed by the size of the vegetables: one potato was so big it could take care of a whole family – I'm telling you it was a giant. I asked how in the heck it got that big, and they said they used human manure. We saw some giant celery too: I was astounded. I also remember getting some beautiful leather boots made there – in less than twenty-four hours.

After doing shows in Korea we went to Okinawa, Japan. We laid over there, but we got word that things were red hot in Vietnam and the military people were concerned about our safety. We'd all been excited to a certain extent before we left that we were going to visit Vietnam, but when we heard that things were hotting up we got worried. That's when the military people said that only seven of us could go; it was too dangerous for everybody. And you should have seen the looks on people's faces: a mixture of fear and relief. They were scared, but they were too scared to say that they didn't want to go. It was funny how some people said, 'Oh, I wanted to go so bad,' but you knew they were lyin' through their teeth. Some were so glad they didn't get picked that they didn't know what to do with themselves. It was also kind of funny because people didn't know whether to say yes or no, because they was afraid of James's reaction.

Anyway, it ended up with me saying I'd go. I've often asked myself why, and these are the reasons I've come up with. The first is that I'd heard how black men were suffering over there on the front line. They were dying, and all they got for entertainment were Oreo cookies that didn't want to be bothered with them. For those that don't know, an Oreo cookie is black on the outside and white on the inside and it was a term used in the '60s for people who know they're black but act like they're white. They walk, talk and try to look like the words 'black people' don't apply to them. They're phoneys. So my heart went out to black soldiers: I wanted them to see that somebody cared. Second, I'd sensed that there was a problem between me and James. We wasn't getting along too well. I didn't hate him, as he could be a likeable person – but he was often such a dog with women, and crude too. I felt that something might change within him if he could see the sacrifice I was making by going to Vietnam: I was hoping he'd realize I really cared for him because I'd volunteered to put my life at stake for him. What more could I do as a human being? You know, death is death: it's the ultimate sacrifice. Also, I felt that if I didn't prove my loyalty he'd treat me worse. I wanted to get that mental and physical abuse off my back.

I weighed it up, looked at the cost, and said, *Well, he can't really take a dancer.* But I thought he had to have a woman there. I thought the soldiers would appreciate a young woman singer, one who was up and coming.

I don't know whether the fellas volunteered or whether they were handpicked but there were certain people that James had to take: a drummer, a bass player, a guitarist and of course a horn player. In the end it was decided that James would take me, two sax players, Maceo Parker and St. Clair Pinckney; two guitarists, Jimmy 'Chank' Nolen and Alfonzo 'Country' Kellum; trumpeter Waymon Reed, bassist Tim Drummond and drummer Clyde Stubblefield. Folks called us the 'Saigon Seven.'

Tim Drummond was the first white musician in James's band; he replaced Bernard Odum, having played with a Kansas band called The Dapps that James produced. I don't know if he was there because James wanted to draw larger, integrated crowds or just to aggravate his black musicians. James never did anything without a reason to boost his career. The bottom line, though, was that Tim was an out-of-sight bass player and a wonderful person. He was bad, bad, bad. As we used to say, that is one bad white boy. He could really lay down the funk. After coming back from Vietnam he got hepatitis and was replaced by 'Sweet' Charles Sherrell. I might have seen him twice since I left.

We all had to do double duty once we got to Vietnam. Especially me. I became a beautician all of a sudden. I was also the iron-ee and boy, let me tell you, I don't like to iron! I also had to tend to James's hair, which in the stifling heat wasn't easy. After each show he left the stage dripping with sweat – more so than usual because of the intense heat and humidity. Then I had to wash his hair, roll in curlers with a little setting lotion, and then he'd go under the drier for about an hour. He combed it out hisself. Then he'd change his clothes and freshen hisself up. He never went anywhere or did nothing without having perfect hair first. His hair was really clean, 'cause he washed it every day, sometimes several times.

When we flew into Saigon the city was being attacked. We had to wear green camouflage uniforms with tin helmets and heavy combat boots, and we were each given a card that stated our name and gave our army rank: I was a general of some kind. This was so that if we were captured the enemy would know we were high-ranking officers and would hopefully give us good treatment. I don't know if this would have worked, but it made me feel a little more secure. We were told we couldn't venture too far or we'd come within range of enemy gunfire. They didn't care who you was – you was going to get shot at even if you was just there to entertain the troops. The US Army made sure we were protected but it was a scooting game: we just kept our heads down and scooted from one place to another. When we got out of buses and planes there was no stand-up walking: we had to duck and run.

The first thing that struck me after we got off the plane was the smell. I guess what with the heat and all the animals – lots of cows, hogs and chickens – the place gave off a really strong, heavy, earthy kind of smell. It really hit your nose hard.

When we got to the hotel, which was the Continental I think, Mama San and Papa San were trying to sell their daughters to men. They'd say, 'Pretty women, very cheap! Want my daughter?' I was shocked: they were pimping their own children. We were warned to be very careful not to mess with the Vietnamese, even to the extent of buying things in the hotel – because, I was told, the people who smiled at us in the daytime become the enemy at night-time. Sometimes you could buy something as a souvenir and it'd have a bomb in it. So you had to be very careful. I bought me a beautiful doll, but James later insisted that I paint its face black.

The hotel was our base. From there we took buses – which had wire screens on them to protect against grenades – and were taken by plane or helicopter to the army camps. At night there was always a curfew. It was common sense: the day we arrived there'd been a huge explosion just down the way from our hotel and some people had been killed. That's where the scooting came in. You prepared yourself ahead of time so you wouldn't be a sitting duck.

James, like all of us, was concerned about being attacked, and said to the military people that he had to have something to protect hisself. He was so insistent that they gave him a gun. In past interviews I've always said that they gave him a stick, but I said that because I wanted to protect him and I didn't want to get the generals into trouble: it was against government rules to give a civilian a military weapon. James took that gun everywhere with him, and he said, 'Man, if they come I've got to have something to fight with.' James was no punk. He'd been a boxer and was used to the ways of the street. He'd mastered the art of self-preservation.

As I said, we scooted everywhere keeping our heads down. But once we got inside the camps, where our soldiers were, we felt safer.

They were so glad to see us all, but especially me, a black woman. They told me this to my face. They said that other soul sisters had been there but hadn't wanted to talk to them and didn't want to shake their hands: their noses was up in the air. I'm not that type of person. I'm always up front. If you ask me something I'll try to answer you straight: I'm not a phoney. I was always taught by my family that humble is the way and that your gift will make room for you. If you do the right thing within your heart then something good is going to happen. So when we arrived in Vietnam the soldiers felt like they was back home for a minute. That made me feel glad.

Mostly we did two concerts a day, one in the morning and one in the afternoon – when the heat and humidity was at its worst. It was draining. James had to have shots after each show because he'd lost so much body fluid. With all the noise and commotion the enemy probably knew what was going on. In fact, I remember some of the soldiers telling us that the Viet Cong knew we were there. I suppose it was very risky, especially when thousands of soldiers were off-duty listening to us. If they'd attacked they could have wiped us all out.

There was one time you could hear explosions and the rattle of machine gun fire from the stage. We were performing at an army base they called Long Binh, which was like a huge outdoor amphitheater cut deep into the side of a hill; apparently they'd used bulldozers to make it. We played to forty thousand troops that day. It was incredible. James brought the house down when he sang the patriotic song 'My Country 'Tis Of Thee'.

We also played at a large base called Camp Martin Cox, home of the 9th Infantry Division and known to most people as the Bearcat. It was 40 miles or so east of Saigon, close to the town of Long Thanh. And we did shows at Tan Son Nhut airbase, just outside Saigon, and the Phan Rang airbase.

Every night we flew back to the hotel in Saigon. Quite often we heard bullets being fired at the plane: you heard that ping, ping, ping sound. I was afraid but didn't like to show it. I said to myself, *Lord keep me, Lord keep me*. Back at our hotel, in the daytime you could see bunkers outside, piled high with sandbags. Common sense told you to keep your head down at night and stay away from them.

As we couldn't drink the water we drank Coca-Cola. Lots of it. If you were going to have a little ice to cool you down you had to put some Coca-Cola with it, otherwise you'd get sick. I kept hold of the Coke bottles and at night in our hotel room – James and me shared a room – I'd put them in strategic places, at the door, at the windows and across the entrance in case someone came in. The rooms wasn't heavily carpeted – I think the floors were concrete – so if a bottle fell you knew somebody was there. You slept light and just the slightest noise disturbed you. You got used to it, because self-preservation is the first law of nature. Although I didn't get much sleep I rested easier with those bottles around. And James slept with his gun under the pillow. That made me feel better too.

We were always on our guard. Danger seemed to be everywhere. We'd only been there a few days when our plane, which was to take us over the jungle, almost crashed. It was a grass airstrip, damp and marshy, but I guess the military people knew the wet ground underneath could hold the plane. I think I saw more fear in some of the fellas than I felt myself, especially the first time we had to walk through the marshes to get on board: they didn't like that. Hell, I didn't either, but I wasn't going to complain. I knew I had to be tough, because the last thing anybody wanted was a sniveling woman.

We took off OK but wasn't airborne for long. I didn't see any smoke, but I heard this strange 'ping' noise. It sounded like somebody had hit a piece of iron but it was a very low sound. In those days my hearing was good and I could hear the slightest sound. Something was obviously wrong. James was sitting next to me. I said, 'Did you hear that?'

He shook his head. 'No.'

I shouted to the rest of the fellas, 'Y'all hear that?'

They said, 'No, uh-uh.'

When I heard that ping sound for a second time I asked them again. No: they hadn't heard it.

The next minute the pilot made an emergency landing in the marsh, bringing the plane down quickly. As we bumped to a halt I heard a man shout, 'Get out, an engine's caught fire! Everybody get the hell out of here!'

We were sitting in the back next to the door. Everyone was panicking and started running so fast down the aisle that they passed me and James. I was on the inside of the seat and James was on the end of it. He was nearer the door and leapt out ahead of me after everybody else had gone. I got to the door and there were no steps: you had to jump out. So I got ready, and was expecting a helping hand: I wasn't so sure I could make the jump by myself, without falling on my face or falling down. But no one reached up for me; they'd all scattered and run off. Nobody really knew what to do, but we instinctively knew we had to get away in case the plane exploded. James was down the way, running like a headless chicken. I was afraid, but I kept the Lord on my mind as I jumped down about 4 or 5ft onto the soft, marshy ground below. The water came up halfway between my calf and ankle – just enough to make your feet wet and your steps heavy. Some of the band was going one way and me and James was going the other way. And then it got funny, because the fellas – I don't know why I wasn't that scared – were running for their lives and saying, 'Oh man, we can't go through this!' And when we were at a safe distance from the plane they started lighting up. They were so scared and their nerves was so bad that they was shaking and had to have a hit of marijuana to get high. I didn't need that, though – I didn't smoke or do anything at that time.

This wasn't the first time that James showed me he only thought of hisself in front of danger. Once we were in his Learjet flying over the Colorado mountains at night: me, James, Mr Bobbitt and the two pilots. There was suddenly a noise like a big bang and the plane shook. Mr Bell, the pilot, shouted to us that the engines had failed, and we dropped like a stone. 'They'll never find us if we crash,' he said, and started calling mayday on the radio. James went into a trance. I had my mouth shut when we dropped, so the air pressure went to my head and I was in dire pain. Me and Mr Bobbitt struggled to get the oxygen masks to come down, which should have automatically dropped. He had a little pocket-knife, which he started using to free them. Eventually he managed to get them out, and we put them over our faces. I had to put one over James's face. He looked like a ghost, his skin pale and clammy. He was still looking blankly out the window, unresponsive to the drama around him: it was like he was paralyzed by fear and his mind had gone. But that wasn't the end of our ordeal. When we went to breathe some air, none was coming out of the oxygen masks. Somehow, thank God, the pilots got the engines going. Afterwards James said, 'I want two brand new engines.' He said to the pilot: 'Mr Bell, what was wrong with them engines?'

Mr Bell said, 'Nothing. Mr Brown, I checked them all out. We went through the whole thing twice. There was nothing wrong with them.'

James said, 'Maybe we was flying too high.'

It was a really scary moment in my life. When everyone jumped out of the plane in Vietnam leaving me to fend for myself, I immediately thought of that incident. But although I'd jumped out of the tail end of the plane I was OK: no bones broken or cuts and bruises.

Later on during the tour we was transported by helicopters. It was the first time I'd ever been in one. I never knew they could be so loud. We had to put ear plugs in to block out the noise but you could still hear things. One time we were flying back in the dusk after a concert, and when we looked out of the window all we could see were bright orange and red lights below. The soldiers were fighting down on the ground, and there were like millions of little red dots flying about – tracer bullets. Although they looked kind of pretty at first they started coming towards us and riddled our helicopter. The pilot started calling out, 'Mayday, mayday, we're being attacked!' We had to lay belly down on the floor until he got us to a safer area.

I wasn't sorry to leave Vietnam. It was the toughest two weeks of my life. We got back on 17 June, and I seemed unscathed from my experience at first – but about six months later I was walking down the street in New York City during a shopping trip when I started shaking uncontrollably. That's when the shock finally came: the stress of my experiences hit me that day. But despite all we endured, serving my country in Vietnam is still the highlight of the time I spent with James Brown.

Although he didn't say it publicly, James was very disappointed by his experiences in Vietnam. He didn't think some of the senior military people showed enough respect for his and the band's sacrifice. In particular, he wasn't pleased about how the band was treated: they didn't seem to be respected. Even at a time of war, when we were doing our duty for the country, the ugly head of racism seemed to reveal itself. I wasn't really aware of this. As the only woman I had my own dressing room, and to be honest I was treated like gold.

You might have thought there'd be some perks for putting our lives on the line and going to Vietnam, but the truth is the United States didn't give us our full cheques for the thirteen days we were away: we were told before we left that our pay would be cut.

Afterwards, though, we all got certificates from the government. I've still got mine and I'm very proud of it. It's from the Department of Defense and says: 'United States Military Assistance Command, Vietnam Certificate of Appreciation is awarded to Marva Ann Whitney... For your outstanding contribution to the morale and welfare of the United States and other free world military assistance forces in the republic of Vietnam while touring the command, entertaining personnel of all services. The significant and lasting impression you made enhanced the morale of the fighting forces and reflects great credit upon yourself and your profession.' It's dated 15 June 1968 and is signed by Creighton W. Abrams, general, United States Army Commanding. I've also got a Certificate of Appreciation from the 9th Infantry Division, the 'Old Reliables,' dated 14 June 1968 and signed by Julian J. Ewell, Major General, USA Commanding Officer. It was good that we were recognized for the work we did in Vietnam but although James was called into the White House several times, and was given special favors and a special this and special that, the rest of us got ignored. We didn't get to meet the president. It's a damned shame.

I'd hoped that going to Vietnam with James would improve our relationship. Although I'd put my life on the line, sadly he didn't treat me no better afterwards. In fact, when we came back it got hotter on me instead of better. In a way I felt betrayed, for me and the band went through hell in Vietnam, and he acted like it was just another gig. I felt that if he couldn't be more open and loyal to me or the rest of us in the line of fire he could just kiss my butt. I think that's when my soul truly had had enough of him, and the end was near. And his behavior towards me got ugly and uglier.

Years later, when I talked to James about our experiences in Vietnam, he seemed to remember it fondly, and his heart went tender for a few minutes. A few minutes after that: next! He just put it out of his mind, like he forgot. He remembered what I did over there, but it didn't change a thing. He was the same man.

I don't have one picture of myself in Vietnam. I know James had some 'cause he told me, and made fun of me because I didn't have any mementos of our time there. But he wouldn't let me see them. I've written to *Jet* magazine to see I can get some photos but so far nothing has turned up. I've even called Washington DC and they couldn't come up with nothing neither, not even military films sent by the soldiers for their museum.

CHAPTER 19

Say It Loud – I'm Black & I'm Proud

When James first got the idea to do the 'Say It Loud – I'm Black & I'm Proud' record – I think Bobby Byrd was with him at the time – he was so excited he couldn't sit still. We were on the west coast, and all I heard that night was how this song was going to be a monster. His mind was just a-clicking. He kept saying, 'Baby, this is it, this is it!'

I directed the children who sang the chorus, but I got no credit for it. Often James didn't give credit where it was due. When we got to the studio, which was in Van Nuys in LA, a bunch of black kids was already waiting for us. They were proud little children and so well-mannered and well-behaved. Patient, too.

After James cut the song he was over the moon. He knew he'd got something special in the can. And, of course, when the record came out it was just like he said, a monster hit. It gave black people a new sense of pride and self-awareness. Some people have even said it was the first rap record. At the same time, though, it was the record that killed James's crossover career. That record scared white people and put an end to his ambitions to be a black Sinatra.

I had to laugh, though, because although James got into the 'black is beautiful' thing he was the last one of us to get an Afro-style hairdo. He found it very hard to stop having his regular hair perm every day, and he wouldn't do nothing until his hair looked right. When the band began to get Afros he laughed at them, ridiculing the new style. But that stopped after he had a meeting with some Black Panthers, who made some kind of instant believer out of him. When he turned up with an Afro we all knew who'd got a hold of him. Of course, once he changed his hair he ordered everyone who hadn't got an Afro to get one right away. In the dressing rooms we laughed, like I'm laughing right now just thinking about it.

Only a few people could make James do anything he didn't want to do. I remember there was a time in New York around the same period when he gave out food baskets at Thanksgiving. He wasn't happy about how much it was costing him, and I remember him saying, 'Hell, why can't they have hens instead of turkeys?' Of course he ended up getting turkeys, and I knew why. The Black Panthers made him.

Despite the odd occasion when he bowed down to pressure from others, James was his own man. The authorities thought he had too much power for a black man – that if he said, 'All right black people, let's kill all the white folks,' he could make it happen. It was when he helped stop rioting after Martin Luther King's death that they saw how much power he actually had, and it scared them. If he could stop a riot then he could surely start one as well. The people in government believed that the majority of black people would do exactly what he said, so they had to bust him. James's people, his advisors, tried to tell him not to go and see President Nixon, but he didn't listen. If James thought something was possible then nothing would stop him from trying to do it. I think he really wanted to help black people and help them rise to a certain standard, but in the end the system stopped him.

I remember there was a heated exchange between James and some folks on the Mike Douglas TV show in '68, when James had just brought out 'Say It Loud—I'm Black and I'm Proud'. Mike and his guests was talking about prejudice, and it really got heated. James was trying to explain why black people in America didn't like what was going on, like Vietnam, and in the end he stood up, 'cause he was so adamant about the way he felt. You could see he was frustrated that he wasn't being understood.

A lot of things frustrated James. One thing in particular that pissed him off was that he never made number one in the Billboard charts, although he topped the R&B charts many times and had lots of gold records. He'd say, 'With all the millions I've sold and all the hits I've had, you know they won't give me a number one spot.' It bugged the hell out of him. As I've said, he was also pissed because he didn't achieve the across-the-board appeal of Sammy Davis Jr and Frank Sinatra. He tried going to Vegas and doing Sinatra-style standards during the time I was with his show, but he bombed out and got poor reviews. Hell, people didn't want to see him doing songs like 'That's Life': they wanted to hear funk and see him do the mashed potato and boogaloo.

CHAPTER 20

Devil's Den – Living the High Life in New York

It's been said by some people that I eventually left James Brown's revue because he wouldn't marry me. That's not true. James asked me to marry him when we were out walking one day, while I was staying with him for a month in New York City in 1968. At that time we were getting kind of close. I really cared for James.

He had an old Victorian house on Linden Avenue in St Albans, Queens. It had turrets like a castle and a moat: you had to cross a little bridge to get to the door. It was very classy. At one time Cootie Williams, Duke Ellington's trumpet player, had lived there. I think James acquired it in the early '60s; he'd spent a lot of time and money renovating it.

It was a beautiful and really warm house. All the carpets were white. When you went in you took off your shoes and put on these Japanese slippers. I think there were four bedrooms in all. When I stayed there my room was next to James's. I think I slept maybe just one night in his room, which had a round bed and glass ceiling. He had a maid and a butler, who were his friends, more like kinfolk. I wasn't the roaming type and didn't like to explore the house on my own. Usually we'd sit in the kitchen, rather than the front room, and went downstairs where the band used to rehearse. That's where James had his own beauty shop and where all his gold records were. It was the coziest place.

That's when I really got the spoiled syndrome, because everywhere

I wanted to go there was a limousine waiting to take me. They came almost every other day. I got used to having people wait on me. I didn't have to go shopping: the shops came to me. When people arrived with carts of clothes on racks, James would say, 'Miss Whitney, pick out whatever you want.' Then he'd send me to the Great Northern Hotel where all the soap opera people went to get their hair done; later he sent me to a woman hairdresser who did Diana Ross's weave. So I got spoilt real good. I was like Queen Bee. James said we could bring Sherrie, my daughter, to New York, and she could have this and she could have that. He gave the word to his staff to take care of me, which meant there was no doubt in his mind that I was number one in his life at that point. But it was a set-up. I was tasting the good life but he had a hidden agenda. What he was doing, I realized when I sat down and thought about it, was mentally trying to put me in a spot that I didn't ever want to come out of. He wanted to make me comfortable and relaxed and put me off my guard. What he really wanted was for me to sign a new contract with him. The current one still had a year to go with a year option – and, as I mentioned earlier, it wasn't even valid; he'd never even signed it, so I officially belonged to King Records, not him. Knowing what I knew about James Brown, I figured the only way to get to him was to say that if we got married then I'd sign. In the meantime he went on about the future, saying, 'We're going to get married,' and I said OK. In my mind I told myself to tell him that if we got married he didn't have to worry about a contract, because he'd automatically have certain rights.

I suppose I was just whistling in the dark trying to find my way and to protect myself, so I said, 'If we get married then you don't have to worry about any contract.'

He said, 'Yeah, that's right.'

Then he said, 'I want to marry you, but I've got to get a divorce and I'm not divorcing Velma yet.' Velma was his first wife. And so we kind of let it go at that, and then no sooner than I left that house in New York than a new woman, Miss Deirdre Jenkins (they called her Deedee), got in that house and got pregnant by James within thirty days of him asking me to marry him. Then he divorced Velma and married Deedee.

I heard that Deedee thought she was headed for the losing line when James and me spent a lot of time together. I was a threat to her.

She got afraid that James was going to marry me – little did she know that I was sleeping in another room. The girl hated my guts with a passion, and she's supposed to have said that her ambition was to get herself a rich entertainer. And that's what she did.

I knew nothing about their marriage until after it happened. James never told me until he had a party when we had a few friends over in my apartment in Kansas City and they was fixing to watch a TV show, one of them award shows. He said to me, 'Marva, they're going to announce Deedee as Mrs James Brown.' I was speechless. Dumbstruck. But I knew I couldn't do nothing about it, and told myself I had to go along with it. But the thing was I was about a month pregnant with James's baby. I never told him, as I wasn't sure how he'd feel about it: I knew he didn't like children. Because I'd already had a child I knew the signs, I'd started to get morning sickness and could feel changes happening in my body, but I went ahead and had it checked out anyway, and it was confirmed. A couple of days after James said he was marrying Deedee I miscarried. Mr Cooper helped me get to a hospital, and because I wasn't that far along it wasn't really too hard on me physically. I think I had a couple of days off, that's all. Again, James never knew. I really believe the shock of hearing about Deedee brought on the miscarriage.

I remember the night that Deedee had her baby. It made me feel relieved I'd never had James's baby. He didn't want to be with her. Even though she didn't like me, I tried to persuade James to go and see her, and to be with her while she was giving birth to his baby. But he was determined not to go. I told him that he should, because it was his child. I said, 'Mr Brown, if you won't go to see Deirdre, will you please send her some roses and tell her how much you care for her?'

At first he wouldn't, but eventually he called his father, who at that time lived on the East coast, and Papa Brown, who was beautiful, said, 'You go sit with Deirdre.' So that was it.

I found out that Deedee had been dating James since she was sixteen, and she was the kind who could do the dirty work with him. That's another reason why I think I lost out, 'cause of the way I was raised: I wasn't going to do no dirty work for him. It was bad enough for me sitting in the plane and see him kicking the hell out of her when she did something wrong. And I'd had enough of being around his other women: that kind of stuff was messing with my mind. Even so, I think James cared for me. I really do. I was told by others who knew and worked for him that this was true. And I cared for him some; OK, maybe a little too much. I don't think James knew how to really treat and love a woman, because he'd never seen or experienced it. You cannot do what you have not seen. Although I think he really cared about the wife who died, I heard that even she caught him at times with other women. He just wasn't capable of being true to someone. I think his attitude to women comes from his mother abandoning him when he was about three years old. He never forgot it, and used to talk about it to me all the time. He said, 'My mother told me, "I got to leave you, James. I can't take care of you. I'm leaving you with your father."' And he said he clearly remembered standing on the step as she walked down the street waving goodbye. When we were working at the Apollo Theater, his mother would be in the next room, and nine times out of ten he wouldn't even acknowledge her, because he said he never saw her until he made it big. He didn't want to see her: he was bitter. He wasn't too keen on his father either, but he was closer to him. I'm so glad that he ended up taking care of both of them.

When you didn't know James you'd think he was the greatest gentleman on earth, because he didn't let you see his dark side. But when you got to be with him you soon found out that he had a violent temper and would play mind games with you. He humiliated me and hurt me, the same he did with Lyn Collins. Later on, in the 1990s when Lyn and me became good friends, it got to the point that we'd sit up and laugh because the same play was given to both of us. Every woman that's been with James, they'll tell you that they had to do and suffer the same things. Lyn figured like I figured: if you're going to be stuck in jail and you're going to mess with somebody, hell, you might as well mess with the boss. That made sense to me then.

During the month I stayed in Linden Avenue a strange thing happened. One night I was sleeping and I heard something go BAM! I mean, it was like a doggone bomb going off: I felt the floor shake. It had to be about one o'clock in the morning. I jumped up and went to the door. 'Stay in your room!' James barked. 'Stay in your room! Shut the door!' So I shut the door, wondering what on earth was going on. I heard scampering going on throughout the entire house. Scampering, scampering, scampering. And then it got quiet. James didn't tell me nothing, so the next morning I asked somebody else what happened. He said that the walls downstairs in the basement had collapsed. James had hidden his gold records and all of his money, his cash, in the walls, and they'd collapsed under the weight.

Papa Brown told me that James had got all his money in the ground. 'Let me tell you one thing, Marva, James is gonna die broke. They tell me he ain't got as much money as he used to have and that he buried his money out here. He ain't gonna be able to find it. I told Junior, but you can't tell Junior nothing.'

Here's another funny thing. James Brown was under the impression he owned that house and had bought it from Ben Bart, owner of Universal Attractions. Little did James Brown know that all of Mr Bart's big artists stayed in that house and thought they were buying it for themselves. That's why James and Hank Ballard – who used to be good friends – fell out. Hank, who with his band The Midnighters had enjoyed some big hits in the 1950s, was still with James when I left, but I later heard that when James showed Hank his house, Hank said, 'Man, is this where you live? I lived here once. This used to be my house.' And they say that's when James went crazy. He picked up an axe and started breaking the house up he was so mad. I think it was a little bit after I left, about '70 or '71. Although he tried to tear the place up, I believe it's still there today.

CHAPTER 21

My Family and James Brown

James came home with me to Kansas a couple of times. He always brought lots of gifts. We'd play the piano there. He loved my family and knew they was a Christian family. I'd tell people, 'Don't say a word: he's sneakin' in and sneakin' out.' But nobody could keep a damn secret. As soon as we got out of the car the whole block was there to greet us. It was a happy time for the neighborhood.

One time I remember saying to Mama, 'We're coming to the house – please don't tell nobody we're coming. Right?'

'OK, I won't,' she said. But when we got near the house, our street was packed with people. I know now she told my baby brother and my daughter. Oh Lord, it was just like we were surrounded by people block to block. I wasn't mad because I knew the people was happy. This pleased James too. He was smiling and happy. We did autographs and he handed out records. Some people there talk about it even now.

I didn't get carried away with all the fuss people was making. Mother told us, 'Don't have no uppity nothing – just be yourself and be humble. Humble is the way.' I try to be that way with all people, and I don't like people with a bunch of airs. You know, I can't take it: that's not my kind of people. I like people who act natural. Just be yourself is my motto. Some people think just 'cause they've got a nickel over a dollar they're a bag of chips.

James used to bring my father watches and different things.

Daddy got to the point that he said, 'Look at all these doggone watches he's given me. I don't know why but none of his watches won't work on my arm.' We used to have a good laugh about that. James was also kind enough to buy my parents their first color TV, and also a beautiful glass set and silverware for Mama. But often he did these things to make himself look good. One time we were at a private airport and he pointed to a big box that was sitting there. He told Bobbitt to pick it up and open it to see what was in it. It was filled with men's shirts for the fellas. I figured that was a plant, to make him look big.

James really liked my baby brother, Winfred, and gave him around $400 to buy his first car.

When we visited my family, they saw the stress in me. I couldn't hide it. My father saw I was troubled and started asking questions. He couldn't stand James because he saw the change in me. He knew I'd always been my own person, and could now see a certain stiffness in me. He knew I wasn't free and could sense my unease. Daddy could see that things was getting worse instead of better with my attitude and then he didn't like it when I brought home a Vietnamese doll that James had made me paint black. I'd bought it as a present for my mother. They said, 'What the hell is this?' That didn't go down too well, though I think they appreciated that I'd thought of them.

But it was the way that James looked at my mother that really incensed Daddy. James always had twinkle in his eye when he looked at Mama. Back then she was fine – and she's still gorgeous now, even with arthritis and aged eighty-four. She had wide hips, big legs and a pointed nose, and was a pretty chocolate brown color. And one day my daddy saw James looking at her with his roving eyes. James was a lowlife to my daddy.

Even though Daddy didn't care for James he loved his father, Papa Brown. They'd both been military men and Papa Brown had also lived at one time in Kansas City. They first met when I was with James and he brought Pops to Kansas City with him. Papa Brown wanted to see where things used to be, so him and Daddy got very close.

My mother liked James Brown maybe a little bit. When she came to hear me sing in Kansas City I sat her down and the menfolk that was working the top seats – the stage managers like Jimmy Smith and

Levi Rasbury – were saying, 'Who is that woman over there? Man, do you see that chick out there? Who is that?' At the time she was a size 16 with a small waist, big hips like she has now, beautiful legs; she was near forty. They started whispering, 'Look at that fox! My God, my God, who *is* that? Who's that fine woman?'

And Bobbitt said, 'Her? That's Marva's mother.' They were dumbstruck.

CHAPTER 22

I'm Tired, I'm Tired, I'm Tired

The constant touring and backbiting behind-the-scenes combined with the abuse I endured took its toll. I was so exhausted that I was doing things that I shouldn't have been doing. One time I was in a hotel when James had a meeting – Hank Ballard, Bud Hobgood and the rest of the clan was there. I started taking off my clothes and found myself trying to go out with just a slip on to where they were. I realized and stopped myself just in time. That was when I came to the conclusion that it was time to go, or else my mind would leave me first. It's true: during the second half of '68, after I'd come back from Vietnam, I really felt I was losing my mind. I was tired of everything. One day I followed an urge to quit. I just had to get away from James Brown. Above all else, I wanted freedom from his tyranny, and I was tired of all the bullshit. I wasn't going to take it no more.

I was in Cincinnati at the time. James often sent me there when we had a few days off. Sometimes I'd do some recording at King, and at other times I'd just be there hanging out at the production offices across the street. Miss Sylvia Medford, one of the violin players, was my steady roommate and travel companion. If I had to go somewhere without James she was there, and that was good. We got along pretty well. Every time I was there, Bud Hobgood – one of the studio staff at King Studios – gave me a package to take to James. These were always quite small – say 4in by 5in, like half a shoebox in size, and wrapped in thick brown paper. You couldn't open them because they was wrapped tight, and most of the time they had string around them to hold them together.

This time I was so tired and agitated that I called the airport to see what kind of flight I could get to LA: I decided to run away like a little kid. Luckily they had a midnight flight, so I booked it, hurriedly packed and said, 'Miss Medford, I've had enough, I'm gone.'

She was concerned and said, 'What am I going to do, Miss Whitney?'

'Look, don't worry about it. Just go and do as planned. By the way, give James this package.'

She agreed, and I caught the flight and went to LA, where I stayed in the Holiday Inn. I thought I'd gone to sleep that night and woken up the next morning as normal, but then I realized I'd been so tired I'd slept solidly for two whole days. I felt better for the rest and time away from the organization, and called Mr Bobbitt to let them know I was all right. Strangely enough, when I returned there was no great fuss made about my departure, so I asked Miss Medford what had happened. She said, 'Oooh, James was upset. He was really upset! When I told him he said, "Whit's gone and done what?" So I said, "Yes, Mr Brown, she went somewhere and I don't know where. She didn't tell me. But she told me to come and see you anyway." He was so upset he was jumping up and down with rage. Then he asked if you'd given me anything for him. I said, "Oooh, you mean this?" and held up the package.' She said his face changed instantly, he grinned and his mood softened. 'Yeah, I can understand what Whit's going through. She probably needed a rest. Don't worry about a thing, Miss Medford, just tell her when she is ready to come back to let me know so we know where she's at.'" He wasn't really that concerned about me: he was just relieved he'd got that package, which contained the only thing he really loved – dollar bills. King Records were sending cash to James wrapped up in bundles. I guess quite a few of us did things at one time or other that wasn't kosher. Some, like me, did it innocently, but there was many others on the pay roll that didn't have no moral scruples. If he wanted them to do something they'd do it no matter what, just to gain his favor.

CHAPTER 23

The Band

When I joined James's revue I think the band was suspicious of me. I guess it was the same for all the female singers. It was like, 'The singers think they got it made. Uh-huh, just watch and see. You won't be here for long. We'll still be here after you're gone.' Fred Wesley, who played trombone and later led James's band after Pee Wee Ellis left, agrees that this was the case:

The musicians in the band kind of looked down on the singers but that was because most of the singers were not good singers. But Marva was excellent. We found out later that she could really sing. I went to the *Joey Bishop Show* with Marva and she sang (Burt Bacharach's) 'A House Is Not A Home.' I said, this girl can really sing. James Brown usually had her not singing – just screaming like he screamed. It wasn't any kind of singing at all – just a bunch of yelling. He picked singers who yelled real loud and molded them into his way of singing. But Marva could really sing. The band looked down on her, but when James wasn't around we got to be good friends.

I wasn't aware that the gents in the band knew to what degree I was suffering, but I never bothered any of them. That's not even in my system, to pick on people. I wasn't raised that way.

When I first met Fred Wesley I didn't think he liked me at all. I saw him happy-go-lucky with Maceo and the fellers but with me his attitude was different; he never looked at me directly, but kind of sidelong. He didn't realize I was a singer when he first joined the band in 1968: 'When I first saw Marva she was in a car with James Brown and I didn't know what the deal was. I thought she was just his girlfriend, but then I found out later she was also a featured singer on the show.'

I realized that he and many of the other fellas in the band were cool with me because James didn't want any of them looking at me. Knowing that I was James's woman, they were wary of talking with me. James once kicked the guitar player Jimmy Nolen in the butt for looking at one of his women, and the band had to stop him from getting a gun to kill him. So the band members felt they'd better not say nothing to me, because they didn't know me and were afraid I might snitch on them to the boss, and I'd been told not to speak to the band. There were stooges everywhere who could get you into trouble: everybody was afraid of everybody.

Fred remembers that James Brown had strict rules that female singers had to pay attention to:

The singers had to sit in their dressing rooms and be quiet. They always had a towel over their knees and I said, 'What's that about?' He wanted the women to appear like ladies. They couldn't be one of the boys, so they had to be a lady, you know. He was a strange man, but that was one of his things, keeping his women close around him. James Brown was a very insecure person, especially with his women. Marva had a chaperone, Miss Sanders, who was also James's wardrobe mistress. She chaperoned the girls when they were around.

I think Fred left James in 1969 because he thought the music was getting stale: James ended up repeating himself through the '70s, following trends instead of setting them. I remember one day Fred said, 'I'm tired of vamping.' James's songs often had the same riff, the same licks, and then went to the bridge section: you'd go from section A to section B back to section A and then you'd vamp on the same thing to the fade. Fred left to join one of his idols, Count Basie, and was away for a year – but he came back, because he needed to earn more money than he got with Count Basie.

John 'Jabo' Starks was another musician I liked. I'd met Jabo first when he played drums with Bobby 'Blue' Bland: Bobby came through Kansas City when I was the female singer with the Derbys.

The band did a little weed to help them cope with the hard work. No one was very out of touch, though – you couldn't afford to be, because James fined every wrong move, deducting money from their paychecks. James was sincere about his anti-drugs stance in the '60s. He meant it. That's why we foundation people – the people on the show in the early days – were so surprised when he went on the hard stuff in the '80s and '90s. When I was with him only very rarely did he hit the marijuana, and that was after work when he'd maybe have a couple of puffs to relax. Usually, though, he preferred a Heineken or a glass of Ripple – a popular wine that the comedian Redd Foxx used to talk about on his show: it was strong but cheap to buy. They don't make it now.

Going back to the band, some lit up a joint after the show to get ready to sleep on the bus, because most of the time there was no time to get to a hotel and rest. Often we traveled through the night to our next destination, where we might be able to check in to take a bath and then maybe – if we were very lucky – get a few hours' sleep. And then it was time for the sound check and the evening shows. We always had to be on the job at 6pm.

If the fellas decided to get loaded it was never on the bus. Ms Sanders always reported any trouble to James. If by chance any of the band got stoned before the gig they walked straight to their seats on the bandstand to rest. They might grumble a little bit about James being so extra hard that night, and even I might grumble, especially when he came on my set and played drums. He thought he could really play, but on my set he massacred every song. What made me mad – though it made me laugh as well – was that he always said my best sets was when he played drums or directed the band for me. We all used to dread this happening.

Although things were often crazy in the James Brown camp, there were times when I found a little solace or what the Bible calls peace in the valley. St Clair Pinckney always had a word of encouragement for me. He played saxophone in the band: a nice man with a distinctive white streak in his hair, he was a gentleman to the bone. He'd been with James since the beginning and I never heard him complain, not once. Sometimes he was disgusted by what he saw or heard, but never to the point that he said something about it: he always kept his composure. He loved James, like we all did in a certain way, but just like the rest of us he knew James was also the devil and that we were all in bondage. A few years after I left the show I called St Clair to see how everybody was doing and what he was working on. He had a production company he wanted to get off the ground: you see, there was no security working for Soul Brother Number One, and he knew he could get fired at any time. The only thing you could be assured of was that everyday hell was on the menu in some kind of way.

St Clair's loyalty was worth nothing to James. It was said that when St Clair died James didn't want to know, but some of his people pushed him to help with expenses to see that he had a proper burial. And that was a man who started out with James. I shall always remember St Clair in spirit.

Pee Wee Ellis was also a gentleman. He'd got his nickname because he was small as a youngster. He didn't show any emotion until you really messed up to a fault, and then he'd look at you as if to say, 'What are you doing?' Other times he'd laugh or give that Cheshire cat grin and try to help you if you were having difficulty. I love Pee Wee, who at the time was married to a nice white lady called Barbara. They had a son and she'd often help Pee Wee with lead sheets. They were wonderful to me. I always felt close to Pee Wee because I felt if he hadn't given me the yes I wouldn't have got the job in the first place. One time after I'd been away from James, Pee Wee told me it bothered him because he didn't know if he'd done the right thing by helping me get on the show – 'cause he'd seen what I was going through. He wrote and arranged 'Get Out Of My Life' for me, which was released as a single. After I recorded it I asked him if that was what he wanted from me, and he said no. He quit working with me on that tune and went on to the next one. He was easy-going that way.

Pee Wee was well respected, even by James, who trusted his musical judgement. I remember one time in particular when we were on stage rehearsing. James had a riff in his mind that he couldn't get quite right, and that's when he called for Pee Wee. Pee Wee wrote down all the riffs and rhythms that James gave give him. James would grunt something, sing a melody or tap out a rhythm and Pee Wee had to interpret the sounds and notate them into a proper score, translating them into music; Fred Wesley had to do the same when he became leader. So James came back, maybe like two months later, and he said, 'You know that riff I gave you that went like this? Da-dada-da-dada.'

Peewee opened up his book and said, 'No, Mr Brown, that's wrong. You went Dada-da-dada-da.'

James pursed his lips, thought about it for a second or two, then said, 'You're right.' There wasn't many people who could correct him – if I'd done it I'd have got a backhander – but on musical matters he knew he had to bow down to Pee Wee's superior knowledge.

I believe one of the reasons Pee Wee left was because of an incident that happened between me and James. Let me tell you about it. While the group was setting up and getting the stage ready at an East Coast venue, Pee Wee and I were sitting at the Hammond B3 organ. We were making small talk when James walked in. When James got to his dressing room he sent for me to come to his office. He started asking what Pee Wee and me had been talking about. He was furious, and before I could answer he hit me on my forehead with his clenched fist, smack-dab in the middle, so hard that it was heard all the way out to the stage. It felt like a sledgehammer had smashed into me. Usually James never hit you direct: he'd give you a backhander, 'cause he was a boxer. But he knew where to hit and make it hurt. He hit me so hard a lump came up that was almost the size of an egg. It stuck right out of my forehead. I was in severe pain, but James told me to do my show that night. As I sang I felt people staring, and could hear people in the first row saying, 'What's that? What's happened to her forehead?' That was the first time I felt in my spirit that the band felt compassion for me. I think that night they felt sorry for me, and began to loosen up because they'd doubted me. They'd thought I was snooty and had it made, but they saw the price I was paying. This is what Pee Wee remembers: 'James Brown thought we were lovers. That's what I think. I do remember that. We were working on a song and I was doing an arrangement for Marva. James was very jealous. He gave her a hard time for that.'

Sadly Pee Wee left James Brown in the summer of '69. He went on to pursue his love of jazz – he was a student of the great Sonny

Rollins – and now lives near Bath, England. We haven't seen each other for many years, but he always has a place in my thoughts.

Fred Wesley was Pee Wee's successor, and he recalls an unsavory incident that he witnessed between me and James:

Once I saw James Brown chase Marva around a car and he was going to hit her. I just turned a blind eye because I figured that he'd done it before and he'd do it again. I couldn't understand why Marva endured that kind of treatment. I don't know why she didn't leave earlier than she did. He had a problem with every woman he was with. He just sometimes got enraged with women. I never understood that about him. They could say the least little thing and it would just send him over the edge. But then a lot of things sent him over the edge for some reason. I guess it was because of the way he was raised. He came from nothing. He started at zero and built himself up to become the number one soul singer in the world. I guess that would cause you to be enraged about little things, like race and manhood, and things like that.

I also got punished by James if my show went down well with the audience. He hated it, because afterwards he'd have to pull all the stops out to win the crowd over. One of James's drummers, Tiger Martin, recalled an incident in his book *Give The Drummers Some*. My set had gone down a storm at the Apollo, and James was so mad that he smashed his fist into my eye and hammered on my dressing room door saying, 'Whit, don't you never sing like that again!' That happened quite often.

As I write this I'm swelling up with anger, disgusted by all the shit that we all endured from this man, who at that time the world thought was so great. I knew it wouldn't be long before I left, for I wasn't the kind of girl who liked being slapped around.

CHAPTER 24

The Sold Brother

I was with James one night, just as the 1968 presidential election campaign was reaching its climax. The then vice-president, Hubert Humphrey (who hoped to take over from the outgoing Lyndon Johnson) was the Democratic candidate. He'd helped James get national exposure for the 'Don't Be A Dropout' campaign a couple of years earlier – when James had released a record urging black kids to stay at school and get an education – and even invited him to the White House.

James had been keen to endorse Humphrey for president at first, but as the campaign progressed, and it looked like Humphrey's Republican rival Richard Nixon was winning, he got cold feet. About two days before the final result I remember Humphrey's daughter calling James at least two or three times in half an hour because it looked like Humphrey was losing votes to Nixon, and the Democrats could see that they needed some extra push because they was in trouble: they was looking for James to help them out and persuade black folks to vote. James said she even offered to spend the night with him if he did. But James said, 'Oh no, I'm not gonna do nothing, 'cause I think Nixon's going to win.' The people around him – including me – said nothing, but secretly we all thought James was chicken shit and a backstabber.

Humphrey had done several favors for James, and James owed him big time. Without James there'd have been no trip to Vietnam and he probably wouldn't have gone on the Ed Sullivan show.

Humphrey had helped James reach a bigger audience. But still James refused to help.

Then Nixon got in. I was told that James's advisors kept telling him, begging him, don't go to Nixon because he thinks you have too much power over black folks. People close to James realized that Nixon couldn't be trusted, but he thought he knew best and had to have it his way. So he went to see Nixon at the White House. A lot of black people thought James was selling them out, and that's when they started calling him the 'Sold Brother'. James's power gradually began to slip away, partly because African-Americans had lost faith in him. They didn't like him buddying up with Nixon. But James saw the power he had and felt, I think, that he was going to be able to continue to use his power against the system and get things done.

When Nixon became president, me and James performed at the All-American Gala Inaugural Ball, held at Washington DC's National Guard Armory in January 1969.

James arrived in a limo. He was all decked out. He really did look better to me with his Afro. On his arm was his new wife, Deedee, who wore a multi-colored dress. It was a glitzy, star-studded affair, mostly attended by white people. The jazz vibraphonist Lionel Hampton and his band played, followed by Tony Bennett, Dinah Shore and Connie Francis. Then James appeared and performed 'Say It Loud - I'm Black & I'm Proud', and the place exploded. When he retired for a costume change I went on stage. I wore a gorgeous long black gown with matching gloves that came up to my elbows. A picture of me at the ball appeared in the February '69 issue of *Jet* magazine. Unfortunately I didn't get a chance to meet Mr Nixon. But that didn't surprise me: James never let me be around anyone who might have the power to help.

Afterwards James turned to his wife and said, 'Ms Whitney out-dressed you tonight. She was sharp. I didn't like your dress, Deedee.' I was embarrassed for her, even though she hated my guts.

CHAPTER 25

I Sing Soul

I had my own way of singing soul music, which was a cross I would say between Aretha Franklin and Dionne Warwick. But when I joined James Brown that style was closed off, because he never gave me enough time to let the songs I recorded become part of me. I could always sing high because I was a first soprano in a gospel group. I could hit it, but it wasn't me. A lot of the songs I cut wasn't in keys I was comfortable with. James often had songs that was already in the can that somebody else had done, so you kept using other people's tracks. When I joined the show and went into the studio the whole way that I was singing before I got with him was erased.

Even so, I did the best I could with what I had. In the write-ups they say I'm a little 'brassy'. That's because when I'm serving my God I just let my emotions, whatever my soul is feeling, come out. I don't hold back. And back in the '50s when I started singing they didn't have microphones in church, like people do today: you had to sing real loud in order to be heard. You had to really project your voice to stand out and make a difference. But as I got older I learned to let the microphone work for me, so I could preserve my voice much longer.

When I look back, I realize my recording sessions were always too hurried for me. Most of my songs for King were recorded in just an hour or two. I couldn't live with the song for a few days – hell, no! Sometimes I only got to hear a song about an hour before, so I had to learn it very quickly. Sometimes there wasn't even no words. I always tried to do my best, but for a long time I couldn't listen to the records I cut with James because it was almost embarrassing. I was ashamed of most of the songs King put out: it was like carrying a heavy burden. James never gave us the time to learn a song like he did before he went the studio. If it was one of his own records he'd rehearse songs for a whole month, more or less until he had it tight, and the band knew it like the back of their hand. James's other female singers, Vicki and Lyn, were in the same situation: like me, they got berated by James, who was hard on singers in the studio and at rehearsal.

Says Fred Wesley: 'We didn't do a lot of rehearsals with the singers, but when we did rehearse it was very intense. James Brown would tell them that they wasn't doing something right and they never would get it and that they was useless. Something like that. It was really a put-down kind of a thing for the singers. It was just how he was.'

Another reason why I couldn't stand to hear myself sing was because I thought my records was mixed wrong. I felt like crawling under a rock and hiding. I'm high in the air all the time – and my people at home knew that wasn't how I really sounded. But with the new engineering they can do, I sound like a human being now. After modern remastering I don't mind listening to my own music.

What was also difficult for me as a singer was the fact that James never used background singers. I think there's only one song I recorded for King that's got background singers on. It's hard: you've got nobody to work off. To tell you the truth, I'm surprised I lucked-out with a few hits.

The first time I appeared on an LP was when King released an album called *James Brown Presents His Show Of Tomorrow* in 1968. There was two songs by James on there (a version of Frank Sinatra's 'That's Life' and another remake of James's first ever hit, 'Please Please Please') and a couple of songs each from me, Vicki Anderson, James Crawford, Hank Ballard and Bobby Byrd. I performed 'If You Love Me,' a soul ballad, and a funky number called 'What Kind Of Man'.

Somewhere between the end of 1968 and the first few months of 1969 I recorded some tracks with Dee Felice and his trio. He was a jazz drummer and his group –with pianist Frank Vincent and bassist Lee Tucker – was signed to King's jazz label, Bethlehem. James also cut some tracks with them in the Cincinnati studios, and I did a duet with him on the Bobby Hebb-penned song 'Sunny'.

It was around this time that James was appearing on a lot of prime-time TV shows in America; as I said earlier, he was trying to portray himself to whites as a versatile night club entertainer like Sammy Davis Jr. I remember we did a TV show hosted by David Frost, an Englishman. Dee Felice and his band (which included a guitar player as well as his usual trio) backed us. James opened with the Sinatra standard 'It Had To Be You', after which he was briefly interviewed by David Frost, who a few years later was engaged to Diahann Carroll.

Mr Frost said, 'That gorgeous lady I saw backstage. Tell me about her.'

James said, 'She's a young lady originally from Kansas City, Kansas. She's from a large spiritual family. She answers to the name Miss Marva Whitney. She's doing a fantastic job.' He then motioned me out on stage. I had a big Afro hairdo and wore a long, elegant flowing dress with blue and green flecks in it. I sang 'Somewhere Over The Rainbow', and when I'd finished I got a big ovation from the studio audience. Then Mr Frost asked James to do a duet with me. So we did 'Sunny', just like we recorded for the album. James kissed me at the beginning and at the end of the song. We were getting on well at that time and seemed real close.

'Sunny' eventually came out on James's 1969 jazz LP *Gettin' Down To It*. The songs I recorded with the Dee Felice Trio were supposed to come out on an LP too; its title was to have been *I Sing Soul With James Brown*. My good friend, Alan Leeds, who worked with James as a tour manager between 1969 and 1974 and is an expert on all things relating to James Brown, actually has a copy of the album. This is what he says:

It was an odd compilation to begin with – combining previously issued instrumental tracks by the Brown band with various Whitney vocals even including those recorded with a jazz trio (Dee Felice Trio). Particularly odd being that I believe that King had enough Whitney vocals 'in the can' to fill out an album without resorting to the instrumentals. Several thousand records were pressed (and scrapped). The artwork for the cover was designed and slicks were printed but no covers seem to have ever been assembled – suggesting the record was canceled before full albums were ever packaged. I actually have a pressing with the blue King labels – not a test pressing. There probably aren't very many others that survived.

I certainly never saw a copy at the time, and I clean forgot about it until I went back on the road in the '80s and '90s. When I chatted with fans after a gig they'd always ask about *I Sing Soul*. I've asked the people at Universal Records in the States, who own all the King recordings that James produced, and they say they know nothing about it. I've heard that James took a lot of masters from King Records when he left. The story goes that he kept them in a shed, and one day a bunch of tapes were stolen. Maybe *I Sing Soul* was among them.

It was a compilation rather than a solo album. Counting the duet 'Sunny', there were eight vocal tracks in all featuring me – including the previously issued singles 'Your Love Was Good For Me' and 'I'll Work It Out' – and four funky instrumental tracks by the James Brown Band. It was mostly standards, the kinds of songs I was doing when I studied with Willie Rice, well-known songs like 'My Funny Valentine', 'The Masquerade Is Over', 'People', 'Somewhere Over The Rainbow' – which they added strings to – and even a jazz version of Aretha Franklin's 'Respect'. I really get to show the full range of my voice on that album. If people heard it they'd be surprised. It's so different from everything else I've done. It was a strange mixture, though, and the instrumentals had already been released on an album called *James Brown Plays Nothing But Soul*.

So why did *I Sing Soul* get canned? I don't know. Maybe it was too different from the funk stuff I had been doing. Perhaps King thought it would confuse people who'd been used to me doing heavy funk songs like 'Unwind Yourself'.

One of the songs scheduled to be on *I Sing Soul* was 'I'll Work It Out', which originally came out as a single in the late summer of 1968. It was an interesting session because it had little to do with James. It was overseen by the great arranger Sammy Lowe and was recorded in New York with a studio band, not the usual James Brown crew. I remember the session well. I usually felt more relaxed when James wasn't around, but on this occasion I was a bit apprehensive. I'd gone to New York all alone, and I felt bad about my performance without a producer to guide me. Sammy Lowe had done that terrific arrangement on James's classic hit 'It's A Man's Man's Man's World' a few years earlier. He was just beautiful; a fine, courteous gentleman, but he didn't give me much direction. The tracks were already put down so I had to overdub my vocal. In the past I'd always had a producer to direct me, offer advice and so on. I remember the music being loud, and I had no control over it. I didn't like the mix at the end with all that hollering from me. Perhaps I wasn't used to his method of working, and in any case I hadn't really had enough studio experience: I think Mr Lowe thought I directed myself. His string arrangement was on the money, though, a beautiful piece of music: I wish I could have done it more justice. This might sound crazy, but if it was ever possible I'd like to do it over.

CHAPTER 26

It's My Thing

In the spring of 1969 the Isley Brothers were hotter than hot in the US with 'It's Your Thing'. James couldn't stand it. Everywhere he went he heard it, and it irritated the hell out of him. It was a thorn in his side, and in a way I could understand that – because the Isleys' new sound was a threat to his popularity. And they were from Cincinnati too, the home of King Records. When James first heard the record he said, 'We gotta break this.'

I remember at the beginning of April we had a layover in Atlanta, Georgia. It was still early, and he said, 'Whit, we're going to record this morning.' I was still half asleep. 'You got to do a song,' he said excitedly. 'I got an idea for you. We're gonna do an answer to "It's Your Thing" and you're gonna write it. We're gonna change "It's Your Thing" to "It's My Thing".' So I looked at that song and thought hell, there ain't nothing you can really do with this song but say 'It's My Thing'. So I wrote it, and we did it that morning at about 6am in Master Sound Studios with a couple of other tunes.

The session was fantastic, even though it happened at the time of day when a singer's voice is not usually at its best: it's usually very gruff and hard, and it's almost like you're half hoarse because you're not rested. My voice don't wake up till twelve or after. But I was used to this kind of thing with James, like I was used to singing in an uncomfortably high key, and the ridicule and put-downs. This session, against all the odds, was one of my better ones, and to my amazement James put me and him down as the writers. He often gave out writer credits to other people. He did this on a whim, usually without consulting us because we was just a piece of property to him. To this day some people in the James Brown organization have ownership of Lyn Collins's songs that they didn't sing or write. Like Charles Bobbitt, who got credited for 'Give It Up Or Turnit A Loose' and James's wife Deedee, who was credited as the songwriter of a 1974 JB instrumental, 'Rockin' Funky Watergate'. Even Bud Hobgood, who'd been a production manager over at King Records in the '60s, was often credited as a co-writer of a song when it was obvious to us that he had nothing to do with songwriting. A lot of us were naïve about the music business back then and were powerless to stop James. We signed things we didn't know anything about, and sadly we're still paying for our mistakes in later life. I remember Lyn told me that after she left she called James's manager and asked to get one of her songs back: she'd written a song called 'Wheel Of Life' with Joe Valentine before she joined James. She cut the track when she joined him, but when it came out it was credited to Valentine and two other people. Her name was nowhere to be found, so she didn't get any songwriting royalties from it.

If James did give us a piece of a song it was just luck. I guess the Lord was blessing me that day when I recorded 'It's My Thing'. Within twenty-four hours of cutting it, James got a record pressed up and sent some promos out to a DJ friend of his in San Francisco. He told him to play it on the air and see what kind of response he got. In those days James had all the DJs and promoters in his hip pocket; he had them on the pay roll. When he got the news that the radio station was getting a lot of calls for the record he knew it was a hit. The response was far out.

Well, back then James could get inside of King Records: he had the power to start or stop the presses. On Brewster Street they had a melt-down plant for records that didn't sell: the old vinyl was melted down to make new records – and all James had to say was 'I want the presses stopped and I want this pressed right now.' So when he got that response from San Francisco he got excited and told them to stop the presses and press up 'It's My Thing' instead.

The record was released and sold like wildfire. It was my first hit, going into the Billboard R&B chart at the end of May in 1969 and spending seven weeks there. It broke into the top twenty, peaking at no. 19 and even crossing over into the pop charts, making no. 82. On the B-side was a song called 'Ball Of Fire' recorded at the same session and written by Charles Spurling (who co-wrote 'Unwind Yourself') and Louis Innis. This is what Charles, now a good friend of mine, remembers about the song:

'Ball Of Fire' was about the first girl that I went with. She wasn't really true to me but she was a ball of fire in all kinds of ways: she was good-looking, had a fiery temper and everything. And that's what inspired me to write it and the rest of it is all self-experience. I co-wrote it with Louis Innis. He was Syd Nathan's partner at King Records. He's the one that signed me up. Mr Nathan owned us all but Louis was a very nice guy and he gave me some opportunities to help other people from the South and write them some songs. A singer called Connie Austin recorded 'Ball Of Fire' first. She was a street girl and she was very young. She moved to California, where they later found her in a plastic bag in the trunk of a car.

Marva didn't know she'd recorded my songs for a long time. She didn't know it because James had told her that they were his songs and they had them in the can. So Marva never knew I wrote the songs until they got out and had a label on. She didn't really know that I had anything to do with it.

Today when I ask people overseas about 'It's Your Thing', they look like they don't know what I'm talking about. But if you say 'It's My Thing', they *know* it's Marva Whitney. That's the response I get.

That song started the ball rolling for me. James began referring to me as Soul Sister Number One – which was a title I wasn't comfortable with – and reviewers gave me the nicknames 'Miss Excitement' and 'Marvelous Marva'. Everyone wanted to know about me. I was featured on the cover of two top black magazines in August –*Jet* and *The Scene*. This is what *Jet* magazine wrote:

MARVA'S MUSICAL MISSION

Singer uses lyrics to bring hope and pride to blacks in US

by Ermerta Black

A Kansas City maiden who nearly lost her life when a troop plane was fired upon while she was on the musical mission in Vietnam last year to entertain US soldiers is still on a mission carrying musical messages to her black soul sisters and brothers via the stage and television.

Like her current hit tune, *Things Got to Get Better*, marvelous Marva Whitney, 25, who began her singing career at age 5 with her parents, triplet brothers and twin brothers under the Manning Gospel Singers banner, has been making a steady climb toward stardom.

From her early training with her pianist mother, Mrs Willa Manning, and Grammar School music teacher, Mrs Thelma Hamilton, to her team up with James (Soul Brother Number One) Brown two years ago as road secretary and featured performer in the James Brown group, Marva began to rise to what she is becoming now – a polished star and successful singer.

The fame, the talent and the will to achieve could be expected. One element, however, which could not be calculated and which may set Marva apart from much young talent is her sense of destiny and commitment. 'I was blessed,' Marva reflected during an exclusive interview for JET. 'If it hadn't been for Mr Brown, I'd probably just be wandering now. All I want to do now is to show black women the way, the way he (James Brown) showed me,' Marva confided.

One of Marva's most perilous missions was her tour of Vietnam with the James Brown group. Out of 20 females in the Brown group, at that time, she was the only woman who made the trip. Marva, explaining why she was pleased that she was chosen, said, 'I wanted to go. I felt like I had to do something for our people. I know that they wanted to see somebody who would make them feel good – somebody who was black.' Although the group narrowly escaped violence twice (once when under enemy fire, the motor of the plane in which they were traveling caught afire; and once again when shortly after they had left their Saigon hotel, the building was destroyed), Marva felt that the mission was necessary to express concern and identification with the brothers who were fighting there. Pleased to tears sometimes by the reception of the black GIs, Marva commented, 'They needed it. They were so glad to see Mr Brown, it was like Jesus Christ had come there. And I felt like I could sing,

sing, sing, sing; I was so happy to do something for my brothers. It was worth it and I would do it again,' Marva said in describing crowds of GIs that were so large that the shows in themselves could have been personnel hazards had the enemy decided to strike.

Aside from her Vietnamese performance, which Marva says she would like to repeat, and road tours with James Brown's group, Marva has appeared on numerous network TV shows, including the *Joey Bishop Show*, the *Donald O'Connor Show*, the *Ed Nelson Morning Show* and *Playboy After Dark*.

'I prefer a song with good lyrics, that have a message. Some songs,' Marva observes, 'tell people what they need to know, like how important it is to 'get yourself together.' 'Who Can I Turn To' says this for me. Who can I turn to if I don't have the right education, if I don't try to learn and do the right thing? Who am I going to be?' Marva said in noting that the most important things that she felt was for black people to establish a base which they could move from and fall back on.

Working with James Brown increased her consciousness, she says. 'He is a great image,' she told JET, 'as a black man willing to stand up for his rights with the white man.'

Speaking for how her understanding of social responsibility evolved, Afro-coiffed Marva recalled how she didn't understand at first 'the natural bag'. But when she started wearing one she says it seemed just 'the natural thing to do. It seemed like my understanding changed. I began to talk different, I became what I am – a black person and proud to be black. Money isn't the whole thing,' Marva observed. 'It would be just beautiful if black men and black women could have love, understanding and respect for one another. Things would be better all around,' Marva observed in pinpointing another base which helps bring cohesion and stability to black people.

Recalling her first appearance in EBONY (February, 1951) as a 'Pet Milk Baby', Marva says she now looks to that magazine for information on black history and culture. JET, the sister magazine, she says, is needed as a pocket reference guide to what's happening now and JET'S Soul Brothers Top 20 chart provides information she needs in knowing what black people want to hear.

Marva, who does not see plans for marriage in her immediate

future, told JET that she wants to keep developing her skill as a singer and imparting message music to thousands of black folks who want to keep on hearing it.

I'd been featured in *Jet* before this article came out: my first appearance was in a centerfold picture showing me in a bikini, wearing a hat and holding a golf club. It was the March 1968 issue, which had Diahann Carroll on the front cover. The caption read: 'Singer's A Swinger. Dressed in a bikini and clutching a golf club, shapely (34-23-38) Marva Whitney, a 23-year-old Kansas City, Kan., lass hardly looks like what she really is: A James Brown vocalist. But the sultry singer is a "soul happening" in her swinging performances.'

A year later, in August 1969, the entertainment magazine *The Scene* included this feature on me:

James Brown concerts are always a study in frenzy, a test of how long the audience can last before the King comes on.

Midpoint through the miscellaneous warm-up entertainment, practically unnoticed by the crowd, Marva Whitney slips on stage and wrestles attention from the wiggling crowd.

Some of the chatter about the hot dogs ceases; kids point and ask Bobby about the pretty lady and Marva pours her soul into her songs.

Her distinctive voice doesn't suit her body at all. She should be barrel shaped and heavy, swinging pounds around like the old singers in the South. She's sleek and young, more mini than mighty, and people have to shake their heads and blink their eyes to make certain that sounds are really coming from that girl.

Some were born with it and some wasn't. Marva was! Although she sounds like Mississippi or Georgia, she was raised in relatively sophisticated Kansas City, MO. At 25, she's been trouping with the James Brown show for over two years.

James found her in Kansas City (until JB, she'd never been far from home), singing in a nightclub and taking music lessons in the daytime. She was discouraged and bored, though she'd only been singing professionally for a year. When her manager said she had an audition with Mr Brown, her reaction was typical. She didn't believe it.

However, the next afternoon James Brown was leaning on the piano, waiting to hear her wail. She threw her heart into it and by the end of the session, she was wondering where to pick up a suitcase before the next morning. She'd been hired on the spot to sing with the band, starting immediately.

Marva had the voice but she didn't have the delivery or the style or the stage presence. Her apprenticeship with the James Brown band was a 'learn while you earn' proposition. Each performance was a lesson. Needless to say, Marva was a little insecure . . . if she flunked, she did it in front of thousands.

Like the cigarette commercial says, 'Marva's come a long way, baby.' She's into feature spots on national television and not too long ago stayed on the charts with a solo record. Each disc she cuts, in fact, is better than the last. 'One of these days,' James says, 'she's gonna hit it!'

Who's this girl with the charmed life? Marva is really Marva Ann Whitney (or Marvan if you're too lazy to say Marva Ann) and still single. She is the star of the family now, but depending on how you look at it, her mother or brothers used to occupy the spotlight.

Marva, the oldest child and the only girl, has six brothers – one set of triplets, one set of twins and 10-year-old Winfred. Kansas City talked whenever her mother went to the hospital.

'Marva doesn't get home much now. She's wrapped up in show business and has time for little else except sleeping and eating,' she says. Sometimes, if she can find a kitchen, she cooks soul food and maybe a few burritos.

She sounds like the old-time singers and quite naturally, the late Dinah Washington is one of her favorites. No one could sway her from the opinion that James Brown is the greatest – 'no one else gives me all that action!' she insists.

Quiet and proper on the outside, one always gets the feeling that Marva is a real swinger on the inside. But generally, after the show means a late dinner and a little television.

She worries a lot about her freckles and very little about her repertoire because she digs any song that gives her a good groove.

Her groove's pretty good the way it is anyway. I think how many women in the US would like to trade places with Marva, just for a day. She thinks about it often, that's why she works so hard. You know it isn't easy being second billing to James Brown!

Given all the press and TV coverage I was getting on the strength of 'It's My Thing' climbing up the singles chart, King released my first album, also called *It's My Thing*. On the back cover it had some interesting liner notes, which you'd often find on a new album in those days. I'm not sure who wrote them – probably Bud Hobgood, who often did liners for James Brown albums on King – but it looks like they were adapted from some that may have been intended for the scrapped *I Sing Soul* album, as they mention the song 'Sunny'. They also refer to *It's My Thing* as my second album.

IT'S MY THING

Here is a little girl with a great big voice and a bigger future. Her style is all her own – her sound distinctive and exciting. Marva Whitney is a bright young star and is destined to be a big star. This, her second album, is aptly titled 'IT'S MY THING,' because soul is Marva's thing!

Marva was in college in Kansas City singing in local clubs, churches, and other social gatherings when she went to see Mr James Brown. Mr Brown talked to her, liked her attitude and gave her an audition with his band. The rest is history . . . Marva joined the James Brown Show as featured girl vocalist replacing Vicki Anderson. She has appeared with the group in concert ever since, and on the trips to Vietnam, Africa, and other parts of the world.

In talking about Marva Whitney and her talents one has to mention her power – her driving style – her dedication to the strong melody line. Blessed with an exceptional range, she blends perfectly with James Brown on duets – they team together on SUNNY in this album.

Her recent credits include featured appearances of the *Joey Bishop Show*, the *Steve Allen Show,* the *Donald O'Connor Show* and others.

Dig this girl – she's groovy – she's a bright new talent who was destined to be around for a long time. She sings soul – sings it better than most – plus she sings soul with James Brown.

Critics generally agree that *It's My Thing* was one of the most consistent LPs that James Brown put together. I think it was strong because most of the songs on there had been cut as singles. It collected some of my earlier funk sides like 'What Do I Have To Do To Prove My Love To You'. I know that tune is particularly popular with my fans. I co-wrote it with James and we did it in just two takes. I remember I wanted the part where I sang the word 'what' to be right on the money.

As fans of my music will know, two tracks on 'It's My Thing' didn't feature me at all. They were the instrumentals 'In The Middle', which appeared on James's instrumental LP, *The Popcorn*, around the same time, and 'Shades Of Brown,' with James featured on the organ. When the album came out I was surprised to see them on my album and didn't like it. It didn't seem right. It was like he had to steal part of my limelight. But you got used to the unexpected in the James Brown show. I often felt like a slave instead of an artist. That man had too many personalities and you had to be ready for which ever one was out.

The album's front cover picture – showing me in a mini-skirt and a floppy brimmed hat – was taken in Nashville, Tennessee, at Mr Hal Neely's ranch. That white gown I'm wearing on the back cover was so beautiful and cost over 500 bucks. I wanted to wear it home for a Kansas City show, but when I put it on I realized the darn thing hadn't been hemmed. I couldn't believe it, but it was too late to change and I almost stumbled as I walked out on stage in it. That was at the Municipal Auditorium in downtown Kansas City, Missouri. I remember my audience that night didn't give me my props – in fact, at no time did I get a hearty response from a Kansas audience: I could feel the chill. My mom tells people there now that's why they don't see me much – I'm in and out and not in love with Kansas City at all. I don't feel no warmth from the city. Even my manager, Mr Cooper, pissed me off as he got a key to the city for James, but not even an appreciation letter for me. James was always uneasy about Kansas City, because they once accused him of rape behind the Blue Room. He always felt they were watching him after that.

To be honest, I didn't feel any real joy when *It's My Thing* went big. I wasn't bubbly or that excited: my worsening mental condition from the torments James Brown was giving me overrode the joy I should have had. Of course James really bragged about my success to other people, and there were even times he'd tell me I was bigger than some other artists, like Diana Ross. I never believed a word of it, though. My mother always taught me never to give my all to anyone but God, so when the unexpected came it wouldn't kill me. After all, I'd seen James start projects and then pull the rug out from under people. That happened a lot. He'd build a person up only to knock them down. And because of that and his treatment of me I was always on edge.

I also made lots of television appearances around this time. I appeared on *The Mike Douglas Show* several times, the *Merv Griffin Show*, Dick Clark's *American Bandstand*, Hugh Hefner's *Playboy After Dark*, a new music show called *The Scene* (where I wore a big blonde Afro wig) and numerous others. The thrill of appearing on TV was always tainted by James's mind games. Every time he'd make damn sure that a few minutes before I went out on stage he stopped by to see me. But it wasn't to offer words of encouragement. Instead he'd browbeat me to death over something – just some little thing that irritated him – so that I was nearly in tears when it was my turn to go on stage to sing. People probably heard me and said, 'Oh, that girl can't sing, poor little thing, and she looks so thin and James Brown is helping her.' He wanted to unnerve me so it affected my performance and I wouldn't be able to compete with him: he didn't want any of his singers looking or sounding better than him. That's why I wasn't allowed to move on stage, or smile. I remember one time we was doing a rehearsal for a TV show and when I didn't think he was looking I smiled at the camera and tried to look pleasant. I got back in my dressing room and he came in: one of his snitches had told him I'd smiled. He gave me the third degree, demanding to know why I was smiling and accusing me of 'Tomming'. He was obsessed by the notion of black people coming over like Uncle Tom to the whites, and was always saying, 'Don't you be doing no Tomming.' It was crazy. I couldn't express myself at all on stage. Sometimes it was difficult remembering the songs, 'cause what he'd said beforehand was playing on my mind.

The only time I was relaxed on a TV show was probably Hugh Hefner's *Playboy After Dark* series, but that's because I'd taken a nerve pill to get through it – and James and I were getting along much better than usual. Also on the bill was the comedians Bill Cosby, Soupy Sales, Jack Carter, Clay Tyson and the rock group, Three Dog Night. *Playboy After Dark* was beautiful and the atmosphere was out of sight: it was a great show. Mr Hefner was so classy: he ,was gentle, appreciative and a wonderful host. We recorded it in November '68 and I think it was broadcast in the summer of '69. James sang a couple of tunes and I performed 'Who Can I Turn To' and 'Your Love Was Good To Me'. When I finished my spot I went and sat alongside Hugh Hefner on his couch. I'd made up my mind that I was going to do my best on the show even if anything happened along the way. When I saw how it was laid out that put me in a better state of mind, and with some of my comrades there in the audience it felt good to me. I remember I wore a shiny green dress with sequins that James had bought for me. I had to have it shortened at the tailor's shop across the street from the Great Northern Hotel in New York. The people in New York know just how to make clothes look their best. It was a comfortable dress too. I don't know what happened to it; I think it was probably left with a lot of my things on the James Brown truck when I left. They never sent any of my things back; didn't even ask me if I wanted them shipped. And I was just one phone call away. I've lost a lot trusting people over the years.

Despite being thrilled to meet people like Bill Cosby, I often felt I was making a jackass out of myself. Of course, to the rest of the world it looked like James Brown was trying to help me in my career, but he was only trying to make hisself look good. The truth was, he couldn't stand anyone else being successful – especially one of his own singers. But in '69 he couldn't stop my success. I had three songs in the Top 100 list that year and was voted number two in the R&B poll for the Most Promising Female Vocalist held by the magazine *Record World*. In August 'Things Got To Get Better (Get Together)' made no. 22 in *Billboard's* R&B chart and later on, in October, 'I Made A Mistake Because It's Only You' reached no. 32. 'I Made A Mistake' was another song credited to me and James, but in truth I wrote that whole song: there was no co-writer. With the lyrics I was trying to appease James and stop him being mean to me. The pressure was getting kind of tough at that time.

Also on the *It's My Thing* LP was a song called 'I'm Tired, I'm Tired, I'm Tired (Things Better Change Before It's Too Late)'. It started off as a version of the Smokey Robinson Motown song 'Here I Am Baby' (as recorded by Barbara McNair), and I remember performing it at the Dallas Memorial Auditorium in August '68. It was an awesome show, I think the first time that James performed 'Say It Loud – I'm Black & I'm Proud' live. The concert was recorded, but was only released a few years ago. The backing track for 'I'm Tired, I'm Tired, I'm Tired' was taken from that very same concert, but because of the political stance that James was beginning to take at that time – and of course, the huge success he was having with 'Say It Loud—I'm Black & I'm Proud' – he wanted to give the song's lyrics more of a social message. If Soul Brother Number One had a message song out then it was inevitable that Soul Sister Number One had to follow him. So it changed from 'Here I Am Baby' into 'I'm Tired, I'm Tired, I'm Tired'. But I hated to sing it: for one thing it reminded me of a Martha Reeves tune I'd heard. Because it reflected the social and racial unrest in America at that time, I've got to confess that it was a really hard song for me to sing. Not because of the music, but because I'd really never had any bad trouble with whites. Of course I sometimes got carried away by the spirit of the times and looked at white people meanly when they stared at my blonde hair, or when I expressed my opinion during those days when I worked in an office. It puts me in mind of something my dad used to say: 'If you're black, get back; brown, stick around; yellow, you're mellow.' I told Hal Neely this a few years ago. He just laughed and said, 'I never heard of that.'

I don't think James liked the success of *It's My Thing* very much. When he got a sales report for that record he saw I was outselling him. You might have thought this was good for us both, but no – he didn't like to be outshone by anyone, especially someone from his own revue.

It was the same thing when I won the Golden Mike award in 1969; this was presented by the National Association of Television and Radio Announcers, based in Washington DC. It was a total shock: I'd no idea I'd been nominated or anything. One day Bud Hobgood just turned up and handed the award to me: a gold-colored microphone – it wasn't real gold, of course. Sadly I lost it in the shuffle years ago. I was disgusted that James hadn't told me, so I couldn't go in person to receive it.

166

Although *It's My Thing* did well, I've not seen much money from it. As I was signed with King Records the royalties should have been paid directly to me, but all through the years the owners of King sent everything to James. Because they could never find me James received all my money. The same thing happened to Lyn Collins.

Another thing: when I went to the studio with James and the band to record some songs under my name, we often worked so quickly that there'd be time left for the band to do a couple of tunes, and quite often James would do a tune himself during my studio time. The band all were union workers, and being dumb I never knew what was going on money-wise; I just know I stayed in the red. At no time did James actually say to me that the session was costing so much and he'd charge it against my future royalties. Being naïve, I didn't ask how the cost of the sessions would affect royalties, but I suspect he charged me for the whole session instead of part of it. Looking back on it, I wonder if me and the other featured singers like Vicki Anderson and Lyn Collins were tax write-offs. But then again, James had no accounting system at King Records – which is probably why he got into trouble with the IRS years later.

CHAPTER 27

Big Trouble at the Beverly Comstock

I tried to leave James Brown's revue again a few months later. He was continuing to torment me and make my life hell, and I'd had enough. I was tired and ready to go. We'd been doing some shows out in California, and I knew people there who would rescue me if I could just get to them – including Tuttie and The Derbys, some schoolmates and Jimmy Lewis, who wrote many songs for Ray Charles. We had been doing some shows out there.

I remember it was late in the evening, the very same night that Deedee was having James's baby, and we were outside the Beverly Comstock hotel in Beverly Hills, Los Angeles, which is where James and I usually had a suite when we went out to the West Coast. There were three of us: me, James and Charles Bobbitt. James was laying into me about something I'd done wrong and I said, 'Mr Brown, I've had all I can take. I think it's best if I leave. I've got some friends out here in California. I'll just take me a cab and go my own way.'

His mood changed in a blink of an eye. 'Ah, Whit, Whit, why you going to do that?' Just before this he'd been talking to me like I was a dog; now he started talking nice. 'Come on, Whit,' he pleaded. 'I'm sorry. I ain't gonna do that no more. I'll treat you right. Don't go.'

He begged, apologized, then smiled and turned on the charm. Like a fool, my resolve melted right there: I gave in and was suckered back to him. I thought that if he knew I was considering leaving it would calm his cruelty. 'OK, Mr Brown, maybe I'll stay after all.'

So then all three of us went into the hotel. Bobbitt got the keys as we walked to the elevator; I remember one man, a bellhop, on duty. I went to the elevator and went in first. It was quite small – almost the length of me – without windows, and was able to hold perhaps four people at most. As I walked in I felt a hard kick on my backside, which knocked me over and threw me to the floor. I was face down as James started to kick me over and over. He had always hit me and Lyn Collins on the backside, apart from the time he hit me in the middle of my forehead and made me go out and sing. When the elevator stopped at our floor Bobbitt stepped over me and went about his business like he hadn't heard or seen nothing: he most certainly wasn't going to say anything on my behalf. I thought he'd help but he just left me. I was James's woman, and he thought it wasn't his place to get involved.

James pulled me to my feet. I stood up, smarting from the pain, and we got out of the elevator. No one was around. He marched me to the suite and he shut the door. Then he pulled a gun on me and shouted, 'Get your hands up!'

James didn't often carry a gun, but Bobbitt usually had whatever his boss might need if a situation demanded it. One time I remember Berry Gordy's people had a party. A woman asked James for a signed picture and he ignored her. She called him an ugly black gorilla and said she didn't really want his picture anyway. A fight broke out, and James ran back to his suite where I was and said, 'Give me my gun, baby.' I found it and gave it to him. I stayed in the suite and couldn't see well what was going on, but they were fighting like gangsters – and Bobbitt or somebody jumped off the rail to the next floor.

James pushed the gun against the back of my head. It hurt. I was terrified. He was very smart: he didn't let anyone see his dirty work – unless it was staff who knew to ignore the situation. 'So you was gonna leave, Whit? I'll see about that.'

I felt the barrel pressing into my head. I was scared out of my mind: I thought he was going to kill me right there. I said, 'Yes sir, yes sir,' to whatever he said.

'Don't shit and fall back in it,' he kept saying. 'I'm bigger than The Temptations and all those other groups.' He went on and on, telling me how great and how big and how powerful he was. I was so scared that I went into a kind of trance and began speaking in tongues. He knew I was from a church where the congregation often did this. Many people find it difficult to understand this. We're what are called the Holy Rollers, and that's the way we talk to God spiritually, from the spirit of our hearts. We have a mindset of what we think we talk in, but we don't really know what language it is. We could be talking French, we could be talking anything. It's a dialogue between my spirit and God, a revelation that comes when you're in a certain state of mind. So when James would get me to a certain state of mind and cause me mental and emotional stress, I would go into speaking in tongues. James never understood this. It scared him and it always calmed him down. He'd visited the church with me, and used to make fun of me 'cause at one time I used to carry my Bible with me everywhere we went. He'd laugh, show me money in his briefcase and say, 'This is my god, Whit. Ha, ha, ha.' But even though he wouldn't admit it, James knew my God, and I've heard there were times he'd gotten down on his knees to pray. One of these was when he knew he was responsible for the comedian Clay Tyson's death: Lyn Collins told me about this, as they were together when it happened. More of that later.

So I began to speak in tongues for quite a while and James put the gun down. He settled a little and had a Heineken – that's the beer he drank then – and kept saying, 'Don't shit and fall back in it.' And so the night went on like any other night: that is, we stayed up till daylight. He was always hyped up and would talk everybody to death: everybody had to be at his beck and call until he felt like leaving. When the sun came up was the only time I could get some sleep: I was averaging maybe three or four hours a night back then, if I was lucky. I was like a doggone zombie a lot of the time.

Anyway, that particular night I was exhausted and managed to get some sleep, but I always had to wake up ahead of James to help him get ready. He'd eat cold steak and a baked potato: that's all he ate in that hotel. They'd send a portable warmer, but the food was always cold. I got to the point where I hated steak.

I knew by now I was on my way out. It was just a matter of when and how. I couldn't take a whole lot more of it. Hell, my daddy never hit my mama, and I was not going to take that. Even Ben Bart – whom I called Papa Bart – of Universal Attractions told me before he died in August 1969 that he knew what was going on, and he tried to get me out. When he came out to see the show once in a while James would laugh at him behind his back: he'd say, 'He used to be my manager but I control him now.' He'd brag about how a black man owned a white man. But Papa Bart got the chance to tell me when we were alone for a second or two that he knew what was going on. 'Just hold on. I'll take care of it. Don't worry: it's going to be all right.' I believed his assurances and surmised he was going to get me bookings so I could establish myself and not be hooked on James's coat tails. When he passed away suddenly I was very sorry and sad. He was a nice man. I knew it was going to be tough without him, but I knew my days with James were numbered with no one there to protect me.

By this time Mr Cooper had stepped out of the picture really. I later found out that he was going to sell his interest in me to James, though in the end they never signed a deal. See, James was very smart. He was an astute businessman who knew how to get the best out of any situation. I remember there was a time he was having problems with King Records – a few years before I joined the show – so he made a deal with another label, Smash. He recorded 'Out Of Sight' for them and it became a big hit. King took legal action against Smash, stopping them releasing any records with James's vocals on, but James came out laughing. He'd outsmarted them both, and gave himself more bargaining power with King as a result – so he got a better deal.

Here's another example of how smart James was. One day the IRS turned up unannounced. They wanted to seize some of James's assets to cover unpaid taxes and tried to impound all his road equipment, including the truck, the PA system, the lighting and all the band's instruments. But as soon as James realized they were sniffing around he sold everything to Mr Moore, who sold posters and programs, for just $1. When the IRS tried to take the assets James told them they didn't belong to him. They left really pissed. As soon as they'd gone James bought everything back – for $1.

CHAPTER 28

Live & Lowdown

Live and Lowdown At The Apollo came out in November 1969, just before I left James Brown and when he was pressing me for another contract, although the one I had wasn't up. On the cover I'm wearing a blonde wig. I don't think any songs on the album was actually recorded at the Apollo. One of the songs, 'I Made A Mistake Because It's Only You', was cut in King's studio and then had audience applause added: James often did that in those days. As far as I remember, the rest of the tracks were recorded at the Bell Auditorium, Augusta, Georgia on 1 October 1969 – the same concert at which James recorded most of the tracks for his famous *Sex Machine* album. I didn't know they were going to record me until maybe the day before.

I can tell you how I felt that night: there was a determination that I'd never had previously. I told myself to do the best job I could; I sensed it was going to be my last album with James and I gave it all I had. It seemed that the band felt something too, for they kicked and played like never before, especially on a version of Aretha Franklin's 'Respect' and 'You Got To Have A Job'. I got over with the crowd: I got applause, applause, applause. I felt like I'd taken enough shit from James Brown and was in form both mentally and musically.

A lady called Ruth K. Abernathy wrote the liner notes for the album. This is what she said:

MARVA WHITNEY –
LIVE AND LOWDOWN AT THE APOLLO

Marva Whitney – better known to many as 'Marvelous Marva' and given the title which she so greatly earned as the most promising vocalist for 1969 to 1970, is, as the album title implies, LIVE AND LOWDOWN AT THE APOLLO THEATER – in her own way. Marva has, for some time, since her team up with James (Soul Brother Number One) Brown, been on the rise to what she is becoming now – a polished star and successful singer.

The fame, the talent and the will to achieve could be expected. As Marva puts it, and I quote, 'I prefer a song with good lyrics that have a message. Take the tune, "Respect" . . . one has to have respect for the other. Some songs,' Marva observes, 'tell people what they need to know, like how important it is to "Have A Job".' 'Things Have Got To Get Better' says this for not only Marva but all of her listeners.

Performing at the Apollo was a challenge as well as a thrill for Marva. She was given a spontaneous ovation by her audience when she so rousingly performed 'It's My Thing'.

Marva Whitney's first few notes will immediately tell you into what camp she falls. It's always pleasant to hear a good voice and hers, with its lively individuality, assuredly commands your attention. To sum up Marva's style is difficult, but a listing of what makes her unique is perhaps easier. In the meantime turn your turntable over to Marva Whitney and be tantalized by her way with this collection of great soul hits she so excitedly performed at the Apollo Theater, Live & Lowdown.

CHAPTER 29

Get Out of My Life –

Leaving the James Brown Show

The straw that finally broke the camel's back happened in December 1969. By then I'd been with James just two and a half years, but with hundreds of shows under my belt and so many bad experiences it seemed more like a lifetime.

I remember we was doing a series of shows at the Apollo. There was a little man who was crazy about me called Jack Fink, a small man in his forties. He was so warm and friendly. It was like, 'Look at this little girl, she sings so well and I really like her.' He was really fond of me and always made his way up to my dressing room. I was so happy to see him, and he always went out of his way to come and see me when I was in New York, even if it was just for five minutes. He was a fine gentleman to talk to and he treated me so royally. He was the one who was pushing for me to get on the TV shows back then, because he was *the man*.

Mr Fink always used to call me Marva, and it got back to James that this man didn't address me correctly as Miss Whitney. As I said, for some reason he believed that people should always be addressed as Miss or Mr. So James called me in and said, 'When Mr Jack Fink comes you'd better tell him to straighten up and call you Miss Whitney.'

My heart was heavy. I knew it wasn't the right thing, but when Mr Fink came to see me later on I said, 'I'm sorry, Mr Fink, but Mr Brown says you have to call me Miss Whitney from now on.' I could feel the hurt and humiliation that came through that man's eyes – it nearly killed me. Years later I heard that Mr Fink's son, Jack Fink Jr, worked at the advertising agency William Morris. I wrote to him and apologized for treating his father like I did. It had haunted me for almost forty years.

Later on that same night at the Apollo, James came up to my dressing room on the third level of the theater. He knew I wasn't pleased about being asked to correct Mr Fink because his snitches had told him so, and he came purposely to pick a fight with me. He asked me to step outside the door. There were people coming back and forth, either going on stage or to their dressing rooms, and I think they were aware of what was going on. Some probably stayed in their rooms listening, 'cause they knew the shit was about to hit the fan. So I stepped out and James started threatening me: 'I'm going to put you back in the gutter where I found you. I'll make sure that you never work again.'

But I wasn't going to take his insults lying down. I said, 'Mr Brown, I come from a well-respected family in Kansas City. I may not have been rich but we wasn't so poor that we lived in the ghetto. Before I came to work for you I was working in a credit bureau in Kansas City, Missouri, and you couldn't be no dummy to do that. I've got secretarial skills.' Before I knew it he'd kicked me on my legs and started raining blows on me. He had a face like thunder, his eyes were bulging with anger and he used the same phrase he'd used at the Beverly Comstock when he pulled a gun on me: 'Don't shit and fall back in it.' He could see I didn't like what he was saying, but he could also see something in me that I guess he hadn't seen before: determination and defiance. And that's when he backhanded me and kicked me.

A young man witnessed all this. Ron Taylor was in his early teens: he'd started as a kid, maybe eight or nine years old, working for James when he came to the Apollo. He was standing right there as James was reading me my rights and low-rating me. Ron says to this day, 'I felt so bad because I knew I should have helped you, but I was too young and I knew I couldn't do nothing. I wanted to kill that man.'

That's how I felt too. I wanted to kill James. It wasn't just the kickings and beatings but the mental persecution too. I'd suffered so much that I was ready to give it all up. People reading this must remember that women's liberation hadn't arrived at this time, and people in the music business didn't want to help me because they thought I was James's woman and didn't want to interfere in case it affected their relationship with him. They knew not to mess with James's 'property'.

After that final pre-Christmas date at the Apollo I finally decided to quit. With three R&B hit singles under my belt, an award and a new album in the shops, I'd achieved a hell of a lot that year, but the bad things outweighed the good. The terrible thing was that the Lord had blessed me to become big enough that my name was going to go up on the marquee on the strip in Las Vegas in January 1970: I was scheduled to appear with James at the International Showroom. But I couldn't take no more. It had got to the point where I suspected that I'd be murdered. I feared for my life. I really did. With the Vegas dates on the horizon I began to get worried. I'd heard too many people went missing up in Vegas, buried in the desert and mountains where they ain't gonna find you.

But there was still work to do. After those dates at the Apollo I was sent out on a two-week tour to the kind of nightclubs that were on skid row. It felt like a punishment. James was trying to humiliate me. And I think he was scared I was going to leave and was tightening a noose round my neck, so to speak. He was hoping I'd fail and come back crawling.

Our relationship had been made worse by a frank interview I'd given a few weeks before to *Soul* magazine – the first I'd ever done without James being present. Maceo Parker was supposed to do it with me but he never showed. I remember that the girl who interviewed me recorded the whole thing on tape. I talked openly about my problems with Soul Brother Number One; I told the truth about how James ran his show. I was trying to help everybody, the whole band, the whole outfit, because everybody was going through the same thing: we were all James's slaves. It was naïve, I suppose, but I thought it would help things rather than make them worse. After the article came out – I remember the magazine had Jesse Jackson on the front cover – *Soul* mysteriously went out of business. I've always thought that James was so furious that I'd dared to criticize him that he used his influence to close down the magazine. Later somebody told me – and I don't know how true it is – that it was James's magazine anyway.

Anyhow, I went out and did the tour dates on my own, but more and more I thought about how to escape from James Brown. I was backed by a young Cincinnati band that he was grooming called The Pacesetters. They'd been a studio band for King Records, and although they wasn't as slick as James's own band they was incredibly funky and enthusiastic. Not long afterwards, when James's band rebelled over pay, he made The Pacesetters his backing band (re-naming them the New Breed Band, then The JB's). They was so talented that this didn't surprise me.

Me and The Pacesetters had been out on the road together twice before. One time I remember we did some tour dates that included a show at the Apollo Theater with Wilson Pickett, Doris Troy and Brook Benton, who did 'Rainy Night In Georgia'. The band featured William 'Bootsy' Collins on bass – who later went on to become a funk pioneer and played with George Clinton – and his brother Phelps, a guitarist with the nickname 'Catfish'. The Pacesetters went with me and my aunt, Margaret Collins, who also lived in Kansas City. She traveled with me to make sure that I had a companion, as I was the only lady on the show. For some reason my aunt helped to make a bond with Bootsy and the guys, I think because her last name was Collins: we all felt like kinfolk. They was a great bunch and we had some good times together. Aunt Margaret was crazy and had fun with them too. I remember we'd congregate in my room every morning and watch a cartoon show on TV called *Casper The Friendly Ghost*. It was Bootsy's favorite, and his wish was my command. He was so cute and so crazy and I had to fight hard to keep our relationship strictly professional, for he was a teenager and I was in my middle twenties. I was raised strict, and fooling with a teenager at my age was a no-no. We struggled at first on the road, but in the end we persevered and made it. They were nice young men – kids really – and boy, could they funk: they could really play their behinds off. I have a special feeling in my heart for them always.

The places we played on our second tour were so rough that anybody with any sense wouldn't come. I told Bootsy, 'I know we've not made much money, but I'll send you your cut.' We took care of business and got good reviews, although James had thought we were going to flop. I remember that one time James and me appeared separately at different venues in the same town. I think the town was Cleveland, Ohio. James's house didn't draw, and after he got off his show he came to where I was: it was jam-packed to the brim. He didn't like that; not one bit. He brought us in off the road after that because he wasn't going to be upstaged by his own people.

Me and Bootsy have remained friends to this day. This is what he remembers about our days together:

We met up with James Brown in 1968. There was my brother Catfish on guitar, Tiger Martin on drums, Clayton 'Chicken' Gunnels on trumpet, Robert 'Chopper' McCullough on sax, and myself Bootsy on bass. Bud Hobgood and Bobby Byrd really liked us as a group and suggested to JB that he should check us out. At that time we were recording a lot for King Records, especially the artist records that Henry Glover and Gene Redd was doing. The word started to get around about how great this new young rhythm section was and JB got interested. He decided to send us out with Hank Ballard first, so we went on the road with him for about three months. But we didn't even make wine money with that mutha. We'd originally wanted to do it because we thought it would be fun, it was Hank Ballard, and we got a chance to get out of Cincinnati – plus people would get a chance to behold the new funk, or at least that's what we thought. But after we got all our equipment stolen and Hank didn't show up on a few gigs that we had to play anyway we went back home and licked our wounds. We told Bud Hobgood that we couldn't go back out with Hank, so the gig came up about going out with Ms Whitney, and we said heck yeah!

I personally couldn't wait to funk with Marva: she was raw and sexy. This was in 1969 and we went on to do some dates with her. We played auditoriums, clubs and ballrooms. The audiences loved her, and we got a little play on the side: you know, I met a few young girlies while out with Marva (I couldn't crack on the boss so I kept it real).

We were all dirty young boys, and were at that age when if you see a fine young lady you're automatically in love whether she notices you or not. Marva was bigger than life to us – not only a star but with James Brown. So Ms Whitney had it going on and we didn't want her to know how nervous we were because we had a rep to uphold. I couldn't let her see my weak side and that I was in love with her. I was sixteen years old when I got with Marva. I think she had a little boy crush on me as well, but she was a professional. We knew her records and everything JB put out on her. We didn't know she was being punished by JB – we just thought he wanted her to do some gigs on her own and were glad because we got a chance to play with her. (This is when we also met Danny Ray. I guess he was on punishment as well.)

Playing with Marva was a much better situation than Hank Ballard. At least we didn't have to jump out of hotel back windows because we couldn't pay the bill. So that was a big plus for us. JB was supposed to pay us but we never got paid by his guys. We wasn't expecting to get paid anyway and we knew Marva had nothing to do with it so she was still the Soul Goddess to us. Remember we were fresh off the streets when James started messing with us, so we were very hip and knew all the tricks in the book. But we were playin' just to play.

We'd drive to and from gigs in a car rented by James Brown Productions. We partied like a mug but never missed a gig or a rehearsal. The gigs and rehearsals were sacred to us: we had to be the best and wanted to make a name for ourselves as well as please the people we were playing behind, in this case Ms Whitney. Marva had a lady named Ms Collins as her assistant on the road and we thought that was cool – after all Catfish and I had the same last name.

Marva never told us about her problems with JB, but when we saw her come to a gig with really dark glasses on and she didn't take them off for the show we knew what was up. We knew a lot about James Brown and how he treated people and his stable of women so it didn't surprise us, but at the same time we asked ourselves why he'd do that to our girl. There was always tension with JB and anybody. We were outsiders so we could see right through a lot of stuff: we always knew what was up.

Christmas was coming up, and after I finished those dates with Bootsy and the guys, I decided to go home as normal for the holiday season but vowed never return to the James Brown show. It really hurt to leave just when I felt I'd made an important breakthrough by having my name on the marquee in Vegas, but I had no alternative.

CHAPTER 30

Free at Last, Free at Last!

When I got on a plane to fly home to Kansas no one on the show knew I was thinking of quitting. I went to my parents' house. I needed time to think, to weigh the pros and cons of my situation. I had to take many things into deep consideration. Money was one. At the time I was making $700 a week, which was pretty good for those days. But money doesn't necessarily buy you happiness. My mental outlook wasn't good at all. I felt like a fugitive on the run.

I felt really blessed to have gained some real stature in the world of show business, even though I'd suffered greatly and paid a hell of a lot of dues. But I had to make a decision. Over the two-week Christmas vacation I thought deeply about things. Christmas came and went, and so did the New Year.

In the first few days of January 1970 James had Mr Moore call me. I've mentioned him before: he sold pictures, posters and other things of interest for the James Brown show, and he was a fine gentleman. When I was part of the revue I'd sometimes slip away and say hi to him and his staff. During our phone conversation I didn't reveal to Mr Moore that I was thinking of leaving.

A few days after I'd spoken to Mr Moore, Bud Hobgood from King Records called and told me that the next record – my funky version of Burt Bacharach and Hal David's 'This Girl's In Love With You' – was ready to be released. I pretended that everything was all right and that I'd be back in a few days. I certainly didn't want the big boys – the promoters – to be mad at me, but I had to make a decision, even though it might cost me dearly in terms of developing my career. But I'd gotten so tired of the pain and hurt and I wanted it to end. And I want to tell those promoters, whoever they are and wherever they are, that I'm tremendously sorry for letting them down, but I was a nervous wreck and I was scared for my life. Despite the temptation that a new record and shows at Vegas offered, I just couldn't go back. I decided to lie low so no one could contact me. I didn't take any more phone calls. If anybody called I got Mom or Dad to say I'd gone out.

Alan Leeds joined the James Brown organization in 1970 just after I left. This is his perspective of how people inside James's camp saw my departure:

After her increased popularity in 1969 via *It's My Thing*, Marva wanted the opportunity to break away from the James Brown show and accept some other bookings. Reluctantly James agreed, but he avidly retained complete control over when she was free to work away from his show and under what circumstances. Her lack of control and flexibility frustrated Marva no end and her relationship with JB suffered accordingly.

A much-discussed article in *Soul* magazine included an interview with a frustrated Marva and brought her differences with JB before the media and the public. James was furious to be publicly discussed as a sexist tyrant of a boss. This was near the end of 1969, just as I arrived in Cincinnati. When Marva was appearing away from the JB tour, Brown brought back Vicki Anderson as a replacement and began recording Vicki again.

The feelings among the staff were divided. Some JB loyalists seemed to view Marva as a malcontent who was ungrateful for the opportunities James had provided her career. But most of us, including many in the Brown band, defended Marva's right to pursue her career. There seemed to be a window of opportunity for Marva to grow from a perpetual support act on the James Brown Show to a star on her own and most of us were rooting her along.

While the precise nature of their dialogue is between Marva and James, it seemed clear that the dispute over control of her career was at the center of their difficulties. James could be a very territorial and manipulative boss. King 6327 would have been scheduled several months after Marva had departed the company and been replaced by Ms Anderson. Brown probably just decided it was foolhardy to continue promoting Marva via old records when she was no longer part of his company, and canceled the record.

What Alan refers to as King 6327 was a track I'd recorded just before I left James, called 'Just Won't Do Right'. Apparently King was going to issue it as the follow-up 45 to 'This Girl's In Love With You'. It only got as far as the test pressing before they decided not to release it, and Alan has one of the few surviving copies. A couple of years later Lyn Collins revived the track for her debut single. I think they used the same backing track.

Back in early 1970 James's camp still hadn't given up on me. They were really concerned at my silence and called out for me on KPRS, Kansas City's only black radio station, announcing on the air for me to call James Brown's office: 'Marva Whitney, Marva Whitney, call King Records,' the DJs said. This went on all day long but I didn't respond. Even back home I didn't think I was safe. At one time I thought someone was following me; that's how paranoid I'd gotten from being with James. I felt that wherever I went, whatever I did, he always had his finger on me.

I guess that when I couldn't be contacted James knew I probably wasn't going back, and I expect he was mad for a while. I guess he felt he'd been wronged because of all the time, effort and money he'd invested in me.

It was when I was in my twenties rehearsing with the Derbys at Tuttie's house that I'd first noticed Ellis Taylor, who was a very good-looking young man and always drove a new car. We started talking and he told me he was an electronics engineer, which was unusual at that time for a black man. He helped set up the tower for the first black radio station in Kansas City, KPRS, which was owned by Ed and Psyche Pate who lived on 23rd and Bent. I don't know whether Psyche is still alive: she was a beautiful woman with a beautiful personality. I think they had either one or two children. When we were kids, our family, the Manning Gospel Singers, used to have a fifteen-minute Gospel Hour sponsored by Standard

Improvement Company (a building firm) on KPRS. Chuck Moore was the station manager, he still lives today.

Anyway, Ellis used to come over to Tuttie's house when we were rehearsing. He'd never really come in, but he'd stop for a few minutes and say hi. When I saw him I thought, *Wow,* because he was good-looking. But he never flirted with me and I never flirted with him. He had a quiet air about him, and lots of Indian in him: he could walk up on me and I wouldn't even hear him. And he was a very deep thinker, soulful and a good writer. Ellis played piano and could write notes; and that man had a sense of timing I never could pick up.

He was an intelligent, ambitious man and considered a black pioneer as far as the radio and television industry was concerned. He was an electronics genius: they said that if he couldn't fix it, it couldn't be fixed. They'd send for him to fix jobs at the TV stations in Kansas City when they could not find the trouble. He was held back because he was black. Ellis was the staff engineer at KMBC radio for a long time, and helped to found the United Minority Media Association as well as serving on the Kansas City Missouri Education Video Transcription Advisory Board. He also ran a television service in Kansas City for years. He also ran a television service in Kansas City for years. Ellis got elected to the Executive Board of Directors of the International Brotherhood of Electrical Workers in broadcasting, and he did a lot of good work helping black kids get into the electronics industry. He was also a musician, had once been a jazz DJ, had ambitions to be a record producer and owned a local record label called Forte Records, which he'd started in the 1960s. I remember that towards the end of my time with James Brown I was at my mother's house when I received a note from Ellis. He knew of my disillusionment with the James Brown revue and suggested we should work together. This offer showed me there was light at the end of the tunnel and that there could be life after James Brown. But before I teamed up with Ellis Taylor I received another offer to record. It was one I couldn't refuse.

When I left James Brown the first people who helped me was the Isley Brothers. At least I thought they was trying to help me, though I never personally met them. They had their own label called T-Neck, and in early 1970 a man named Gene Smith representing the company called me after he'd spoken to my manager: 'Marva, come over here,' he said. 'We'll help you. The Isley Brothers want you on their label.' So I went up to Chicago, where they wanted me to record, and signed with T-Neck. Gene and Floyd Smith co-produced a session I did for the company that produced two songs. Floyd was a jazz guitarist who later managed and married the disco singer, Loleatta Holloway. The songs he cut with me were 'Giving Up On Love', a really lively funky number written by William Durham, and 'This Is My Quest', a slow, soulful ballad penned by Floyd with Lennie Satin. T-Neck released 'This Is My Quest' as a single with the faster 'Giving Up On Love' on the B-side. I thought those two songs were really good, and I felt positive about the record because it was my first taste of freedom. Also, T-Neck was distributed by New York's Buddah Records, which was another plus. But it wasn't long before my hopes were dashed: the record was a complete and utter flop. Although T-Neck pressed up the record I never actually heard it played on the radio. Not once. And because of that it never hit the charts. T-Neck asked me to send about fifty pictures because they were going to do some promotional work on me, but I don't think the record ever got properly promoted. I don't think they were serious about it. Because it didn't sell back then it's hard to find now, and funk collectors will pay a lot of money for it. Of course, I didn't get paid. When I asked BMI through lawyers they told me that too much time had elapsed for me to make a royalties claim.

I was bitterly disappointed by the failure of 'This Is My Quest', as I thought it was better than most of my James Brown-produced records. I even wondered if James had used his influence to stop my record getting airplay. After all, he'd said that if I ever left the show I'd never work again. His power in those days was great, and he bought the loyalty of DJs and promoters, even radio stations. If you think about it, most people who left James's show didn't achieve much afterwards, except Tammi Terrell. He made darn sure of it. He could ruin an artist's career with just one word.

What I didn't figure out until some years later was that the Isley Brothers had probably used me to get back at James Brown. They'd been pissed when James released 'It's My Thing' on me. I heard they all had a row because 'It's My Thing' was so close to their song 'It's Your Thing'. It was said that the Isleys went to see James and they had a fight in James's backyard over it. There was certainly a dispute over the writing credits, and the Isleys apparently wanted some money and residual royalties from it. Only a few words were changed on 'It's My Thing' from the Isleys' original, and I think as a result they thought they could use me as a thorn in James's side – but I don't think he could have cared less. In the end I suppose I was written off as a tax loss by T-Neck. I didn't record for them again.

Around the same time I was thinking of ways to make myself different from other female singers. I wanted to create something new, especially because I was having trouble getting work. I'd heard that in the 1940s there was an all-girl rhythm and blues band that had been bad, out of sight. Inspired by them, I tried this group of local young ladies out as a backing band. They were called The Sweethearts and they were sisters: one played piano, while the others played guitar, drums and bass. Another sister, Marian Love, had a couple of records out for Capitol at one time. In rehearsal The Sweethearts sounded good. They'd previously worked with Ellis, so I didn't have no worries about their abilities. So we rehearsed and then we had a concert in Kansas City. It was a complete disaster, so bad I wanted to crawl under a rock and hide. They acted like they'd never rehearsed in their life: they got complete amnesia up there on the bandstand. I believe now that they purposely sabotaged me and tried to make me look bad. Maybe James had got to them in some way, slipped them some money to ruin the show, perhaps, to make sure I didn't get any more bookings. I never used them again.

It was hard after I left James. Really hard. Only a few DJs, promoters and journalists seemed to remember me, because as I said earlier James prevented me from meeting these people and establishing some kind of relationship with them. Fred Wesley sympathized with my plight. To this day he believes James helped ruin my career: 'I really believe James had a big hand in Marva not making it after she left because she was an excellent singer and she could have made it if he'd allowed it. But he just wouldn't allow it. I've had trouble getting record deals myself because I was with James Brown. They don't think you've really left him and stuff like that.'

After the T-Neck fiasco Mr Cooper tried to get me more work. But let me tell you, it was like my name was bad news. When I left James in January I knew I was in big trouble, but I told myself it might blow over in six weeks or so. But I was wrong. I couldn't get a job. The comedian, Redd Foxx, offered me work in his club in LA, but Ellis didn't want me to go there so I didn't. The only places I could get work were down South, where I think they hadn't heard that I'd left James Brown. Being James's road secretary at one time had its advantages: I knew all about booking artists, and made contact with some Southern promoters. A gentleman in Florida, I believe his name was Fisher, he and his family booked me; then a radio personality called Dr Daddio booked me too. He was the first black owner of a radio station in Denver, Colorado. His real name was Jim Walker, and he was a pioneer in black radio – the first African-American to get a job as a DJ on KDKO, which was originally a country station. In 1989 he bought the station – and I believe his son's the president of it now. Dr Daddio also had a nightclub called Showtime. He booked me a couple of times because, hell, he wasn't scared of James. I also worked at a black club in Texas a couple of times: I can't recall its name. They were nice people to work for.

Jimmy Smith, a former road manager for James Brown, booked me out of Atlanta when he found out that I'd left James. I think he'd got fired. He had a gangster image, and if you didn't know him you'd be scared to death. We had another female singer with us. I can't remember her name; she was fresh trying to make it. We worked the South and did pretty good until someone got sticky fingers and took off with the takings. After that I joined forces with another James Brown refugee, Hank Ballard. We played Grambling College in Louisiana as the Hank Ballard and Marva Whitney show. Someone stole all of my clothes there. I mean all. I offered a reward but no one came forward, so I performed just wearing the mini-dress I had on. We went down well as I recall.

Other than the people I've mentioned, no one helped me or came to my rescue. I was locked down on many fronts, but I was a fighter. Mr Cooper and I tried to start a production company and booking agency in Kansas City, but it was a no-go. To get it off the ground we had a business partner called Dr Fuller, who was my dentist, and reputed to be one of the best black dentists in the city. He had ambitions to get involved with the local football team, the Kansas City Chiefs, as one of his best friends was connected with them. They were college players and the best team in Kansas City, Missouri: they won the championship for the first time round about this time. Anyway, Dr Fuller ended up siphoning our funds and using some of the money we'd saved to try to buy hisself in with them. I think it was to help set up a nightclub for the Chiefs. I was sent out on the road, and when I came back I discovered all these expenses put on me that he couldn't account for. Dr Fuller eventually lost his license, his wife and everything else to drugs and women.

I also got ripped off by Jimmy Smith. One time he was sending me to a gig and I asked him to send a deposit from the venue to our office. But I didn't get it. I called the venue and said, 'Y'all didn't send a deposit to the office.'

They said, 'Miss Whitney, we sent that deposit two weeks ago.'

So I called Mr Smith and he just said, 'No they didn't.' But the people at the venue showed me a receipt for it. We knew right then Jimmy Smith was lying, so we stopped using him. Maybe that's why he stopped working for James Brown: you can't tell me he wasn't taking a little bit off the top, 'cause he was the one handling the money. And he had a bad attitude, too, I remember: he had a short fuse and could be intimidating. So me and Mr Cooper was glad to wash our hands of him.

After that I took it easy for a while and watched a lot of TV. I enjoyed being a part of the community in the south of Kansas City, Missouri, and spending time with my daughter Sherrie. We had a lot of catching up to do. I also had time to grow a vegetable garden and planted flowers. That's when I began to date Ellis Taylor: though my career was in limbo, romance blossomed. I'd known him a long time, and my mother had known his mother, Dezzie Taylor, Ellis and his sisters when she was young. They'd come to Kansas from New Hebron, Mississippi, and they lived in Armourdale, where I was raised. My mother and her baby sister became very good friends of the sisters, who died an early death. My manager, Mr Cooper, couldn't stand Ellis, though. I thought it was jealousy initially, but I found out that they'd done a few business deals in the past. Mr Cooper kept telling me that Ellis was no good, but I figured it was just a man thing and I didn't pay him no attention. Within a year my manager said if I had to be with Ellis he had to go, so when I married Ellis in August 1970 Mr Cooper faded into the sunset. Mr Cooper's position in the music business had been weakened by my leaving James Brown; his name didn't carry the weight it once had. Maybe it was for the best that we parted company.

Ellis was twelve years my senior. He was my third husband and I was still only twenty-six. I was hoping it was going to be a case of third time lucky. On 14 July 1971 – the same day as my baby brother Winfred's birthday – I gave birth to Ellis Taylor Jr. Winfred, of course, became his godfather.

By the end of 1971 my appetite for music had returned, and Ellis had high hopes for me with Forte. What little bit of money I'd gotten from the James Brown show I began to put back into the company. We also set up our own publishing house, Ellshermar (the first letters of Ellis, Sherrie and me), and Ellis taught me about the business as we went along. We even took a course in lyric writing.

Ellis had other artists besides me on the label. There were The Bloodstones, James Whitney – my ex-husband Harry's baby brother – Lee Harris and The Teardrops, Tommy & The Derbys, Gene 'Mr Super Soul' Williams and The Rayons – a girl group that did some background work. We eventually got a national distribution deal with Nashboro, a Nashville-based record company set up twenty years before by a white businessman called Ernie Young. I think it was a gospel label originally, but when we joined forces with them they had a soul label called Excello, which released a couple of records I did with Ellis for Forte. A man called Bud Howell, the president of the company, signed us.

The first single released on Excello was a funk tune called 'Daddy Don't Know About Sugar Bear,' a fantastic song that Ellis wrote for me. It didn't have the James Brown flavor but was funky in a different way.

'Daddy Don't Know About Sugar Bear' featured musicians from Kansas City, Missouri: I think the backing was provided by Lee Harris and the Teardrops and some of the Derbys, including Chisholm, their saxophone player. On the B-side was 'We Need More (Somebody Gotta Sacrifice)'. It was a joke tune, in which I just talked with Ellis. The song talks about a bum's automobile and me getting a job. It has a social message that's still relevant today, especially given the state of the world right now. Ellis produced 'We Need More' and came up with most of it, including the lyrics and sound effects (like the cranking of the car). He acted silly, changing his voice by talking a little through his nose.

I remember one Halloween Ellis made a tape. He waited for a bunch of kids to come on our lawn and then he turned on the machine: there were monitors in the bushes. The noise and the sounds scared the hell out of most of the kids, and they ran off screaming. We went out and gave candy to the strong ones who braved it enough to come to the front porch.

Because my hometown didn't have too many up-to-date studios Nashboro sent us to the producer, Oliver Sain, in St Louis, which is about a four-hour drive from Kansas City. Sain was a saxophone player, drummer and bandleader who was recording for Nashboro's A-Bet label when we worked with him. He also discovered Fontella Bass, the singer who hit big with 'Rescue Me' in the '60s, and he and Ike Turner worked together a lot. He had some big hits himself, including 'Bus Stop', his biggest hit, and 'Booty Bumpin', which he cut for Excello's sister label, A-Bet. Oliver was a nice person. He died just a few years ago. Oliver and Ellis was friends, and they got together when Nashboro asked Oliver to re-produce some of the songs on the album I did for them. Ellis produced most of his own songs, though Oliver did a few in St Louis. He used his musicians on the ones that wasn't done by Ellis.

I think we recorded about nine or ten songs with Oliver in his studio on Natural Bridge Road. They were intended for an album but it never came out. Several have never been released, although over the years some have come out on compilations. One that was left in the can to gather dust was discovered and eventually released by the British company Ace Records in 1996; it came out on a CD they called *Funky Tales*. 'Do Your Thing' was a track that Ellis did with me. It was a punchy, uptempo number, and I think Oliver Sain had a hand with the horns. I shout out the names of cities like San Francisco, San Diego, Oklahoma and so on. The order of the towns is improvised – they just came out in that sequence. I just said what came to mind.

There's one song in particular from those sessions that I know could be a smash, but it can't be found. It's called 'Touch Your Woman' and was written by my favorite country singer, Dolly Parton.

I thought my first Forte/Excello single, 'Daddy Don't Know About Sugar Bear', was a great record – but it didn't sell well. I still do it today, often as the opening number of my show. In 1972 Excello released another 45, 'Don't Let Our Love Fade Away' with 'Live & Let Live' on the B-side. Again I thought it was a strong record – and probably one of my most soulful – but it did nothing.

In February 1972 I performed at the Landmark in Kansas City's Union Station on a Sunday jazz bill that included the Bettye Miller Trio, Four Plus One and a group led by trumpeter Gary Sivils, which included the young guitarist Pat Metheny, who went on to become internationally renowned. I performed as a guest vocalist with the Warren Durrett Big Band, a nineteen-piece jazz orchestra, singing standards like 'All Of Me' and 'Kansas City'. The show got a favorable review in the *Kansas City Times*.

But my records still wasn't doing that well. They were good, I think, but the promotion was poor. I thought Nashboro were just releasing them in the States but in the 1980s when I went to Europe I found they were coming out in other countries as well. People kept asking me where 'Gripey' Taylor was (that was Ellis's nickname), and said they wanted to hear 'Daddy Don't Know About Sugar Bear'. I was really surprised to discover that the song came out in England on Mojo, a short-lived label run by the UK magazine *Blues & Soul*.

Of course we didn't see any royalty payments from Nashboro. They'd originally wanted to do an album with me, but when the singles failed to take off they wanted to wash their hands of us. Our relationship with the company soured when one day Bud Howell, President of Nashboro, who was a balding white man with thick black glasses, started bawling me out like a dog about singing the word 'choo', which sometimes soul and funk singers replace the word 'you' with. It seemed really petty, and something that could easily be fixed in the studio even in those days. But it was his excuse for finishing with us.

I felt that Bud Howell and James Brown had something going on, especially after I found that Nashboro had done an album for Maceo & The Kingsmen and that they wanted to sign Lyn Collins after she left James. I don't know for sure, but I kind of felt it. Maybe it was a coincidence, but one day Bud Howell had tried to get me to go down to Nashville by myself. I had a feeling – a strong one – that James was gonna be down there, and that he wanted to get me by myself to talk to me. Ellis and I decided we'd go together. Nashboro only expected me, and as we were coming into the airport Bob Patton, one of James Brown's promoters, was leaving and we bumped into each other. He said, 'Have you seen James? He's here.' It was a strange coincidence. Even stranger was that when we got to Nashboro's offices we wasn't made to feel welcome. Or rather Ellis wasn't. In the end, Nashboro had nothing constructive to say. It was a wasted trip, especially after all the fuss they'd made about me going to see them. Maybe James wanted me back or maybe his people wanted to set up a deal. Who knows?

After Bud Howell chewed me out for singing 'choo' we didn't work with Nashboro/Excello again. It was a frustrating time.

CHAPTER 31

Lean Times

In 1973 I finally got the nerve to go and see James Brown. Every time I heard he was coming to town I suffered mental anguish and felt that if I actually laid eyes on him I'd end up doing something bad to him. The words from the Bible 'Vengeance is mine' always echoed ominously in my mind. Anyway, about two or three years after I left him, James was doing a show in Kansas. I plucked up the courage to go and see him. I plucked up the courage to go and see him. To tell you the truth I went along with the intention of putting a bullet in him. It sounds crazy but I really did: I had a .38 pistol in my purse. I was going to shoot him 'cause I couldn't make a dime: I was struggling to put food on the table for my family.

As I walked in I felt nervous but James's reaction calmed my fears. He flashed that famous toothy smile of his and genuinely seemed pleased to see me. My resolve to shoot him faded. He was very cordial, as he always was in public. 'Miss Whitney, I want you to meet my new singer, Miss Collins.' Lyn was sitting down the way. I smiled and walked up to her to say hello. I'd heard about his new singer, and although I felt a twinge of jealousy I knew full well that she didn't have anything to do with my leaving. She was very beautiful, but I could see she had the same haunted look in her eyes that I'd had when I was with James. It reminded me of the song 'Just One Look' by Doris Troy: with just one look I could see that the miserable look she had on her face – and tried to hide – was the same one I'd once had. Poor child. It was a look of pain, tiredness, torment, frustration and resignation. I sat down next to her. We were both ladylike and dignified – like two statues or pieces of stone really. We made small talk, and then I said this to her: 'Honey, when you feel tired and your nerves get bad, you got to go fishing.' I love to fish and found it gave me great solace in moments of stress; there's a calmness when you're near water. 'There's peace in the water,' I said to her. She nodded.

As we shook hands and exchanged pleasantries she was trying not to give me too much of an 'I gotcha' look, but I knew she understood what I meant. I could see what she was going through. I didn't see her again until the '80s, when our paths crossed again.

Before I left I was given one of Lyn's records, 'Rock Me Again and Again And Again'. James said, 'We came here to Kansas City to the Cave Recording Studio and cut this smash hit.' His words stabbed me like a knife. Even after I'd left the show this man was still trying to jab me and cause me pain. But I concealed my feelings and didn't let on how much I was burning up inside. *Of all the places,* I thought, *you have to come to Kansas City to record.* I thought about the gun in my purse, but told myself he wasn't worth it. Thankfully I can laugh about it now.

A few months after I'd been to see James he called me. He said, 'Leave your husband and come back to me.'

He upset me but after I calmed down I said, 'I can't do that – I'm married and have a baby.' He called another time and asked the same thing. I turned him down again. I think James, in his own way, loved me, though I know he would never have stopped his whoredom.

The same year, in June 1973 I think it was, I was saddened when I heard that James's son Teddy was killed in an automobile crash. I liked Teddy: he was a nice kid, one of the sweetest young children I ever met in my life. I felt like crying sometimes when I saw him. He used to say, 'Miss Whitney, I wish I could talk to my daddy like I can talk to you.' Teddy went through mental hell because he loved his father, but his father had no emotions to give back to him. James just didn't seem capable of returning love, even to his own kids.

When his father was around, Teddy often acted like a backward little kid. All of us who worked on the James Brown show knew why – because he was programmed, like we were all programmed, to say what his father told him he'd better say. It was strange: Mr Bobbitt's oldest son died within a year or so of Teddy's death. They were best friends on the road, and always stayed around me like they did around Lyn Collins later on. We showed them love and they could be free around us. But around his father, Teddy was always half-trembling. He was a sad little kid.

When Teddy died he was running away from his father. He'd had a big bust up with him and was picking up his friends; they were going to go to Canada. Ron Taylor, the young man who worked at the Apollo and witnessed James beating me, was one of them.

CHAPTER 32

Family Tragedy

In December 1973 an incident happened that shook us all. One day Grandfather Collins – who was then about seventy-three years old – had driven out to the church where he was pastor. It was about two or three degrees outside, as cold as hell. When night came he decided to go home. It was so late and dark that I tried my best to persuade him to stay with us for the night – we were closer to the church than his own house – and go home the next morning, because Ellis and I had a two-storey colonial house with plenty of room. But my grandfather could be stubborn, and as he got older he seemed to grow even more so. It was just dirt roads by his church, which could be treacherous in winter. His eyes wasn't the best and he had a limp because one leg was shorter than the other. This was because back in 1960 when he wasn't familiar with a new car, he put it in the wrong gear, and panicked when it took off. He tried to get out while it was still going, and ended up being dragged underneath it for about a block. He was knocked out and when he woke up he was in St Margaret's Hospital. I talked with him and he said he remembered nothing. The doctors put a pin in his leg and he walked with a limp afterwards. They gave him a good pair of shoes, one taller than the other, but you know what older people can be like; he didn't wear them. He used a cane for a short while, but he soon put it down and walked without it for the rest of his life. As he got older we all had to look out for him, as by this time his second wife had died. But he was very independently minded. He didn't care what time it was: if he wanted to go to church and it would take him a long time to get home then that's what he would do. As I say, he was stubborn.

So, preferring to go home rather than stay with us, Grandfather got in his car to drive back. But he didn't make it. He had to pull up on the way back because of a problem with his car. Unfortunately he was in Shawnee Mission, an area of Kansas where blacks didn't go: if they did there was always trouble of some kind. We think that Grandfather heard his car make a noise and thought he had a flat tire. So he pulled up in the car park of some type of club where there was lights on. There wasn't many cars there – I guess it was the time of night when they was closing up. It turned out that he didn't have a normal puncture: two men, one aged nineteen, and the other twenty-something, had taken a shotgun and purposely shot out my grandfather's tire. They left and went on up the street. Perhaps seeing that my grandfather was an elderly black man on his own, and therefore an easy target, they doubled back and beat him with a car jack, knocking his teeth out and making a hole in his head. Grandfather had been roughed up twice before; one time he was robbed on the same street, so it seemed like death was on him.

My mother told me that she had a premonition that something bad was going to happen. When she got a call in the middle of the night, she told me she knew what it was. The KU medical center called her and told her that they wanted her to come. She said, 'It's my father isn't it, Nathaniel Collins?' They said it was. She went down there and identified the body. They'd beat so many holes in his head that it was a wonder that you could recognize him in the casket. Mr Hobbs, the black funeral director at Hobbs' mortuary, was a friend of my mother's and he did a very good job of patching Grandfather up.

The community of Shawnee Mission, where the incident happened, didn't want the stigma of having a man beaten to death in their district so they put out a $3,000 reward for the killers to be found. But they knew racial prejudice ran deep in the area and that it wasn't the first incident. Given that my grandfather was an elderly church man maybe they genuinely wanted to right that wrong and help bring the killers to justice.

Both men were found and arrested on the day of my grandfather's funeral. I think the Lord had a hand in their capture. Someone who knew the men came forward to the police. If that person hadn't told, one of the killers would have never got caught because he was on furlough from the army. The other was somebody who lived in North Kansas City, a predominantly white area with a history of racial hatred against blacks. It turned out that after the two men had killed my grandfather they went and told a friend of theirs – who'd been to prison – what they'd done. They gave him the shotgun to look after, but he went and gave it to some old people. He told them what the two men had told him and that they'd told him to keep the shotgun. Then the man who'd been given the shotgun to look after told his wife what had happened, and she told him that one of the men had raped her one time. That's when he decided to turn them in.

The older one, who was in the army, confessed to it and gave up the information the police wanted. I think he got between three and seven years. The young boy was given a life sentence. But for us that wasn't enough. I said to myself that even though we've won he's still got a chance to breathe air. Not like my poor grandfather. After seeing the pictures of what they did to my grandfather and the brutal way they beat him I really felt he should have got the death penalty. I said that to the prosecuting attorney, and he looked at me strangely and said, 'Well, he got life, didn't he?' It was like we should be satisfied with that. It rubbed me the wrong way. What also irritated me was the deals they tried to make during the trial, hoping we'd agree to something so they'd serve less time. We said no: we wanted them to get what they deserved.

The Reverend C.N. Rooker was a great help. Every day they had court he made sure there were carloads of black people sitting there listening to what was going on and making sure that everything was written down in the local newspaper.

After several years had passed the young man's time for parole came up. Every time this happened the Shawnee Mission police sent a letter to our family to ask our opinion. We gave it the thumbs down for several years, as we thought a life sentence should be a life sentence. I was surprised the authorities gave us a say in the matter and actually heeded what we had to say. When we said no, that young man never did get parole. One day, many years later, Mama told me he was asking for parole again. Something came over me and I talked to her about it. I said, 'Mama, you know he's been in there sixteen years? That's more time than I thought he'd do. That's a long time for the powers-that-be to keep a white man in prison for killing a black man. They usually get out quick.' We always knew that in America there are two kinds of laws: one for whites and one for blacks. If a black man killed a white man he usually got a longer sentence than a white man did for killing a person of color. If you're black you're gonna get the book thrown at you. That's why we were surprised that they listened to us when we didn't agree to the young man's parole. I said to Mama, 'If that young man hasn't learnt his lesson by now he never will. I don't know why, but I think it's time to let him go. Let's not say no this time, 'cause he's served more time than I would've ever thought possible. Perhaps justice has been done.' She discussed it with the rest of the family and they agreed we wouldn't try to block or fight his parole. They let him out then. I don't know where he's at, or whether serving time helped him or not.

We still have lots of prejudice here in the United States of America. It's more prevalent here. Over in Europe there's a different feel in the people. Racism is the ugly side of America. My grandfather used to tell us about lynchings down south, when whites talked about going to a hanging like they was going to a picnic.

CHAPTER 33

Payola

In 1973 and '74 I recorded a couple of singles, which Ellis released locally in Kansas on Forte. We put out '(Hey You & You & You) I've Lived The Life' backed with 'Nothing Rather I'd Be Than Your Weakness' under my married name, Marva Whitney-Taylor. We did that because we thought that if I changed my name we'd get some more airplay and get around James. It didn't seem to improve things, though. My final Forte single was 'All Alone I Have Loved You', a duet with my brother Melvin. He was in the war in Vietnam and later he was with a group called Touch Of Gold. Touch Of Gold would have made it, I think, if they'd not had the wrong lead singer – the group's organizer, Ernest Malone. The best singers were my brother, Melvin Manning, and a young man by the name of Larry Brown. They can still sing and they're still out of sight. They traveled a lot in the United States and they had a song called 'I'm So Lonely'. They also got an album out, done by J. Bridge Productions, which was one of the first big productions during that time that I felt might have a chance. They really tried, but they didn't make it.

On the duet Melvin sang with me for Forte, backing was by the MWT Express. We came up with the idea for Marva Whitney-Taylor Express because of the TV show *Soul Train*, which was coming on strong in the early '70s. I'd never done that show but we listened to it, and we thought that by calling the band the MWT Express it would give us some attention. The B-side was '(Get Ready For) The Changes', which used the same backing track as 'Daddy Don't Know

About Sugar Bear'. As we was unable to get a major distribution deal, it was hard getting radio airplay outside Kansas, and the records didn't make much noise.

James, of course, was doing much better than me in the mid-'70s, but even he was struggling to match his earlier achievements. I always tried to keep abreast of what he was doing, which wasn't that difficult – especially in 1975. That was when there was a high profile payola scandal involving the famous New York DJ Frankie Crocker, who allegedly received illegal payments to play records on his show. James got drawn into it after his manager, Charles Bobbitt, was subpoenaed to appear in court. He testified that he'd paid Crocker a large sum of money to get James's records lots of prime-time airplay. James, of course, distanced himself from this, saying that he knew nothing about it. But I was told by people inside the Brown camp that James asked Bobbitt to take the hot seat for him, and that if he did so James would make it up to him financially. I think James knew that if he was on that witness stand he might end up going to jail. It didn't look good for Bobbitt, but in the end I think the case collapsed.

Mr Bobbitt had to put up with a lot. He was very loyal, but by the mid-'70s he'd had enough. I believe he left James after they visited Gabon in West Africa in early 1975, when James was invited to play at President Bongo's birthday party. They had dinner with the president, after which James and President Bongo had a private talk. The president didn't like what James said about Mr Bobbitt, who he could see was loyal, and afterwards he told Bobbitt what James had said and offered him a job. Mr Bobbitt thought about it and decided not to go back to the States with James. He wrote a note telling James of his decision to quit, gave it to one of James's lackeys and told him not to give it to James until he was up in the air.

Bobbitt went along to the airport like he was going home, and when they got ready to board the plane James apparently said, 'Come on, Bobbitt, we got to go.'

He replied, 'Mr Brown, thanks, but I think I'm going to stay here for a while.' James was mystified, but got on the plane. As soon as they left the ground he was handed Bobbitt's note – and when he read it he went berserk. He must have been mad as hell. When I picture it I can't help but laugh.

So Mr Bobbitt stayed with President Bongo for some years,

helping to train his son who wanted to be in show business – but I think he was grooming him to be a future leader. After this he went to work for Michael Jackson. After Michael Jackson, and as times began to get kind of lean, he and James made up and he returned to work for him.

CHAPTER 34

California Dreaming

My marriage with Ellis Taylor lasted seven years. Although we split up in 1977 the judge didn't sign the final divorce papers until 1980. I suppose some people will think I'm like a black Elizabeth Taylor; I expect they're gonna say, shit, she ain't got no sense at all. But Ellis had turned out to be a jealous man, one of the most jealous I've ever seen. I remember once I told him I was going to see Bootsy Collins who was bringing his show to town. Ellis didn't like it at all, so on that particular night he came home filthy drunk: he had a lot of Indian in him and couldn't hold his drink. He started being verbally abusive, telling me that all entertainers were low-lifes. I said, 'Well, you married one.' See, I never did take it lyin' down: that's another thing men don't like about me. And I'm not one that you can possess. Since my time with James Brown I've become worse, I think. My experiences with him toughened me up, made me harder. James showed me the best of life but he also he showed me the worst; and he showed me what not to take. And when men get to a certain place, uh-uh, I ain't taking no shit. I ain't gonna take it. Some of them have lied down to their teeth till they couldn't lie no more, and expect for me to take it. I had a couple of men in my life that were married, but told me their wives were their housekeepers. And when I found out the truth they was still lyin' to protect themselves. When I went with them they'd sometimes mess up and call me their old lady's name. After they were exposed as liars I said thank you, Jesus, for letting the truth come out.

Most of the men in my life have been insecure about my being in show business, but Ellis was probably the most affected by it. I remember one time I came home from a weekend job with maybe $1,000. Ellis was an A1 engineer and he was making pretty good pay, bringing home about $300 a week – but I came home with a grand for a weekend plus expenses. I've always been the kind that lays my money on the table so we can take care of business. I think that was a mistake. He couldn't stand that: that I could earn more than him kind of humiliated him. And he also resented that he was seen by many people as Mr Whitney rather than Ellis Taylor. In my experience, if men can't be in charge they mess up and are hell to live with. That's what happened with Ellis and me. I've been with a lot of shysters and players, and he was no different really, except he was sneakier. It was after I separated from him that I found he was cheating me out of royalties.

After Ellis I dated a fella called Gorgeous George, who was Marvin Gaye's MC. George came through Kansas City with Marvin one time in the '70s and we entertained them. My pastor cooked a full meal for Marvin. He was half-loaded, but he had sense enough to know that it was good home-cooking. 'Oh this tastes so good,' he gushed, 'it tastes just like my mama's cooking.'

After he'd eaten I remember his manager said, 'Marvin, you've got to go for your run now.' That's because he was so down with booze and dope they had to run him, like for an hour or so, so that when showtime came he'd be halfway sober and awake.

When it came to the show, Gorgeous George announced him on stage: 'Put your hands together for Mr Marvin Gaye, Marvin Gaye!' He looked back and there was no sign of Marvin. 'Just a minute, we'll be right back!' he said, and went off stage. When he found Marvin he said, 'Man, come on! You've got to go out there.' When Marvin finally agreed, George did his announcement again: 'Ladies and gentlemen, are you ready for a soul superstar? Here's Marvin Gaye!' After one or two false starts they finally got Marvin out there. Once he sang his first song he was at home, but he always suffered badly from stage fright.

I decided to head for California in 1977 after Ellis and me split up. I tried to get work as a singer but nobody cared about what I'd done in the past. They wanted me to audition. It was humiliating. The hits

I'd gotten less than ten years previously counted for nothing. They did Lyn Collins the same way: we were locked down. But we were fighters: we never gave up.

I thought I'd got a break when I met up with Marvin Augustus. He was from Detroit originally and a couple of years younger than me. He was a fabulous arranger and a conductor who'd started out as a trumpet player. He got his big break in 1972 working with Gil Askey on the movie about Billie Holiday called *Lady Sings The Blues*. Diana Ross played Billie.

I finally got a chance to do an album with Marvin. It was awesome. We cut the tracks at ABC/Dunhill's studios, but before we could complete the project they closed the studio down because the company, which also had the Four Tops on its roster, ran out of money. Lamont Dozier was there and he helped too. I think he was working on his own project for them. I was so hurt when we had to leave the album unfinished, as I really believe it was some of the best work I ever did. It was a whole different bag from what I'd done before. It had its own soul style and would have fitted in with the Top 40 format too. I wish someone could find it: it's a winner, a beautiful piece of work. Marvin Augustus has a style the world needs to hear. He loves to use a big musical canvas: using a symphony orchestra is a piece of cake to him. I must have had ten violins on one piece. Some of the titles were 'Feeling The Love, Loving The Feeling', 'Was It You On My Mind', 'I'll Do Anything For Your Love', and 'Let Me Live In Your World'. After this Marvin worked with Gladys Knight, Lionel Richie, Mavis Staples and Anita Baker, as well as writing scores to the movies *Which Way Is Up*, *Outrageous Fortune* and a TV series about The Temptations.

Around 1977, while I was out in LA, I hooked up with my old buddy Tuttie from the Derbys. We formed a five-piece group and had some promotional pictures taken. Getting gigs proved hard work, and we eventually went our separate ways.

CHAPTER 35

The Late Seventies – The Platters

When I think about The Platters the words life and lies comes to mind. How does that mix with The Platters? Well, you'd probably be surprised if you sat down and thought about the stair steps in your life and how the truth reveals itself. Let me explain.

I'd not long moved to LA when I met a gent by the name of Alton 'Ray' Brewster, who'd been in the music business since he was a teenager. He was in the group The Penguins, who sang 'Earth Angel', and had been a member of other groups, including The Cadillacs. Through Ray I met some people who was opening up a new recording label by Bobby Day, the man who sang 'Rock-in' Robin'. Bobby was crazy but a very likeable gentleman who liked his drink. They were putting out some good songs and were serious about their business: just being at the studio was a joy. I can't really remember how I met the people from his organization but I stayed with them about a year. One thing I do remember is the pain. That you never forget.

Ray was tall and handsome and highly intelligent. He was also very shrewd, but I found that out too late. When we first met for some reason I didn't care for him; something, which I couldn't put my finger on, just didn't feel right. But after a while we got friendlier and became close – real close, in fact, and the relationship that developed ended up causing me physical and mental pain, which it took years to get rid of. I thought we were in love. I trusted him completely, but I realized from the things his mother and daughter said that he was lying to me about certain things. Of course I don't automatically believe everything everyone says, but when his mom and daughter began to talk I had to listen, and my eyes were opened to the person he really was. In the end I came to the conclusion that he was stringing me along, as he preferred rich and highly educated women. And they had to be white too. I was none of those things.

I wasted too much of my time with Ray. It didn't help that we kept in touch from the late '70s to the '90s. He said he loved me, but his other interests kept him so busy that he had no real time for me.

When my auntie came to LA and visited me he never came around. I guess he knew she might be wise and see through him – and in fact when she did eventually see him she gave him the thumbs down in a split second. Yeah, he did a few nice things but he was a pain, because there was always a lie at the end.

Through Ray I got to work with The Platters. I joined them in 1978 and stayed for about three years. When I wasn't with them I worked for the Task Force Agency, a temporary employment agency that I'd worked for in Kansas City after divorcing Harry Whitney, as a secretary. They were good to me and very understanding of my singing career.

Ray had known Paul Robi of The Platters from the old days; he was one of his best friends. At this time there were several Platters groups going around, because all the original members who'd left had their own versions. I thought Paul had the best. There was me, Wilbur, Leo and Paul, of course. Paul's wife, Martha, was the group's manager. She was a very strong, beautiful South American woman, and she knew how to handle business. The money wasn't good but it got me away from LA. We traveled overseas and visited places like Japan and Switzerland. We even went up to Alaska for a show.

Paul taught me my part. I took over the role of Zola Taylor, the group's original female singer. Martha designed and made some beautiful gowns for me to wear when we performed, but, oh my God, there were so many beads and bangles that they became a chore to wear: they was the hardest part of the job.

Paul liked to drink but it never affected his performances. He seemed to find peace in that spot, out there on the stage. He was kind to me, but I could see he was unhappy about something, for at times he'd disappear and we couldn't find him. Maybe it was the sickness I heard he suffered from after I left that bothered him (he died in 1989). But despite his troubles he was always kind.

I remember he'd usually open the show by saying, 'Good evening, ladies and tables.' That would crack the place up. The clientele we performed for were often high-up, top-notch people. I suppose they had to be, because you had to pay a pretty penny to see Paul Robi and The Platters back then. Even so, with all that money he made we could never get any raises from him. We never could understand that.

One of Paul's long-running jokes was to refer to The Platters as The Plates, because we played for lots of supper clubs. The songs were so slow I'd almost go to sleep, and the choreography and hand movements were the same on every song. That's why we were so glad to sing a livelier song like Johnny Nash's 'I Can See Clearly Now': I think that was the fastest song we sang. I never worked up a sweat. I sang lead on 'He's Mine' and 'My Heart Belongs To My Daddy'. We never had to carry a band with us, just a young lady called Janet who was very good at getting pick-up musicians from the unions. Once we had had a rehearsal, the musicians played like they had been with the group for years. Janet was quiet but very pleasant.

Looking back, I don't think I ever really pleased Martha, Paul's wife. She never pronounced my name properly: she called me Marba. That letter 'v' she could never get just right. I really liked her, even though we all grumbled behind her back. She was just doing her job, even though she ruled with an iron hand. Her youngest daughter sang in the group in the '90s, and her oldest daughter married Sugar Ray Leonard, the boxer.

I remember several times we got stopped from performing when we were just about to go on stage because of an injunction. These were served by a woman called Jeanne Bennett, who was a secretary for Buck Ram, the man who originally put the group together in the 1950s and became the owner of The Platters' name. With all those different Platters groups, there was some kind of feud going on. But Martha, being a smart woman, called us Paul Robi and His Platters, which was acceptable – so they let us perform.

One day while we were in New Zealand or Australia we started talking about nationalities while on our way to a performance. I found out that Paul was from Oklahoma, and some kind of way I gave the impression that Paul was a black man, which Martha disagreed with; she wouldn't accept he was black. I stood my ground even when she argued me down – but I realized it was time to go; she couldn't tolerate me any more. When she told us about the next job I said I wasn't going to go with them. I think I beat her to the punch – as I'm sure she would have fired me anyway. She took away all those gowns and all the beads and bangles. I wasn't sorry to see them go.

Martha, I'm grateful to you for letting me be in such a wonderful and classy group: it was such a pleasure. But I haven't changed my mind. Paul was a handsome man and he had beautiful straight hair, but it was easy to see he was a black Okie with lots of Indian in him. Paul never said anything about what color he was.

Anyhow, when I left The Platters, the 1980s had already begun. In 1980-81, at the age of thirty-eight, I went to West Los Angeles Jr College to study business administration, which involved English, typing, computer work, psychology, and even anthropology. The course consisted of twelve units and was full-time. But the Reagan government cut off the grants, and because of that I didn't take all my finals. After this I worked full time in the EOP&S department on the campus, as a secretary to one of the administrators. EOP&S stands for Extended Opportunity Program and Services: it's a professional body based in California that gives grants for books to educationally and economically disadvantaged students, helping those without much money to get a full-time further education.

CHAPTER 36

Bright Lights Big City – Las Vegas, 1982

All that glitters is not gold. I found that out after moving from LA to Las Vegas in 1982. Although I tried to resurrect my singing career I found it very difficult. While I was there I hooked up with an old family friend, Alfred 'Pico' Payne, who'd sung with the Ink Spots. Pico and me had formed a group a year or so earlier while I was in LA. It was called Coffee, Cream & Sugar: a white girl called Mary Lou Flesh (a guitarist who played in the clubs) was 'sugar', I was 'cream' and Pico was 'coffee'. We had an awesome sound but only performed one time, in Orange County as I remember, although we practised for about six months. Our first song was 'Up Where We Belong', from the movie *An Officer And A Gentleman.* I've got a practice tape around somewhere. I think we would have been a Top 40 group but we really never got started.

Pico Payne was the group's leader, a heavyweight in slick harmony phrases. I'd known him for years; he was my play father. By that I mean he was like a second father to me when I was younger. He was a dynamite singer, teacher and music director, and on weekends he came to our house to teach us how to sing correctly. I remember he loved my mother's pinto beans and cornbread. Hell, everyone loved mama's pinto beans and cornbread. Pico was from New York, and he was the director for the Metropolitan Spiritual Church. That church scared me when I went in it as a child to sing. It was founded, I believe, by Bishop Boswell, and it was a deep church – like a Catholic one, with rituals and everything. But what got me was that it was half-dark with lots of candles. And when church started, the pastor, Bishop Lawson, who was so good to us, spoke from somewhere up near the ceiling: 'Jesus is the Light of the World'. It was spooky, but after we started singing I relaxed. It was the mother church of the spiritual churches of Kansas City. They believed in prophecy and used candles as symbols, and as a reminder for whatever you was praying for.

Their choir rocked the house, and really got into the anthems. You thought you was in heaven listening to them.

Going back to Coffee, Cream & Sugar, we didn't last long because Pico, who'd sung in the Ink Spots, got a call from one of the original members of the group to go to Las Vegas. And that was an opportunity he couldn't turn down. So when he went to join them I decided to try my luck there too.

While I was in Vegas Pico and I were helped by a nice white lady called Arlene McPhail, Pico's girlfriend. She became a good friend to me too; she was a beautiful person. She knew that being a professional singer was a precarious occupation and she proved to be our angel. Arlene had a beautiful trailer home (it had a fireplace and even a bar) and she invited me and Pico to stay with her until we got on our feet. She had a black poodle, but that dog didn't like me. I guess he knew I didn't take to dogs.

It was hard getting work as a singer, just as bad as LA. I made ends meet by working underground as a general secretary at a business called SIS Services. I was the first black they hired. They were very good to me. SIS handled insurance claims for the show people, like dancers, who worked on the Vegas strip. If they got injured they could claim some money, and SIS determined eligibility for aid while the claimants were off mending. They secretly scouted out people who was jiving about being hurt. It could get funny sometimes: we'd sometimes see movies that detectives had filmed secretly of them picking up groceries when they were supposed to be in a wheelchair with a broken leg or a serious back problem. If that happened they'd be busted and they'd have their money stopped. My main duties was typing letters, sorting the mail and handling the phones, and I also drove the car and made pick-ups at the casinos for concerns that SIS handled. I suppose I was like a Girl Friday. The top secretary sometimes took me home or picked me up for work. They were kind, just a wonderful bunch of people. Most were Mormons.

One time Pico came to the office and asked me for money 'cause he'd found the perfect place to live, one block off the strip. We were staying at a place he didn't like after we thought we should give Arlene McPhail some air: she'd given so much, so long. It was nice and we moved in; we shared the rent. Every so often I got a gig, but most of the time Pico was away on the road. My new job gave us both the support we needed to live. People don't know how entertainers suffer: that is why I always went underground as Marva Taylor. People soon forget but I did not want to use my show name. Sometimes in California I told the people I was Marva Whitney and I got better treatment, but in Vegas I just couldn't get off the ground. It's a tight, cliquey town. I tried a few places, but I don't think I was even able to get an audition.

Redd Foxx, the comedian, was also living in Vegas. His pal Cha Cha Hogan worked as his valet and was a friend of Arlene's too. All of us played bingo. Cha Cha introduced me to Redd, and I tried to get Redd to remember me: when I first left James Brown, he'd been performing in Kansas City. He had a nightclub in Los Angeles and invited me to perform there. He said I reminded him of his first wife, and he was kind to me. Then just after that all that trouble with taxes he owed started on him. When Cha Cha and I became friends, he took me to Redd's apartment. He had a picture of every black artist that he knew and worked with, ranging from Dinah Washington and Sarah Vaughan to Bill Cosby. I mean everyone – he had a fortune on the wall. But he was like us: sometimes up and sometimes down, good times and hard times. We helped one another. When Redd's daughter came to Las Vegas to live I found out she was separated from her husband, who was Ms Daisy Stubbs's grandson. What a small world, I thought. She was somewhat younger than me, and when I finally left Vegas I gave her all I had, even my car.

Cha Cha was a singer with a satin voice. He was classy and old school, but he stayed current in the pop field. His nickname was 'Mr Ink Spot', and he did a lot of overseas work when he wasn't Redd Foxx's wardrobe man. He died shortly after I left Las Vegas.

As for Pico Payne, he stayed there a while after I'd gone; then he ran a karaoke club in Honolulu until his death. I believe he even sang for Queen Elizabeth in England during his travels with the Ink Spots.

CHAPTER 37

Back Home – The Preacher's Wife

In 1984 I'd had enough of Las Vegas and decided to move back home to Kansas City. I was so broke my brother Ray Junior came to fetch me and helped me to get home. The people at SIS made sure I got every penny owed me: they were wonderful.

Then in 1985 I married a preacher, Dr Clarence Lawrence Charles Irvin. Together we pastored about four churches. Churches can be just as hellish as the world, so they say, and I caught hell every which way: for a gospel session I did, I wrote and produced a song called 'Get Up Off Of The Preacher's Wife' – long before Whitney Houston's *The Preacher's Wife* movie and soundtrack came out. I clashed with members of the church, and they also victimized my husband because he'd married me. For some reason most of them thought I was supposed to look like an old lady with long dresses and act meek and humble. I think they expected me to act older than I was because Dr Irvin, like Ellis, was twelve years my senior. Most, I think, learned to like me in time, but it took a while. My singing and piano-playing gave me favor, I think. Some knew I was a professional singer, and when I went away for a while they surmised I was off singing somewhere. I could tell they didn't like it, but they didn't say anything to me. To a certain extent Irvin was proud of the fact that I'd been in showbiz – and many of his preacher friends actually said, with some amazement, 'Man, how did you get her?'

I was tired of trying to make it in the R&B world. Bottom line I was tired of the hard times. I knew church work, and so I think I was a pretty good first lady; however, church people can be very cruel and I think they enjoyed seeing me struggling to maintain my career as a singer.

Irvin tried to sell cars on the side, and in other circumstances he might've proved a good moneymaker – but business was slow. In the end he became extremely jealous of the attention I received, and I had to slip away from him. His jealousy got to the point that I couldn't even go to the store by myself without he was spying on me. I'd look over in the corner and he'd be furtively watching me from the end of the aisle. If my hair was out of place from the wind he'd ask how it got that way and what I'd been doing. If somebody told him anything untruthful about me he always believed them. Between the church giving him a hard time, and him not making enough money from selling cars, he was impossible to live with. I divorced him in 1990.

CHAPTER 38

Back in the Limelight with

James Brown's Funky People

I didn't see Lyn Collins again until around 1988. She'd left James some time before then – I believe it was 1976 – and moved to California. Although I wanted to look her up I was ashamed, because things wasn't going that well for me. Little did I know that Lyn and I stayed within a mile of each other just before I left LA.

After I got to Vegas, Charles Bobbitt called me. He told me that Lyn lived in LA and that she was doing a session with Fred Wesley, James Brown's former trombonist and bandleader. He invited me to the session to meet her, so I could help do back-up work with her. I turned the chance down, saying I couldn't get to the studio. But the bottom line was I was ashamed. I didn't know she was going through the same thing.

I got to know Lyn properly in 1988 after Polydor reissued some of our old songs on a couple of CDs called *James Brown's Funky People Volumes 1 & 2*. Our music is still very popular and highly thought of in Europe, and a lot of young people were interested in James's music again because his old records had been sampled by lots of hip-hop artists. There was also what they called a 'rare groove' scene in England, which helped give my career a boost. The positive reaction to both the *Funky People* CDs resulted in Lyn, me, Vicki Anderson and Bobby Byrd joining forces for a tour of Europe.

The liner notes for the *Funky People* CDs were written by Cliff White, who's a big fan and really knowledgeable about James Brown. It seems that my biggest fans are white and not of my race. Maybe it's my Irish roots that appeal. Cliff's a well-respected English journalist who wrote for the long-running British music paper, the *New Musical Express*. He's family, one of the first people I met when we came to England – in 1989 or thereabouts. I was a little jealous for he knew Lyn better than me, but he made sure he gave us good attention, and besides, Lyn was part of the James Brown era when I left. I love him, and Lyn did too – and when he didn't come to the shows we felt incomplete. Cliff opened my eyes to the world of discographies, which is how I learned that you can go into the vaults and pick up old, often unreleased material and put it out on records.

I got the opportunity to talk to Cliff this year. He hasn't changed. He's still a very knowledgeable man, and he was gracious enough to answer all the questions I had for him about the music business and computers. When I asked him what he was up to he said, 'I'm staying at home with my lovely wife.' She's blessed that he wants to stay snuggled close to his love. Cliff White is a gracious and beautiful man; he's always cheerful.

As I got to know Lyn during our tours in the late '80s I felt a kinship between us. It wasn't just the suffering we'd had at the hands of James Brown that bonded us, but I felt strongly that we were related by blood in some way. Her maiden name was Collins and she was born in Texas; my mother's maiden name was Collins and her family had migrated from Texas. Lyn had hips like my mother and her side of the family, and our family values were almost as one. She was highly educated, and my grandma's folks were highly educated – and they all had an air of class about them.

I was excited about doing the JB's Funky People tour; Lyn was too. But although we'd been invited on the tour by Bobby Byrd and Vicki Anderson, we felt that our presence wasn't welcome. For some reason we seemed to be kept out of the loop: I could sense it, and so could Lyn. Some of JB's people had picked up James's nasty ways. I always surmised it was professional jealousy.

The tour was awful. Bobby and Vicki were just like James in terms of their behavior and attitude. Me and Lyn, who'd had the biggest hits of the Funky Divas and done national TV shows, were treated like second-class citizens. We were left out of things: our sound wasn't up to par, and we discovered that some of the shows were being taped without our consent. Then it was always Bobby and Vicki who had the hotel suite. I'd loan them my iron or something they didn't have and it would come back broke. Do you think they offered to replace it? No. And both of her children used to walk up and down the halls listening at our doors to see what we were talking about. Hell, one time I got pulled on the carpet from Vicki 'cause I was talking to Bobby Byrd. She got suspicious, and Lyn had to jump in and say, 'Oh hell, no, that's not the way it went. Me and Marva was talking and Byrd heard us and he put in his input.' We had to take care of each other.

At the end of the show me and Lyn preferred to go back to the hotel, rather than eating at the club. More than once they said, 'We'll call you to let you know that we're there.' And we waited – and then all the food was gone. There'd be nothing left but maybe the icing off a cake. We had the leftovers if we were lucky, while Vicki fed her kids. She looked after her own.

One time Mr Bobbitt was there, and he ended up sharing a couple of chicken wings with me and Lyn. Vicki noticed, and said to me, 'Oh, I'm sorry, honey, forgive me.' She knew exactly what she was doing, though.

One time a fan came backstage and asked why me, Lyn and Martha High was acting like background singers, and why we wasn't singing more of our original songs: 'That's what we came for.' He also asked why our uniforms were different from some of the other people's. We said we didn't know – but the fans picked up the vibe: they were smart, and guessed what was going on. At the end of one show a bottle was thrown at Vicki's head, and we knew why. Some of the audience was mad because we wasn't getting our fair share of the spotlight.

In some ways this was just like being with James in the bad old days. Me and Lyn got tired of it, and decided we wasn't going to work with Vicki and Bobby no more. We knew it would never get no better. From this time on Lyn and me became buddies who looked out for each other, and we never was out of touch with each other from then on. I talked with her mother and she talked with my mother; it was as if her mother was my mother and my mother was her mother. They told us to stick together, and that was easy to do. We were each other's leaning post with our God in the middle. We cried together and prayed, sang and exchanged ideas. Our phone bill was easily over $100 every month. We used to talk about doing a book. I'd say, 'What we gonna put in it, Lyn? You know how people are. They probably won't believe us.'

'Tell the truth,' she'd say. 'Just tell the truth.' So that's what I've done.

When I wasn't out on the road performing my old tunes as a Funky Diva, I was singing in church at home in Kansas. In 1990 I decided to make a gospel album, which was something I'd wanted to do for a long time. It was a real family affair. My brother Winfred played bass, and my mother played on some of the tunes as well. My daughter, my son and my brother, Marvin, helped out too. A young man by the last name of Green played on it too. I'm hopeful that I can do something one day that'll make people realize I can do something other than be part of the James Brown show, but for now the album remains in the can. Mr Cooper, my ex-manager, was a minister by this time, and he wrote the liner note for it:

The word soulmate merely hints at the relationship between Marva Whitney-Irvin and Rev. Clarence Cooper. Since Marva's debut with the Manning family in the late '50s, I, Rev. Clarence Cooper, have been involved in her life and career as both friend and manager.

In the role of promoter, singer and recording manager, I've been blessed to make important contributions to the development of many talented performers. In a dual role as public relations manager for James Brown and manager/promoter for Marva Whitney, I've had the unique experience of working closely with two powerful talents simultaneously; my steadfast commitment to Marva Whitney assisted to her inevitable rise to stardom.

Although widely known for her secular musicality, Marva's heart and soul remained cemented in gospel roots and inspirational music. Ms Whitney's tours with James Brown took her all throughout the States, and the world. James Brown and Marva Whitney were later to become one of the three Black performing groups that were permitted to perform in Vietnam.

Followers of gospel music long anticipated and have waited for Marva's return to inspirational and religious music. Drawing from her wellspring of faith and her lifelong trek of spiritual development, Marva has forged word, music and her Christian experience into an outstanding celebration of praise and worship.

This collection of contemporary gospel story-telling shares truths and observances indicative of Marva's higher spiritual plateau, and for the listener it's a rapturous experience none can afford to miss.

Sincerely

Rev. C.M. Cooper

CHAPTER 39

Married, Again

In 1992, only a couple of years after splitting up with Dr Irvin, I married again. He was a former schoolmate by the name of J.J. Jones. I think we stayed together almost three years. When that marriage went down the pan it really hurt me, more than any of the previous marriages, because he had been a schoolmate of mine at Northeast Junior High in Kansas City. He was the same age as me. He was in the football team and used to play for the Pittsburgh Steelers, and he had a degree. I thought there was something special, a different kind of respect maybe, because we'd been at school together. But he turned out to be the biggest gigolo of all. Like me he'd been married before, and he hated being thought of as Mr Whitney. In the end he divorced me, although he was unfaithful.

I'm sure people who read this are gonna say, 'Is that girl dumb or what?' Maybe I'm the black Elizabeth Taylor. I say that jokingly. I've had a naïve heart, so maybe that's why things haven't gone right with the men in my life. I've never ever shacked up with anybody: I don't believe in living together without being married. Perhaps that explains why I got married five times.

I've only been able to show affection for one man at a time, but all of my life it seems that every man I've ever had an interest in or thought I could trust tried to use or abuse me. And when you get to my age – I was sixty-eight in May 2012 – you don't want to go through that kind of thing again. I don't have a boyfriend, and it's been over three years. But I'm enjoying – up to a point – being by myself, because I don't have to answer to anyone or wonder about the lies or the bullshit. Basically every young man I went with in my life was intelligent, but when they found out I was broke and nothing was really happening on the entertainment side they lost interest.

Throughout my life I don't think I've picked the right man: I don't even know if there's the right one waiting for me out there. I always tried to judge a man on his own merits, but men have a good side and a dark side, and they only let you see the good side: that's my experience. Then they're with you for five or six months and all of a sudden you catch something. And that has happened to me. I hate to say it but it's happened with every man I've ever had. After the romance comes the reality and often it's not pretty.

I had one, who was a schoolteacher. He was a great saxophonist and guitarist. He still lives and is a good-looking guy. He romanced me like I was a queen. That was about 1982 or '83 'cause I think I came back to Kansas City in '84. When he found that I didn't have no money he asked why I wasn't rich. I tried to explain, but he didn't understand. Like a lot of people, he thought that if you was in show business you must be rich. If only that was true. I think he was just a gigolo; in fact, I think most of the men I've run into are gigolos. They might be educated and well-groomed but they're still gigolos.

It says in the Bible that 'He who findeth a wife, findeth a good thing.' But I seem to do better if we're just buddies. One thing I know: as the song goes, I will not throw my love in the garbage can. Uh-uh.

My mother gave me some good advice about men. She always taught me to have a safe zone: love a man but leave room, so you can escape and keep your sanity. And that's what I've done. I don't give a man 100 per cent of my heart; he might get 90 per cent, but he's not going to get all of it. I hold back because I don't want to be hurt again: I'm protecting myself. Even when I've given 90 per cent I've still been hurt, but not as much. I mean, I might have suffered and cried but because I've reserved a space I'm able to survive. That's the reason why I thank God I've never had to go out and whore for a living. I've never had to go out looking for a man. If there was a cooling off period then I didn't want to see them. And each one that I cared about I just had to accept disappointment or heartbreak, and move on and find some space. It might take a little time but I get over it. People say not to judge who you're with against the last person you had. I tried to do this, and maybe it takes a little longer for me to get to a certain point with a new person because I try to protect myself.

Frankly, I'm not highly sexed. I can have a very good rapport with a man who just knows how to be nice to a lady. Now I'm going to say something that you probably wouldn't expect to hear from me, because it's raunchy. There's a saying – after the fuck, then what? And that is what these romances I've had have been about. I mean, you can go through the fad of not giving up the goods, so to speak, until a few dates down the road, but hell, it comes out the same. So I'm resolved that it's better for me to have peace and quiet, and no man. I feel that unless God sends my ideal man to me and melts him and pours him over me I'll stay a single woman. 'Cause unlike some women I don't need a man to survive.

CHAPTER 40

The Funky Divas

In April 1998 Harry Weinger at Polygram Records and Alan Leeds, a former road manager for James Brown, co-produced a Polydor compilation called *James Brown's Original Funky Divas*. It was a two-CD set featuring all of James Brown's female protégés – ranging from Bea Ford, Yvonne Fair, Anna King and me in the '60s to Vicki Anderson, Kay Robinson, Lyn Collins and Martha High in the '70s. There was a launch party at the Motown Café in New York, which I attended along with Lyn, Vicki and Martha. It was an exciting release and helped get us back in the public eye again; I recall doing quite a few magazine interviews as a result of its release. But I think it's true to say that it wouldn't have come about but for Lyn. She was originally approached along with Vicki Anderson to do an album together, using songs that was in the can. But Lyn thought about it, and said why not make an album of all James Brown's divas instead? So that's how the album came about. Lyn was so unselfish. Thankfully Harry Weinger had the vision to see it was a good idea. It was beautiful. They even did a remix of the song 'Things Got To Get Better (Come Together)'. On the new version, which me, Lyn and James had recorded separately, they brought us all together: me, Lyn and James on the same track! That was a gas. Every once in a while I put the CD on and listen to it: it brings back a lot of memories.

When *James Brown's Funky Divas* came out they set up a Funky Divas show for us in New York, with Bobby Byrd and Vicki Anderson. Martha High couldn't make it because she was doing work with Maceo Parker – and I think she was better off not being there. We were all supposed to have equal billing, but it didn't turn out that way: it was really the Bobby Byrd and Vicki Anderson show. They took over. I seem to remember that Harry Weinger from Polygram Records (as it was before it became Universal) and the people he had with him left when they saw that Lyn and me wasn't going to sing no more. They was so angry and disgusted at the way the show had been put together that they walked out. Vicki didn't let us do any solo spots. I didn't even sing half a song. Lyn managed to bulldoze her way to do almost a whole song, but it was cut short. The Byrds let their little son, Bart – who plays the organ – sing about eight songs. They had me and Lyn looking like background singers.

The Byrds and us had a fight about it earlier in the day, because we were hoping to rehearse with the band but we were kept waiting. Both Vicki and Bobby told us in no uncertain terms that there was no segment for us in the show. I couldn't believe their nerve, especially when it was supposed to be a Funky Divas show.

After Lyn and me had done our bits in the show we were blocked by Bobby from leaving the stage. It was crazy. They wanted us to stay on stage and provide backgrounds for Vicki. They knew that would be humiliating for us. So I was up there backgrounding and dancing like a hired help: they had to carry me downstairs from the stage because I couldn't walk; my feet were too sore. How I stayed on the stage that long I don't know, but afterwards me and Lyn vowed that we would never work with them no more.

As it turned out, though, I did perform with Bobby Byrd and Vicki Anderson again, but in very different circumstances.

CHAPTER 41

My Baby Sister Lyn Collins

Lyn and I became great friends as a result of performing together. Like me, she had been bullied by and felt backhand licks from James Brown. She told me he went to her dressing room before a TV show and put her down and humiliated her in front of people, just as he did with me. Also like me, her songs were recorded too quickly for her, and she had little time to prepare properly.

James also used his divide and conquer tactics on Lyn and her husband, Bobby Jackson, who worked as a record promoter for James. She was married to Bobby, her childhood sweetheart, but fell weak to the fabrications and lies that were invented by others on the road with James. When they joined the revue in 1971 Lyn and Bobby had promised never to forsake each other, but James made sure they spent little time together. Lyn knew that if they wasn't together working on a show it would be a recipe for the break-up of their marriage. When she found out Bobby had fooled around with someone else she felt betrayed, but she loved him till her death.

Lyn, like me, struggled to make ends meet financially. She lived in Texas, where she was born, and when it got cold in winter there her arthritis gave her hell. It's hard to believe, but she couldn't afford a furnace to keep her warm in her homestead, so she often went to California for the winter, where her son and Uncle Shortie lived. She had a lot of friends there too and they were like relatives to her. James promised Lyn himself that he'd get her a furnace for the winter, but she had to wait three years.

On those tours we did together as the Funky Divas sometimes Lyn really struggled. She was quite weak physically and took time to get her bags packed for our trips. I remember once when we were getting ready to go on tour overseas I'd just gone out through her bedroom door with a suitcase when I heard something go crack behind me, like a twig being snapped, and Lyn hollered, 'OHHHHHHHHHHHHHH!' I came back to the room to find her on the floor holding on to the bed. She couldn't get up and was in real pain. We had to call for help to get her on the bus on time. When we arrived at Atlanta International airport I told Mr Bobbitt about her situation and he kindly got her a wheelchair. A little later he got her started on magnet therapy. At the time Vicki Anderson, who never really liked Lyn, said in a nasty way, 'Honey, are you going to be able to work?' But Lyn made it and never missed a show. She had real courage. She was a fighter.

Lyn decided to leave James in 1976. It was the death of the comedian Clay Tyson that persuaded her it was time to go. She was with James when they heard that Clay had died – and apparently he felt responsible for Clay's death.

Clay was the sweetest person; we all loved him. The same month he died, December, he'd been begging James to let me go on a new TV show he hosted called *Future Shock*, which was broadcast from Atlanta and was a bit like *Soul Train*. James introduced the acts, then performed. Clay's persuasion worked, and I performed one of my Forte songs, 'Nothing But Your Sweetness Is My Weakness'.

Clay was in his forties, and couldn't read and write too well. Because of a stroke half of his body couldn't move – and he had a glass eye. James tried to send him out on some kind of TV comedy show where they did jokes, something like *Laugh In*, but Clay couldn't hold it down because he couldn't read. After that James was really pissed and refused to pay him – but Clay was sick and needed money for medicine. The stroke he'd had affected him badly; he never really recovered from it.

When Clay died I think they were in Atlanta. He was supposed to pick up some woman that James wanted to be with, but she didn't turn up. It was hardly his fault, but even so James took it out on him. Lyn told me that Clay said, 'Mr Brown, you haven't paid me. I need my medicine, and I need some money to take care of my family and pay my hotel bills.' But James gave him nothing, and got in his Learjet and shut the door in Clay's face.

Clay was so desperate that he started running down the runway after the plane, hoping that James would change his mind. He didn't. The plane took off, leaving Clay on the runway. He must have been distraught: he had no medicine and he knew that probably he'd have nowhere to stay because his hotel bills were still unpaid. He went back to the hotel and begged them to let him go back to his room just for one night. The next morning they went into the room and found him dead. Poor Clay had had another stroke.

When James heard about Clay's death he felt bad. When he was alone with Lyn he broke down and said, 'Get on your knees and pray.' Lyn said she prayed to the Lord, begging him to let something touch James – so he really felt what he'd done. Then James started hollering, 'Lord, I'm sorry! I didn't mean it. Lord, forgive me!' Lyn said her prayer was answered. And that was when she knew she had to leave James Brown.

Lyn knew what James was capable of, because he'd already tried to kill her. Once he'd backed her up against a big bathtub full of hot water. 'I know what he was trying to do,' she later told me. 'He was trying to make me fall backwards into that tub. So I picked up a glass Listerine bottle – James always used to keep big bottles of Listerine around – and smashed it on the sink so the glass was sharp and jagged. Then I said, "Come on, come on!" I was ready to whup his ass.' After that, during the last two years she was with James, Lyn carried a gun with her.

There was also an incident between them in Africa in 1974. James and his entourage had flown out to Zaïre to provide entertainment – along with The Spinners and Crusaders – for the famous Muhammad Ali and George Foreman boxing match they called 'The Rumble in the Jungle'. While they was together in a room Lyn did something that James thought was wrong, and he started beating on her. She hollered and screamed to attract attention, and people came running. She quickly excused herself and went to the bathroom to start packing; she felt that if she stayed she was going to shoot him.

Lyn told me she even had to threaten Gertrude Sanders. Gertrude sometimes lied to get Lyn into trouble: James believed everything she said. One time they were flying back from Africa. Lyn was sitting well away from James: he'd got mad at her for some reason, and as a punishment made her sit in the back of the plane with the other folks, which she actually preferred. During the flight Lyn asked to swap seats with someone so she could sit next to Gertrude. She said, 'Ms Sanders, I've had just a damn 'nough of you setting me up and lying on me. Now I'm going to tell you this one thing... and I ain't gonna tell you no more. I've got enough money to take care of you. Do you understand, Ms Sanders? That's right: take care of you.' Lyn said Gertrude looked afraid, and understood what she meant. That's how Lyn got Gertrude Sanders off her back.

After leaving James in 1976, Lyn was approached by Bud Howell at Nashboro about joining the label. She said, 'I asked them how much money they were going to give me for the budget. So they got quiet. And I wanted to know who was going to produce the record.' You see, Lyn had a business head and asked all the right questions, but Nashboro never called her no more after that. They knew she was smart, asking things that most artists forget to ask.

After that Lyn moved to LA, and lived there in the '70s and '80s. Like me she put singing on the back-burner and got a good job, working at a famous recording studio called the Record Plant in 1978. Starting off as an accounting clerk, she worked her way up through the ranks, and by the time she left in 1988 she was operations manager and second in command to the actual owner. A lot of people don't know that Lyn went under the name Cecil Collins at the Record Plant to conceal who she was. It was a high school nickname she got from the TV show *Beanie & Cecil*.

After she left her job there she moved back to Abilene, Texas, and lived with some of her folks. But her mother's family and her father's family didn't get on, and she wasn't treated the way family should be treated. Some of the folks she'd helped when she had money just ridiculed her. But she had a few relatives she could depend on, like one who ran an insurance office and was a bigwig in the local community. He was the pastor of a church that didn't allow musical instruments in the building – but boy, could they sing, in beautiful harmony with their strong *a capella* voices. Lyn also depended on Lafayette, an ex-FBI man, and a lady called Lois who lived down her street.

It's sad that when Lyn went back to Texas she couldn't get help from the town she grew up in. There were many days when she didn't know how she was going to keep the basics going. Her two sons helped her all they could, but they had families and it wasn't very easy for them as they lived far away. Things got so bad I asked her to come and stay with me. Later I told Martha High, and she persuaded Lyn to go and live with her.

During her stay with Martha, Lyn saw some of the old gang, and a few times the JB's asked what she needed. But nothing ever came through. She fought rheumatoid arthritis with all her energy, although doctors deprived her of medicines she could have had, and she didn't get any royalties from the songs she'd written – as I mentioned earlier, her name wasn't added as a writer. We had high hopes of getting royalties owed us from James Brown after Bobby Byrd and Vicki Anderson took a case to court. We knew that if they won then doors would open for us; but they lost, and our hopes sank. During her last year Lyn was determined about getting back the rights to her biggest hit, 'Think (About It)'. She wrote the tune while she was with James, and he was credited as sole author. The only time she got some money from it was when she did it with the reggae artist Patra in 1992, and it went gold.

In the last ten or so years of her life, Lyn lost the people she loved the most: her mother and family members on both sides. It was only in the last year of her life that Lyn began to accept her mother's death in peace. She also lost her mother and father-in-law, Mr and Mrs Jackson, who died within a few months of each other. Lyn's own health was fragile by this time. She got some help with dental, car and house services from certain organizations that helped artists when they wasn't able to look after theirselves properly. I'm very grateful they did that for her.

CHAPTER 42

Back with James

My Aunt Lena, who our family had stayed with during the great flood back in the '50s, died in 1999. She was ninety-two, and had only been in hospital once – at the time of her death. She scared me sometimes because she was so strict. Once, when I was in my early fifties, I remember staying with her and she tried to give me a whipping because I'd been out to see a movie and got back at 10pm, which she considered too late. You should have seen me running from her as she chased me round. Hell, she couldn't have weighed more than 80 pounds. I stayed away from her until her last days, and I remember a few hours before she died, she said to me, 'You'll always be my Armourdale baby.' She had no children; her twin babies had died at birth. After Aunt Lena died I lived about a year and a half in her house, from about 1999 to 2001. It was like a doll's house, just too little for all my furniture and clothes.

In summer 2000 I heard from Lyn that James was giving a concert at the Key Arena in Seattle on 25 June, to celebrate the opening of the Experience Music Project, a new museum using state-of-the-art interactive video technology. Apparently it was going to feature James with the original JB's and Maceo Parker.

Lyn couldn't go. She was waiting for a ticket from Fred Wesley but she didn't really have the money to travel: it was a long way from Texas to Seattle. I didn't have the money to fly, but hell I felt ornery. So I got me a bus ticket and packed me a bag with the sexiest and the finest stuff I could. I checked into a hotel in Seattle and ordered me an escort for that night, someone who knew some friends of mine. I paid him just to be an escort. Somebody on the inside said, 'You know, Marva, we don't think that's right.'

'Hell,' I said, 'I'll just surprise them and show up and see what James'll do.'

So I got my ticket. I knew where they were staying and I called Charles Bobbitt. He said, 'Marva, you here? How'd you get here?'

I said on the bus. 'I've been riding for two days. My feet are swollen. I just thought I'd call you to let you know I was here. Don't tell James.'

He said, 'Why don't you come on over here? I've got some tickets.' I said I'd bought two and had everything set up.

When I got to the concert Bobbitt gave me my pass, and everything for me to get in. I was near the stage but in the balcony. When James came on to do the last part of the show I knew I had to make my move. The knee-length dress I had on was sharp and stylish. I walked down to the stage. I told my escort to stay right there. I said, 'Don't leave until I come back to tell you can leave,' and he agreed. I made my way down; I actually crawled under a rail, like a cat burglar. When I got to the end of the stage I saw Danny Ray. He scoped me and shouted excitedly, 'Marva, Marva!' At first James didn't see me, but then I got his attention and I made darn sure he saw me. I just smiled and grinned, and he about dropped. I genuinely believe the man was actually surprised and *happy* to see me. He invited me on stage and gave me and Martha High more play on the mic than he did anyone else. We did at least thirty to forty-five minutes, if not more. They were filming that night: I saw the cameramen.

After the show was over I made my way backstage to make my little homage to James. I hoped my escort was still out front waiting for me. A new man on the show wanted to give me a hard time and stopped me from going into James's dressing room. 'Mr Brown? He can't be seen,' he said.

But then Martha High came around the corner. She said to him, 'What are you doing? Do you know who this is? Come on, Marva, don't pay him no attention. Y'all leave her alone. She was here before y'all were, leave her alone!'

Before I went into James's dressing-room I saw this lady called

Vonny Sweeny, who had worked with James as a promoter for many a year; she'd just come on board a little before I left. She was out of California, and she worked like a dog. James once put a contract out on her. He told her that if she didn't bring back a car that she had from him – which he bought as a gift and gave to her – that was going to be the end of her. So she brought the car back. She was sweet as ever, but damn, she'd gotten big and put some weight on. But then again, so had I. When I was with James I was a size seven – but I looked sick; I don't want to be no bag of bones. Sadly Vonny passed in 2005. James didn't even send no money to pay for her burial. Knowing how Mr Bobbitt is, I expect he helped her. But here's a woman who worked for James all her life, and he couldn't even be bothered to go to her funeral or send a damn thing to express his condolences. He was the same with all the others who passed before him. Some of his people made him go. But his attitude was that he wasn't giving them nothing.

Anyway, after chatting with Vonny I walked into James's dressing room. He flashed me a big smile and seemed happy to see me. There was a long couch in there where several white women sat. As I said before, James had a thing for white women, which back in the '60s he kept quiet about – but by now he didn't have to hide it no more. He seemed so happy to see me. He got up from his seat and he looked at me. And you know what? That man just had to touch my legs. He ran his hand down my thigh and said, 'Oh, you're beautiful, Marva. You're just beautiful. You got a way home tonight?'

I said, 'Yes thank you, James.' After I left the show in '69 I rarely called him Mr Brown. I respected the man for who he was and what he'd done, although I didn't like the way he'd done it; but to call him Mr Brown made me feel like I was submitting to him. Me calling him James didn't seem to upset him. 'My driver is waiting for me now,' I said. 'I just thought I'd pop in here and say how I enjoyed being here and seeing you. You're still bad and I enjoyed being on the stage with you, but I got to go 'cause we're on a time zone. I really have to go.' And I just got out of there.

When I caught up with my escort I said, 'Let's get a cab.' When I dropped him off I asked the driver to take me back to the hotel, where I immediately started packing. I knew that in the morning I had to get out quickly and get on that bus again. It took me two days to get back home – but it was worth it. Looking back, I think that me and Lyn should have been invited to the show in the first place. After all, it was like a reunion of people from the old days. Bootsy Collins was playing bass (though not on every song – not even 'Sex Machine' that he'd played on originally; there was still some political stuff going on in the James Brown camp even then). His predecessor, Fred Martin, was also present, and Maceo Parker was blowing his sax like there was no tomorrow. His brother Melvin was playing drums alongside John 'Jabo' Starks. The line-up also included Phelps 'Catfish' Collins on guitar, 'Sweet' Charles Sherrell on keyboards and Johnny Griggs on percussion, vocalist Bobby Byrd, who'd been with James Brown since the two formed a gospel group in the '50s, trumpeter Ron Tooley and former bandleaders Fred Wesley (on trombone) and the great Alfred 'Pee Wee' Ellis. It was just like old times.

The same year – 2000 – my first King LP, *It's My Thing*, finally got reissued on CD. It had taken so long to get a re-release that I thought it would never come out. It was issued by an English independent company called Soul Brother Records, who licensed it from Universal and added some extra tracks – old singles of mine – that hadn't been on the original album. I have to thank Laurence Prangell and his brother Malcolm, of Soul Brother, for putting me back in the game again. I was so happy. It seemed like a brand new album. The technical side of recording has changed a lot since I recorded the album back in '69, and the quality of mastering has much improved over the years. The reissue sounds good to me, much better than I remember first time round. It got good reviews in the press and people were interested in me again. Thanks to Mr Prangell I got a booking at the Jazz Café, a prestigious venue in London, and I've played there many times since.

In 2003 a British film company collaborated with James Brown to make a documentary about his life, called *Soul Survivor*. It featured contributions from quite a few people from the old days. Me, Lyn Collins and Martha High were asked if we wanted to be interviewed on camera for it. We all agreed and were flown to Atlanta, Georgia. As I remember we were all paid a few hundred bucks. It was interesting to me because it showed some old black and white film of me and James together in 1968, which I'd never seen before. The film later came out on DVD.

CHAPTER 43

Soulpower – A Brand New Day

One day a few years ago, when Shirley Parks – aka 'Ms Lady' – was my manager, she was sitting on my bed looking through pictures and talking about how we were going to redo my promo kit. Then she turned her head to the north and startled me by hollering. I asked her what the matter was, and she said, 'I've had a revelation and I just saw you making the biggest comeback, and you don't have to worry – everything's going to be all right.' She'd had a vision. She reminded me of someone who felt the Holy Ghost and was prophesying. I knew she meant what she said, for she didn't joke about such things. Then she said, 'Don't worry – James won't bother you.' Ms Lady was not a clairvoyant but she believed in what we call the mystic – something beyond our five senses. I believed her, but I couldn't see how it was going to happen. But now I'm in the midst of her revelation. It was during the last year of her life that Shirley got the vision: she died on 7 November 2001 aged just fifty-three. The number seven is significant to people who believe in a world beyond this one; it's seen as a number symbolizing completion.

A few years later her words began to make sense. And it took a young man, someone overseas, to have the guts enough to try to bring the Funky Divas back. He gave his job up as a newspaperman because he believed in us. In the spring of 2004 I made contact with a young man from Germany called DJ Pari, who ran a Hannover-based organization called Soulpower. He was young, enthusiastic and very enterprising. Above all, he was a genuine fan of my music. His

English, too, was first rate, which meant there were no communication problems. He'd already been in contact with Martha High, who in turn put me in touch with him, and he'd also been in touch with Lyn Collins. Pari had lived in the States for a time, making a name for himself as a DJ; he'd even DJ'd for James Brown. After that he'd been a journalist for a time on the German tabloid newspaper *Bild*. His real passion, though, was soul and funk music, and he began Soulpower to provide music for parties and nightclubs locally. It quickly grew into a global booking and management agency. This is how Pari describes his background:

I started getting into funk in the late '80s through Prince and the Acid Jazz movement from the UK. I started DJ'ing around 1990/91 in Germany, and in early 1994 I moved to the US – Phoenix of all places. I went to college there (my majors were music business and journalism), but within a few months I was a well-established DJ in Arizona, thanks to my Acid Jazz collection (around that time the Acid Jazz hype had started in the US). After a while I hooked up with the Solsonics (they released an album called *Jazz In The Present Tense*) from Los Angeles and started touring with them. It was their lead singer, Kevin Williams, my best friend at that time, who hooked me up with an apartment in Los Angeles – so I moved. With my partner DJ Orb I DJed all over the LA club scene (from the famous Whiskey A-Go-Go to Johnny Depp's Viper Room) and all over California (San Diego, San Jose, San Francisco).

In 1996 Orb and I started our own club night called Groove Lounge in Venice Beach. Our first house band was the Black Eyed Peas. We booked shows for acts like Ozomatli, Big Black and Mandrill. Finally I made friends with the James Brown camp and started DJing at James Brown gigs. I also played at JB's party at 'Billboard Live' in Hollywood, after he was awarded his star on the Walk of Fame. After my move back to Europe I tightened my knots with the James Brown family and traveled with them occasionally. This is how I made friends with Sweet Charles Sherrell and Martha High.

In 2003 I moved to Hannover and started Soulpower as a monthly party series at the Palo Palo club in early 2004. Our first guest was Sweet Charles Sherrell. Martha High came second. She told me that she was still in touch with Marva Whitney and that she'd been sitting home in Kansas City for some years. So I started emailing Marva and booked her for three gigs in Germany for September 2004.

Although I agreed to do the Soulpower shows for Pari in Germany, I felt I wasn't ready. It had been a long time since I'd been out there on the road on my own. Also, I'd never traveled alone to a foreign country before; I couldn't speak German and I was worried I'd get lost. I was worrying about all sorts of silly things, I suppose, because my confidence was low. I never like to travel by myself if I can help it.

'Pari is a nice man and you'll like him,' said Lyn Collins, trying to ease my fears. 'Don't worry, everything will be all right.' *Aw man*, I thought – but I kept my unease to myself. I was immediately reassured when I finally met Pari. He seemed very young to have such a position of responsibility, but he was kind – making sure I was comfortable and that I understood what was going on. I decided I'd have to get him to let me go at a comfortable pace without letting him know. After thirty years out of the big time I'd got out of shape a little, I suppose, and wasn't physically fit enough for doing gigs and traveling all over the place. After all, I was sixty and not really where I should have been in terms of fitness and stamina. Singing in church and clubs are two different things. *Lordy,* I fretted, *I know my keys from playing the piano, but I might have to change them now my voice has got deeper with age.* I was worrying a lot, but for the sake of us three Funky Divas I didn't want the job to be a downer.

My comeback concerts in Germany arranged by Pari and DJ Baba (his business partner at that time) were awesome. I was backed by some wonderful German musicians called the Soulpower Allstars who Pari had put together. I did two sold-out shows in Hannover. One was at an amazing club called Palo Palo, and the other was at a place named the Jazz Club. That's where I met the mayor of Hannover, Bernd Strauch, who turned out to be a big fan of mine. He was so happy to meet me that he invited me to City Hall the next day. I felt very honored. After that I did a show in Hamburg on the coast at a place called the Mandarin Casino. The place holds 600 people but there were only a hundred there that night. Pari blamed it on poor promotion. Even so, the crowd was great; they seemed to love me and made a lot of noise. I really felt I was back in the limelight for the first time in many years.

Although I don't believe in management contracts – I'm just too afraid of being tied down and ripped off – by 2005, with a few more European concerts under my belt, I knew I could trust Pari, and regarded him as my personal manager. To this day I don't have a written contract with him like he does with Martha High and Gwen McCrae: our agreement is a verbal one.

Now I'm real picky when it comes to managers. Let me tell you, there are managers and there are managers. To have a manager or personal manager can be tough: it's a type of marriage – and like a marriage it can get on your nerves at times. It's a powerful relationship. One of the first things you want to make sure of is that your manager's knowledgeable about the music business. They have to know how to think ahead, be bold, and a whole lot of other things besides. Even unsavory things, like sticking up for and protecting the artists even if it means getting into fist fights with promoters over money. These days that doesn't happen so much, but back in the day when I started out I saw managers get into fights with promoters, band members and even people who got too pushy over something. Whatever happens, the ideal manager is loyal, especially to the artist. The trouble is, I suppose, that both the artist and the manager think that they're the boss. Neither wants to feel used or be intimidated. They have to maintain respect for each other if they're to succeed and work happily together.

Sometimes the artists and manager can seem like family and sometimes they don't want to know each other. But the bottom line is, always take care of business and keep it looking respectable to the public. As the artist I might ask to see the books anytime, with all the receipts and everything, so a manager has to be on the ball even if he's tired or having a bad day. It's not an easy job and you have to be nervy and crazy to handle it all. Above all, though, the job's got to mean something to you. Whether you're man or woman, short or tall, skinny or big, it's not a punk job.

My first real manager other than Tommy Gadson, leader of the Derbys, was Willie Cyrus. He got me the deal with Bobby 'Blue' Bland, but I was scared and didn't take it. Toni Sheffield, a female DJ, also managed me. Then Clarence Cooper got me the job with James Brown. I've also had a couple of lady managers: Lyn Collins, of course, one of the most knowledgeable women in the business. She'd act all official and business-like when a gig came up, and she made a believer out of them on the other end of the phone. Oh how I miss her. Before her there was Ms Shirley Parks, better known as Ms Lady, who I mentioned a little earlier. I met her in the mid-'90s when she was a manager for a blues singer in Kansas City called Cotton Candy (her real name was Annette Washington). Cotton was older than me, but I'd known her as a child. She was a singer in the church and my mom used to play for her. She could keep you laughing sometimes.

When Shirley and I met she and I hit it off; of course Taurus and Gemini always get along. That's why I got along with Lyn, who was also a Gemini. To cut a long story short, jealousy set in and Cotton and Shirley broke up because of me. Shirley had taken to helping me, but Cotton felt she gave me more attention. To me that wasn't the case. Cotton was a blues singer and a darn good one, while I sang soul. The only difference was that I wasn't going to work for pennies, and I still remembered what was taught in the James Brown camp. Heck, it cost me nearly $100 to just get ready for a show.

Shirley believed it was time for women to be able to book an artist with respect and a fair price. Most of the vendors didn't want to deal with women agents, so it was hard. I was one of the few young ladies from here in the '60s who made the big time, as they say, but they had no respect for my past because the jobs wasn't there for me. Shirley was a true friend: she told me like it was and looked out for me. She was the mother of five or six children, who she'd raised by herself – and they all graduated and went on to more schooling. All were girls except one. They had good jobs, working for the government, and she kept the young folk in the neighborhood occupied by finding them something to do to stay out of trouble. She was younger than me but carried a big stick. Even though Shirley knew the people, she didn't really fulfil her own dream the way she wanted – although she knew how to make money.

On the side, to make ends meet, Shirley cleaned, cooked, did other housework and cared for the sick. And guess who her relief girl was: yeah, me. I never liked housework and wasn't really used to taking care of ninety-year-old ladies. Shirley would put things in order and say, 'I need a few days off, Marva. Just keep it the way I've left it:

the food's cooked, and if you have any problems call me and I'll be there.' She did just that, and she paid good. Who'd ever have thought I'd be doing homecare? The old ladies could be something else. There was one who was hard-headed at ninety-ish. She was a tough, rich old bird, but I liked her. She could get feisty, and she didn't like to take her nightly bath. We'd try to encourage her. One morning I had a panic attack when I saw what she'd done. She was covered in excrement from her feet to her head, like she'd been playing in mud. It was all over her bed and rug, and they looked like they'd cost loads of dollars. She looked at me – and I went to call Shirley. No way could I clean it up. Shirley came over and took care of it. I had to go into another room I felt so sick, though I did manage to bathe her, fussing all the way. Yeah, the pay was good, but many a time I felt like running.

After Shirley became my manager she kept on knocking on doors, but it didn't do any good. It was always freebies; we turned them down. She was really hurt about Cotton Candy. She'd helped to pull Cotton out of the drunken pit she was in, cleaned her up and found her gigs; but then she dropped Shirley. Shirley had a contract with her but wouldn't act on it; she said that God would sort it out.

Shirley got a chance to meet James Brown, and he told her to take care of me. He seemed to take a liking to her but not enough to throw us a little help. We kept on trying to find work in Kansas City, but my home town wouldn't recognize me. There's not much paid work for performers there, just freebie fundraisers. When I realized there wasn't much future for me there I bowed out. Many female singers worked in the town but not me. I have no great love for Kansas City; it's just another song title for me.

You'd think that people in Kansas City would want to help me – especially as I used to perform with James Brown. But no, it's like I don't exist. I can't even get a job on the large riverboat casinos in my home town, even though I've played everywhere in the world, even Vietnam and Africa.

I had two other promoters who booked me: Roger Neightor and Dwayne Gilley, who I consider a friend. He manages a singer called Myra Taylor, who is in her seventies and still travels worldwide. She can sing her behind off, do jazz and tell real funny jokes. She's fantastic.

There's also a gentleman in Kansas City called Allen Bell who knows a lot about what's happening here musically: the name of his company is America's Best Attractions. He's been successful in the entertainment business and is still responsible for putting on festivals around here. He really knows what he's doing. Today he and his son are attorneys in North Kansas City, and have a thriving business. He just loves me to death. When I go see him he hugs me, he kisses me, he's got to take me to lunch, he got to do this, he got to do that. He says I'm the Tina Turner of Kansas City.

So I've had a few managers in my time, but Pari is one of the best. He's been a Godsend. He's the only person who's tried to put the Funky Divas back in their place. Nobody else has come out of the damn bushes. I respect him a whole lot because he's doing this. At the same time, though, I feel I must stick to my set of principles and standards: I want to be treated with respect and get the money I feel I deserve. See, I'm at an age where I don't suffer fools gladly and won't put up with second-class treatment. It's first class or nothing for me now. That might sound harsh but it's where I'm at. I've been used many times before, and those days are over now.

At my first concert with Soulpower Pari was very attentive. He called me and asked if I needed anything. He gave me all the details of the venue we were playing at, organized rehearsals, gave me a wake-up call if I needed it and asked me what I liked to eat. I felt this young man seemed to have an answer for everything. *So far so good,* I thought to myself. What also impressed me was that he was always on time. He's so professional, like he's been doing it for years. The band he'd got together knew the material and had beautiful attitudes, even when I had to change a few key signatures, to make the songs more comfortable for my range. You see, being a singer is like running track: you have to build momentum and know where you are, but you try not to show it. I wasn't sure at that time which of my songs I should put in my set and what order to do them in. Pari helped me out, and said he knew how the songs should be stacked, if I didn't mind. I was very relieved. Lord, I was glad. I'd no idea of the pulse of the crowd or what they wanted to hear.

Pari is one of the finest young men I've ever met. As I worked with him I began to feel that he was pretty much on the up and up. Maybe he didn't realize, but I was watching him closely, checking him out. I'd met Baba too, Pari's then business partner in Soulpower. I relied on him a lot, for the lighting on stage made it hard for me to see and, hell, at my age I didn't need to fall or bump into anything. I remember Baba saying, 'Don't worry, I'll take good care of you, Marva.' He sure was cute. Both of them were about the age of my son, Ellis Jr.

Pari has been the only man since Mr Cooper that I could see being my manager. I'm proud of him. He knows something about everything. I wondered how he'd handle a situation when I wasn't in the best of moods and dissatisfied, but he's proved himself. He seems to make sure I don't get into those kinds of negative moods: sometimes it's like he's going on fifty he seems so considerate, mature and understanding. I believe a person is known by his words and deeds, and honestly Pari has passed the test. We sometimes disagree, of course, but we always come to an agreement. He lets it roll off his back and just keeps on working and plugging on my behalf. I feel secure with Pari. He always asks before he commits me to something, and explains why it's good for me if I'm not really interested.

I feel I have two sons now. Pari had been just what I needed: someone who's in my corner, God-fearing and upfront. I'm blessed we work good together; I respect him and love him. I feel we have a relationship like James Brown and Charles Bobbitt had: we understand and respect one another.

Now I was getting back in the limelight as a solo artist I wanted to do some more recording. Before I got with Pari I'd been working on a gospel album with Eugene Smiley, a well-known musician in Kansas City. We got a cheap price at a studio and he recorded the songs we wrote onto a reel-to-reel tape machine. We were originally fifty-fifty partners, but when he started working on his own project I took ours on myself. I want to get it redone and add things to it – but the tape's deteriorated, and I've been told it'll have to go through a baking process to preserve what's on it. I think I'm just about half-finished, because really all I've got to do is go lay the vocals down. What I like about this album is that it's all me – it's not James Brown. I wrote half the tunes and Smiley and I kind of grew up in the business together. But what I really like are the words. They can go gospel or they can go R&B. Is there room in the marketplace for something like that? Whether there is or not, it's something that I think is me, because it's soulful and the words are meaningful. It shows a different side of me. I'm not hollering or screaming.

I realized that by joining the growing Soulpower family my ambition to do a gospel album would have to go on the backburner for a while. In early 2005 Soulpower released a compilation CD called *The Best Of Year One*, which featured me doing a live version of 'It's My Thing', along with songs by other ex-James Brown people like Martha High, Clyde Stubblefield and Waldo Weathers. It was intended as a taster of what Pari was doing, and featured words of encouragement on the cover from James himself. It read: 'Hi, this is James Brown, the Godfather Of Soul. Thank you for being so into it. Thank you for keepin' it real. We wish Soulpower the greatest success in the world! James Brown November 2004.'

When 2005 arrived Lyn, Martha and I had high expectations for Soulpower. Personality-wise, we were all different, but the mental suffering that we'd shared united us. We're deeply spiritual as well, and we believe that what God gives to you is for you alone: can't nobody take it or sing it like you. We had this thing, this agreement between us: we don't care who's first, second or third on the bill, but each of us is going to try our best to hit a home run. We're not going to back down because we're singing on the same bill as other soul sisters. We used to laugh about it. We were still competitive but there was no bitchiness or backbiting. I remember once at a show in Paris not too long ago, where it was packed with people, Martha High tore it down. I had to come out after her and I said, 'Oh God, Martha, what are you doing to me?!' But we've got that understanding because Martha's Martha and Marva's Marva. And Lyn was Lyn. We're very close, a tight-knit family. People think that because we're women we won't get on. But we proved them wrong.

In February 2005 Lyn was well enough to go on a Soulpower European tour. She was still suffering, though. There were times she swelled up so badly – especially her feet and her hands – that she couldn't even get out of the bathtub. The doctors were slow in helping her. Our friends Stanley Swift, Charlie Bethea and Mary helped all they could, but I believe not having heat in her house along with mental anguish contributed to the worsening of her condition. Sometimes she couldn't move for months. There was a lot of times she couldn't move period. She'd call me and say, 'My fingers are as big as conies today, and my legs and my feet have swollen up so bad I can't move.' Our lives were similar in that we never really had a companion that we could say actually cared for us, and wanted to take care of us as women. The men we hooked up with thought we were stars, and were jealous of that.

Eventually Lyn was registered disabled by her doctor, but the state of Texas didn't do right by her. We had to send her medicine. I heard that she had to get people that was on food stamps to give her money. But she was determined to try to make it, for she didn't really want to be on disability. She said, 'I got to try, sis.' And she went on what sadly turned out to be her last ever tour. A few weeks after she'd got home she passed away. What shocked me was the fact that I'd been speaking to her on the phone the day she died, 13 March 2005. She called me in the morning. She was so excited, bubbly and full of joy about the European tour. We talked about everything that was happening with Soulpower, and she told me her thoughts on how things should take shape. She was excited because she'd had a new photo set done. I remember her saying that it was great to prove people wrong and show that female singers could get along together without egos getting in the way. See, if Lyn couldn't help you she wouldn't hurt you. If you asked for her opinion she'd give you her best.

Lyn and me was hatching lots of plans, like fixing up a special foundation for people who had been in show business and had fallen on hard times. We planned to get an organization to provide home taxis, dentists and doctors. We talked about doing a gospel song on an album together, because we shared a church background. But none of those plans came to pass.

I was told of Lyn's death by my fellow soul sister Martha High. Lyn had been visiting her son and choked on a piece of food. They called an ambulance, but before they got her to the hospital she was brain dead. It was a terrible tragedy: she was only fifty-six. It's strange, but she'd told me earlier in the year that her former husband, Bobby Jackson – who had died the previous year – had come to her in the spirit and told her it was time for her to join him. Although they'd been divorced twenty-five years she never stopped loving him. I had told her not to pay any attention to what he said. Only those who know the ways of the spirit can understand this.

I've thought about her death many times. I found it hard to take in, especially as she was so happy that morning, a few hours before she passed away. She had no business dying the way she did, especially with the talent she had. One of the last things she said to me was, 'Well, if I don't get the royalties I'm owed for records, my sons will be rich one day.' Me and Lyn had a dream that we were going down the Yellow Brick Road together, like Judy Garland in the movie, and we was going to go down it and everything was going to be all right.

For a short time Lyn was kept alive on a life-support machine. She was in a coma. I pleaded with her family members to keep her on it a little longer. I've known of people who were in comas with no hope and they came back to this world. Our lives are in God's hands, and three more days for Lyn on the lifeline wouldn't have hurt her. But the medical people was so certain there was no hope they turned it off. After that they did an autopsy, which I thought was strange. If they was so certain there was no hope then why did they butcher her and keep her body two weeks after she died?

Lyn's friends Stanley, Charlie and Mary were at her funeral along with Vicki Anderson, Bobby Byrd and Martha High. One of the ladies (I've forgotten her name) who helped Mr Moore sell pictures with the James Brown show in the late '60s took care of the food. We tried to make Lyn look better and more presentable in her open casket, because the hospital had butchered her forehead as a result of the autopsy. We tried to get her hair right, but we couldn't. It was awful. James Brown sent flowers: twelve roses and one tulip. I thought that was strange. What did the tulip mean? He had to work, apparently, so he wasn't able to make the funeral. Some of us were very glad of that, because we was angry with him for not helping her buy a winter furnace.

Lyn's passing did do one thing; it got her mother's folk and her father's folk to come together in a Baptist church. That was a miracle as the families weren't close at all: Lyn had talked about them not speaking. Those two families being together and pleasant to each other was beautiful to me.

The funeral was beautiful, but it was hard. I asked Vicki if Bobby could talk for all of us, but I also wanted each of us to say something if we wanted. We couldn't think of a song for all of us to sing that was appropriate, but the family knew how close me and Lyn was, so I got up first and sang a gospel song. I said that if anyone had anything to say in our group to come up front while I was singing. I got to the piano and played and sang, and by the end every last one of them was up on the front row. Everybody had something to say, and Vicki and Bobby sang a beautiful duet. I think one of Lyn's friends sang a number too.

After the funeral we went to the graveyard. Lyn is buried close to her mother under a beautiful tree. Charlie and I could do nothing but kneel down and rub her casket, our tears running down our faces. We were all suffering. Then we went back to the church, where we, her friends, served a beautiful dinner for all. In spirit she's never left me. I see her daily, for she's my baby sis, my dear Lynnie.

Lyn's death shocked Martha, me and Pari, but it didn't weaken our resolve to carry on. It probably made us stronger. We had to carry on for Lyn's sake, because she was the one who'd set us back on the path to recognition in the first place. When I've performed since I've always done one of Lyn's songs in the show and always dedicate it to her memory.

In the summer of 2005, I traveled to Europe and did several more shows for DJ Pari and his Soulpower organization. We played in Helsinki, Finland, and also in Cognac, France, the place where they make French brandy.

That October, I returned to Europe to step in for Bobby Byrd and Vicki Anderson after their tour was canceled when Bobby was taken sick. I did three dates in Germany – one in Hannover and two in Berlin – and then went to England where I shared the bill with Sweet Charles Sherrell. We did dates in Newcastle and London together.

But at the end of 2005, I had to take time off to have an operation. This put me out of action for several months, which was frustrating, but your health is important. I know that because I've had a few health issues over the years. I was diagnosed with high blood pressure when I was thirty: unfortunately it runs in the family. That, mixed with the downfall of my career, took a toll on me. I'm happy to say, though, that I never took drugs, became a drunkard or a whore. I was blessed to have a family that had my back even though I got on their nerves.

My main concern in recent years though has been my eyesight. My eyes started bothering me somewhere in the mid-'90s. One day my right eye was about to drop on the floor: there was no light going into it, and I saw nothing but blood and had to hold my head down for two weeks to see if it would improve. But it just wouldn't move. I was diagnosed with a condition called macular degeneration, which starts off as blind spots in the eye. It's a condition, I'm told, that comes with age. I've had several laser surgeries to try and correct it but they didn't work. To keep me from losing the eye, the surgeons sewed it down into the socket. You know, God is good because most people don't even notice it. If I didn't take my medicine, about six or seven pills a day for the past few years, it'd affect my eye. I can't see on my right side beyond my shoulder, so I've learned to allow myself extra room while walking so I won't bump into anything. Pari helps to guide me onto the stage now. I tell myself that if it wasn't for my left eye they'd probably call me Ms Ray Charles. I get a disability allowance now because of this.

Of course my voice has been affected by time. I get anxious sometimes because I find the high notes aren't as easy to reach as they used to be. But Pari knows I can only do about three numbers at a time and lets the band play a tune so I have time to get my strength back. He's very considerate.

While my career seemed to be gaining momentum my former husband, Ellis Taylor, was deteriorating. He'd not been well for some time.

He fell down in his home and broke a leg, and when they found him lying on the floor he'd been there three days. After that he had to go to a nursing home because he couldn't look after himself. He was only there a few months before he died. That was 2005. I think he was getting Alzheimer's, because sometimes it was like he didn't know who I was or where he was. He always seemed very fearful about something. He was scared of his own shadow, even scared to sleep: he hadn't had a good night's sleep in years. I don't know what was going on with him but I'm glad he's at peace now.

In his will, Ellis left nothing but 51 per cent of Forte Records and all his tapes to our son, Ellis Jr, who's going to try and do something with it and maybe re-activate the label. Ellis left no one in charge of his business so it's in pretty bad shape. We never got any accounting for the records we sold from the distributor we used. Hopefully together we can bring Forte back. Ellis told me somebody broke into his basement once and took some boxes of records, and more recently I found that his daughter from his first family sold lots of master tapes and records to a man in Independence, Missouri. I was mad at her for that. I believe she only sold them for a few hundred dollars. When I get it straight, my son is going to divvy up the other 49 per cent with the other children. I was Ellis's second wife and he had children outside of his first wife. None of them, as far as I know, was interested in music, just Ellis Jr.

Ellis Jr lives in California. He's a fantastic singer: he sang on the *Men In Black* soundtrack album. He can just stand up and sing and he's in the groove. He does hip-hop but it's a positive hip-hop. That makes me proud.

It was after Ellis's death, in early 2006, that Pari came to me with a recording proposition – a record with a Japanese funk band called Osaka Monaurail. He told me he had a national distributor for the proposed album, which was to be released on a Japanese label called Shout. Pari sent me some material on CD and they sounded just like the James Brown Orchestra under the direction of Pee Wee Ellis in the late '60s: it was hard to tell the difference between them. I asked Pari if they'd put James's old vocals on their tracks, but he said no – it was their singer. Hell, they got it down with the voice and the band too. At first I told them I wasn't interested, as I wouldn't get a nickel until everybody else was paid – and I didn't feel like going through that any more. I was already working on my own gospel project, which was coming out of my own pocket.

As I listened to Osaka Monaurail again I was impressed by their musicianship. They were damn good. Really tight too, with punchy horns. So I reconsidered, and eventually agreed to cut an album with them. Pari felt that with their classic funk sound Osaka Monaurail was just right for me. It turned out his idea was on the money. The plan was that they'd bring some of their original tunes with them and we'd also do maybe one or two tunes I'd done with James. It was also agreed that Osaka Monaurail would let Pari and me contribute to writing the lyrics.

The group, led by singer and organist Ryo Nakata, had nine members. Ryo had a gruff singing voice and to me sounded just like James Brown. The group had a big horn section, made up of trumpeters Kentaro Yamagata and Seiji Sakakibara, trombonist Katsutoshi Hiraishi and saxophonist Shimon Mukai. On guitar they had Dan Hayami and Yuichi Ikeda. The band's heartbeat was provided by Tsuyoshi Ouchi, who played bass, and drummer Kensuke Okuse. They was really together and if you closed your eyes, you would think you was listening to James Brown's band.

The basic instrumental tracks were put down in Japan, then Ryo sent Pari a tape of some tunes and he picked two for me to work on. Pari flew to Kansas with the tapes and we went into a local studio for me to overdub some vocals. Pari had been working on some ideas for lyrics on the flight over, and came up with the title 'I Am That I Am', a phrase from the Bible I always used to sign off my emails. The night before the studio session Pari and me worked on the lyrics and melody, trying to get everything just right. He was able to sleep but I couldn't sleep a wink that night.

The next day, 17 March 2006, we went into 64111 Studio in Kansas City, Missouri. I was calm more than nervous. We worked quickly, and I think we did two songs in less than three hours. I ran through each song twice. The studio was very comfortable, and being comfortable is important for me when I'm recording. I put down the vocals to 'I Am That I Am' but I kept singing it wrong, changing it to 'I Am What I Am.' I don't why I did this but I guess it sounded more natural to me. In the end, Pari let it go and 'I Am That I Am' became 'I Am What I Am,' though Pari was worried that people would think I'd covered the Gloria Gaynor song called 'I Am What I Am.'

After that song was in the can, we started work on what eventually became '(Let A Sister Come In And) Wrapp Things Up'. It was Pari's idea to have me rapping on it. Basically the idea was for me to say whatever I felt. I was a bit stymied at first. I asked myself what I was going to rap about. I know nothing about rapping, except what the young artists are doing – and I don't think I can really do that. I thought I'd feel like a fish out of water, but Pari encouraged me and gave me some pointers. I loved the track, but couldn't find a singing or a rap idea at all for the music. I was in a bind because the clock was ticking away, and time is money when you're recording in professional studios. So I just started praying: 'Help me, Lord, help me,' I said. 'How do I start?' Thankfully Father God gave me favor and an idea came into my head: I would talk about Lyn Collins, and the many conversations we had about life and our shared suffering under James Brown. So, off the top of my head, I started talking. I can be a jokester at times with funny country sayings, so I knew that once I got into it, ideas would start to flow. And they did. I just heard the music over the earphones and began to make up lyrics out of my head as I listened. I talked about us soul sisters and what we'd been through. I was just playing around really. On the first couple of takes I talked about Lyn, but I decided it was too personal for me to make public: my feelings were still too raw. So we did a third version and decided to go with that one.

We finished the album off during a tour of Japan in June 2006. We did live shows all over the country, not just Tokyo. We played in Osaka, Fukuoka, Nagoya, Sendai, and even flew to the island of Okinawa, where we did two shows in a place called Naha.

I'd already been to Japan with The Platters back in the late '70s and early '80s. It seemed to take forever to get to it, I remembered, and I was worried this time that my feet might swell because of my experience with long bus journeys. I was hoping, too, that I didn't have to taste any sushi, as I didn't like the idea of eating raw fish. On the other hand I didn't want to insult the Japanese people.

After landing in Tokyo I met up with Osaka Monaurail, who were to be my backing band. I had a good feeling about them: after initial misgivings about them being a novelty act, I was sold on them. They were a great bunch. I felt a real sense of love and respect from them. I was excited about going in the studio and cutting some tracks live with them. I was met and greeted by Ryo and the rest of the band and we seemed to gel from the beginning. I don't think they could have treated the queen any better; their hearts were true, and we all bonded. Later, when they started bringing their children to the studio, they showed me old pictures of me I'd never seen myself. It blew my mind. I felt like we were family.

The first studio Pari had booked felt too stiff at first. It was big and grand and felt like a symphony room – a little too classy and formal. I was a bit unnerved and said I couldn't record there, but they changed things around and added some homely touches so I felt more at ease. The sessions were wonderful. We had a good chemistry going and were on the same wavelength from the get-go. After cutting a couple more original tunes for the album they wanted me to do some James Brown numbers. I don't know why they wanted that, because I felt it would be good to do some more original songs. Anyway I agreed. 'Mother Popcorn' was suggested first, but I felt the lyrics weren't right for me because of my faith and because it might upset my Mom. So we agreed on 'Give It Up Or Turnit A Loose', one of James's hottest funk numbers. We really got into a good groove and the song ran to almost twenty minutes, which had to be edited down. I also did a new version of 'Saving My Love For My Baby', which I had originally recorded for Federal as a B-side back in 1967. Then I chose a couple of covers: 'Ev'ry Little Bit Hurts', which was originally done by Brenda Holloway at Motown in the 1960s and was later re-done by Alicia Keys, and 'He's Mine', which I used to perform when I sang with The Platters.

After the Japanese tour was over, we went back to Tokyo to finish off the album, but this time in a different studio. It was smaller than the first one we'd visited and I felt much more at home. Except for one thing. There was a small bobble-head figure of James Brown there and it freaked me out. It sounds crazy but I was convinced that James was watching us. I told Pari to cover it up so he put a tablecloth over it. After that, the session went well but as we neared the end of our studio time, we still needed one more song to complete the album. I insisted that I wanted to put a gospel song on the album but as there wasn't enough time to put a full band arrangement together Pari suggested I sat at the piano and did a song that I sang in my local church. I chose the classic Thomas Dorsey song 'Peace In The Valley'. I just sat down, touched the keys and they rolled the tape. It was that simple, and it finished off the album with a nice spiritual touch. I'm glad we included it. It shows a side of me that the world doesn't really know.

I believe this album is great – and it got rave reviews in UK magazines like *Mojo* and *Blues & Soul* – but I believe our next album will be even better, as I feel we'll be able to put more time in it. Ryo, Osaka Monaurail's main man, is awesome to watch. He's a genius and the gentleman in the band. Here in the States, I feel, people can waste a lot of time as they're not on the same wavelength, but in Japan they knew who the leader was, and that was reflected in the spirit of how they worked together. Everyone was well organized and worked like clockwork to get everything right. Everyone worked together, striving for the same goal.

In my experience it's usually one tune that sells the whole album, and I certainly thought we had a good one with the title song, which got released in Japan as a vinyl single before the full album came out. I believe the album will at least pay for itself and put some cash and a lot of dates our way. Pari says that's why I'm picking up more tour dates now.

I'd like to do more recordings with Osaka Monaurail, and my endeavor is to make our next album different, with something in it for everyone. Not just one type of music – for I like all kinds of music and I don't want to be pigeonholed or stuffed in a box.

I'm really happy that my career has taken off again, but saddened that some of my friends couldn't be around to see it. I've lost three of my best friends in the last three and a half years.

Shirley Parks, my former manager, passed. They told me that all of a sudden she fell on the floor from the couch at her home and went into a coma. They called me and I ran to the hospital. When I got there and touched her she was cold as ice. She was out. I kept rubbing her and talking and praying but to no avail. She died later on that night. Her funeral was packed and she looked beautiful. I miss Shirley: she was my friend, and she was a lady.

After Shirley Parks another old friend, Shirley Kidd, went to glory. From the age of nineteen or so we went to clubs when I was singing with the Derbys. Boy, could she dance. She was on her own at the age of sixteen. During that time she met a young man named Henry Kidd, they fell in love and he went to war in Vietnam sometime around '64 or '65. When he came back they got married, and that was the beginning of hell for her – though I didn't know it until she passed. Shirley was a hard worker. She helped run his take-out chicken and sandwich house and after-hours club. Whatever she could do she did for Henry, but he had a drinking problem and a lot of people thought he was crazy, though he never let me see that side of him. I remember when I was coming home from a James Brown show she called me to loan her money to get Henry out of jail. She promised she would pay me back but I said to forget it. We were friends and I didn't need it. She was always so kind to me and so encouraging.

I'd dated her cousin, Ozell, in the early '60s. We were close, and he was so good to me, but he made the mistake of telling me that he was separated from his wife and children. That really surprised me. I scoped his wife one day and she was a nice-looking woman. I told him to go back to his wife and children. He didn't, and I was determined not to be the one who kept him away from them. I heard later they divorced. When I was in town Shirley said all he ever talked about was me and that he missed me. I dodged him, though.

One day in 2005 I got a call from Shirley that Ozell had died, and that she wanted to let me know that he was talking about me just before he passed. He said that because I'd gotten used to big money he knew he didn't have a chance. When Shirley called to tell me about Ozell she told me she was on an oxygen tank. Her breathing was bad. The years had taken their toll on her. By that time Henry, her husband, had retired from one of the car plants. She sounded so bad that I said, 'Shirley, go to your mother's house and stay there for the winter: it's warmer there. You can't take another winter here.' She could barely talk she was so breathless.

Not long afterwards one of my brothers called me. He said, 'Marvan, do you know a girl named Shirley Kidd?' I assumed it was something to do with Ozell's funeral, but I was wrong. My brother said, 'She's dead.'

I didn't believe it. I just knew he was wrong. I called Shirley's mother, Miss Temple. She broke down and exclaimed, 'That so-and-so killed my daughter!'

I said, 'What?'

She said, 'Shirley came over here. I'd been trying to get her to come and stay with me during the winter. She finally came today and went to lie down on the bed. Then she rose up and said, "Henry will never be able to hurt me any more. I'm not going back." Then she passed.'

I went to the funeral and sang and played organ for the service. Shirley had to be a size 22 but she always dressed sharp, and her casket was one of the best you could find. So now my other Shirley was gone, I thought, *Lord, how much can I bear?* Mama and Lyn helped me get through it.

After Shirley, Sharon Hooks, my longtime childhood friend, passed. It was a hard time for me – it felt like all my friends was leaving me. Sharon was two years older than me. She was a timid girl and truly had a humbleness that never went away. I loved her and Bettyan Turner, my other school friend from way back. They say good-looking girls get the good men, but that's a lie in my experience. Sharon got married and the bastard, her husband, didn't help her; he just left her. Sharon was working at the employment office. Someone picked on her, and she wasn't able to work that job or any job after that. She was a walking miracle for what she had to go through. She raised two girls and a boy. She never fought. She was almost too humble. I've been that way too: I don't like confrontations. The only difference is that I fight if there's no other choice.

The church was packed for Sharon's funeral and the service was beautiful. The Mannings was the only other guests on the church music program. Mother designated me to do the talking. My youngest brother Winfred was there too. I talked to the congregation about how we'd made mud pies as children and how we'd talked the last year about how some of her sisters got on her nerves. It brought laughter to the crowd. Then I sang my song 'I Need The Lord To Guide Me'. It was warmly received. I also talked about my upcoming book and how there would be a chapter on the Hooks. I saw a whole lot of Armourdale people that I'd not seen in a long time. It was like a homecoming. One lady whispered to me, 'Marva, you really brought the sermon.' The pastor also had a wonderful message.

At the funeral it was said that when Sharon was ill – she'd been on dialysis – she fought to get better and briefly rallied before dropping into unconsciousness again. We believed that she took stock of her life in those brief waking moments when she called out everyone's name. It was like she had seen or been in the Promised Land and come back. In the end she decided to go to glory because of what she'd been through in this life and didn't want any more. She was blessed enough to make a choice. I cried before the funeral and walked around the house, saying to myself that I'd lost four close friends in about two and a half years. It's lonesome sometimes. God bless Sharon – she's in good hands, with her family on the other side. I spoke to her in spirit and told her to visit me anytime she wanted to and that I wasn't afraid. For me and my religion, the spirit never dies. Our loved ones come and go as they please in spirit and sometimes work and help you. Like Lyn. Her spirit comes to me and we have a mental conversation, and she advises me on certain matters. It might sound crazy to those who don't understand, but I truly believe it.

Thankfully another good friend, Miss Betty Knox, who's a whiz at accounts, is still around. We became friends a few years ago. Around that time she knew of me but we didn't know each other that well; she knew my brother better and my parents, because she helped them with tax problems they had. She's a genius and a hard-working woman.

I talked to her every now and then, and then there came a time when I needed somebody to go with me to the few shows that I have in Kansas City: I never like to go alone. I don't like running with big groups because of the situation that happened when I was in school, when I had a fight and got expelled. So I'm kind of a loner. Betty is too, but she loves to help people. Just as one example, she helped me get my things together when I moved to a new apartment. She's really been a blessing to me.

Let me update you about Bettyan Turner, my childhood mud pie buddy. We lost touch for a time but rekindled our friendship in later years. I've found out that you don't have to talk to a friend every day and run in and out of their house to stay friends. We've made a pact that whenever either of us has a problem we'll drop everything and go to the other's aid. Just a few months ago I got an SOS call, having not talked to her in months. Her baby brother had died. Me and my mom was with her on the spot, and handled what she needed. This has proved to be a true relationship. We both made bad judgements in regard to men, but always knew how to make a respectable living of some kind. Bettyan worked as a background singer for Bobby 'Blue' Bland in the '60s. She loved to cook and invited entertainers to her home, which was New York at that time. Her home was the place you could kick back, eat soul food and have a nice party away from your craft. When I came off the road with James Brown we saw each other for the first time in about seventeen years, for the 1951 flood had split us up.

A few years ago Bettyan retired as a cosmetology teacher. One of her daughters is a pharmaceutical executive in Chicago: she travels far and wide and makes big bucks. The other daughter is a beautician. Bettyan also has a son who's a preacher, another son sadly died.

I remember Bettyan was responsible for putting on a fantastic Thanksgiving Breakfast Dance a few years ago. The late Johnnie Taylor, who was known as 'The Philosopher of Soul' and had a big hit with 'Disco Lady' in the '70s, was top of the bill. I ended up being the opening act for Johnnie, who died the next year. I'd known him as a quartet singer many years before, and had heard him preach his first sermon as an ordained minister as well. He could really preach: the ladies would throw their pocketbooks at him or run up and fall in his arms. Johnnie was a ladies' man. He couldn't help it for he was fine, fine, fine. He was closer in age to my mom than me, and Mama knew his mother and others in his family. Johnnie and his mother are buried in a mausoleum in Kansas City, Missouri, on Meyer and Troost. I have a lot of friends and family in there. I haven't been able to go visit during visiting days because it upsets me.

Going back to the Thanksgiving Breakfast Dance, Eugene Smiley and his band backed me up. Bettyan was so excited about the show, which began at nine o'clock in the morning. She took it upon herself to be the one to fix me up. And she went all the way. She'd bought a big, top of the line car, which was money green. She announced proudly, 'I'm your chauffeur, Marvan.'

For the past fifty years Thanksgiving morning at our church has been a time when people come to party, decked in their finest garb. There's plenty of food and plenty of alcohol too. That particular year it seemed like all of my classmates was there. And God gave us favor. I was gonna get out of the car when we arrived and Bettyan said, 'No, no, you stay right there. You're a star, sis, and we're going to let everyone see a star is arriving.' She parked that green car, opened the door, carried my bags in first, and made it look like Her Royal Highness had arrived. She got me to the dressing room and put up a Marva Whitney sign saying to knock before you entered. That was a day I will not forget. Everyone said we gave Johnnie Taylor a run for his money too.

That's the day I also saw Mr Turner. Bettyan said, 'Daddy, do you know who this is?'

He hadn't seen me for many moons but remembered me and said, 'Yes, it's Marvan.' He was so happy. Then he proceeded to tell me his business. He was in his eighties, had built his own house, which was so beautiful, and raised hogs. Bettyan said that when she was a child after the flood, all the land in the back of the house was full of hogs. There was so many that her daddy didn't know how to get them all to market.

Like me, Bettyan has had hard times, good times and was unlucky in love, or so it seemed. I'm so happy to say that at the time of writing Bettyan has finally been found by a good man. Yes, I believe that if women learn to be pursued we'd fare better. She's now married, and known as the Reverend Mrs Bettyan Turner McConnell.

I also stay in touch with Hal Neely, who used to be an executive at King Records in the '60s and still calls me from time to time. He's about eighty-three years old now. He always says, 'Remember, Marva, the artist always follows the master and you were signed to King Records. You belong to King Records – don't ever forget that. I've got your contract here somewhere.'

I say, 'Mr Neely, won't you send me a copy of my contract?'

He replies, 'Marva, I don't know where it is – all I can tell you is this and don't ever forget it: the artist follows the master.' One time he said, 'Marva, technically these masters we've got you've paid for, and they're yours. But the record companies don't do that. They keep them in their vaults and use them as they may, unless you're somebody big and can raise a lot of hell and can afford to get lawyers, because companies like Universal they got lawyers just sitting there waiting to eat you up. So you don't bother them.' He's like a father. When I try to interrupt him he says, 'Be quiet, Whitney, and let me talk to you.'

Mr Neely took over at King when Syd Nathan died, 'cause they were friends. Mrs Syd Nathan still lives. Mr Neely used to write sleeve notes for James Brown's records, and told me that he'd go in at night into King's Cincinnati studios and remixed all James's songs without James knowing it. He said people never knew that.

I'd also like to mention another good friend, who I consider a mentor. Her name is Pearl Thurston-Brown, and my mother went to junior high school with her. When I got older Mama talked about her and from time to time I saw her on TV. Sometimes she had a band, but mostly she drove all over the US working in white nightclubs and hotels for months at a time. Business-wise she made some good choices. I met her as she was going into retirement in the '90s; before then I saw her picture in the Black Federation Musicians' Union building. She was responsible for helping the union purchase their first piano, a baby grand, which is still in the Federation today. She suffered many prejudices as a black and beautiful lady in those clubs, and some of the stories she's told me would make anyone angry.

When I met her she remarried her first husband, Julius Randolph Brown, who was the first black fire captain of the Kansas City Fire Department: he was assistant chief when he retired in 1988. I still convince Pearl to play occasionally. She's eighty now and as bright as a button. She can play in only one key, F sharp, but this never stopped her earning money and bought her houses, furs and the means to take care of her mother. She's like a queen. I wish I could bring her to London, so they could get a good taste of authentic Kansas City jazz.

I have some good and loyal friends overseas too. Ron Roelofsen from Holland was a fan who became a good friend. He's an avid collector of anything to do with James Brown (he calls himself James Brown Collector #1) and has collected lots of rare film of me on TV. This is what Ron says about how we met:

I've been a James Brown collector since I was twelve. That was thirty-two years ago. I started collecting singles and albums, later specializing in videos. In 1989 (when the boss, James Brown, was in jail) I saw Bobby Byrd and the JB All Stars live in Amsterdam in a venue called Paradiso.

All of the original funky people were there: Martha High, Bobby Byrd, Maceo Parker, Pee Wee Ellis, Fred Wesley, Vicki Anderson, and, of course, Marva Whitney. They played the roof off the building that night. It was a miracle seeing all of these people in one place.

After that tour in Europe everybody went back to do their own thing so it was not until 1998 that I saw Miss Whitney again. She was now part of the 'Kings Queens' tour with Bobby Byrd and again performed at the Paradiso venue in Amsterdam. It was another classic performance.

Marva started touring again in 2004 with the Soulpower all-stars run by a friend of mine, DJ Pari, from Hannover, Germany. In 2005 I checked her and Martha High (touring as The Original Funky Divas) out in Paris, France.

Before the show, I went to the ladies' hotel. Martha, I already knew very well and she introduced us to Marva who welcomed us like we knew her from back in the days. From day one this felt very special and we just clicked. Since then she did a few European tours and recorded a CD with Osaka Monaurail and her career is up again. I feel blessed to say that I am her friend and have shared a lot of thoughts. Marva is always very open and 'tells it like she feels it'. She is what she is.

I've called on Ron for memorabilia I've had stolen or lost during my lifetime: I lent people albums, singles, tour programs and press kits and often they never gave them me back. I stopped lending stuff years ago but my library of memorabilia and mementos of my career is still very lean. Ron has helped me rebuild my collection, and seems to be so happy to do so. He's got material I didn't even know existed. He's been a blessing to me.

CHAPTER 44

Christmas 2006

It's late Christmas Eve 2006. I'm trying to get to sleep but my mind is wide awake. I've been like this for several nights running. I'm restless. I go to bed and lie there churning things over in my mind. I don't know why but there's a lot of fear in me. Although it's the holiday season, I haven't any joyful incentive to go Christmas shopping. For some reason holidays don't mean the same to me as they used to. Maybe it's because my children are grown and gone. Mama, as usual, said, 'I need nothing.' She's really different: she saw a sweater I had on one Sunday and asked if she could have one like it. She was happy with that; it was enough for her. I have such a wonderful, loving and sometimes stern mother. She keeps the family together truly with Father God. I don't know how my family would function without her.

The past keeps flashing through my mind. I think of my father, who we lost about ten years ago. You know, I can't even tell you the year – maybe it was less than ten years. I just blanked it out, I guess. All I know is that he's not here in body and I miss him so much. My mom, thank God, is still alive, but most of the time she's hurting from arthritis.

I'm still wide awake, having thoughts of the past and thinking of Lyn Collins, Shirley Parks, Shirley Kidd and Sharon Hooks. All of my best friends gone.

I'm tossing, turning, saying to myself, *Oh God, I'm so lonely: why did my best girlfriends leave so early and all within the last four years? Lord, I thank you for what you've given me but I'm so lonely. I don't even have a man to date, so I'd rather have peace all by myself – but sometimes the price is high.*

If I'm not on the road you will find me mostly home or at church. And I just can't seem to get my mom to come and spend time with me. She won't leave her house. She considers where I live to be out of town, even though it's in the same county. But still I can be thankful for her gift of playing that Hammond B3 organ and piano. She's still on the one. And I say that not just because she is my mother – the girl is *bad*. She's anointed to the bone. Sometimes I jokingly call her Mattie Moss Clark, one of if not the baddest teachers and musicians in the Church of God in Christ.

I'm grateful my God has kept me these past sixty-eight years, but the truth is I've been so unhappy most of my life. It really started back in 1968, during my first year on the James Brown show. When I joined I was so happy because it was like a dream come true, even though I passed up other offers.

I'm still finding it hard to sleep. I take a hot toddy to help me. It works: I feel I'm almost there, starting to feel drowsy at last. As I'm just dropping off the phone rings. I sleepily fumble for it and pick it up. 'Hello?'

On the other end I hear a woman sobbing. She says 'Marva!' and I hear the distress in her voice. It's Joann Houston, one of the original James Brown dancers. She's frantic, pitiful. I ask her what the matter is. She pulls herself together. 'Marva,' she says, 'I just got a call that James is dead. I know it must be true because they wouldn't play such a cruel joke on me.' Joann had moved to Atlanta and helped James organize his giveaway of Christmas gifts on Friday 22 December. 'He was sick last week,' she continued, 'but he was still adamant about giving turkeys and toys away. The weather was damp and he had his zipper down on his shirt. I said to him, "Zip up your shirt. What's wrong with you? You shouldn't be out here." All James said was, "I just *love* Christmas!"'

As I talked with her on the phone I listened to CNN in the background and heard the news. I could hardly believe my ears, but slowly it began to make sense. In a way I wasn't surprised, for some of us who'd worked with James and kept in touch had a feeling that his time wasn't far off. I don't know why but we did. It was just like him to make a dramatic exit on Christmas Day of all days. There's never much news around at that time so he was able to take center stage again.

As you can imagine, sleep didn't come easily that night. I thought I might hear from someone else when morning came, but I heard nothing – although when I turned on the TV all the news programs were about James Brown.

James's death meant that the media speculated again about his age, with some saying he was older than seventy-three. That doesn't surprise me. Miss Sylvia Medford and me once had a conversation about this. When I was with him in the '60s I possessed two of his ID cards, but over the years they've been misplaced. One of the cards had him born in the early 1920s and the other stated he was born in the late '20s, which would have put him nearer to my mom's age. She's eighty-four, born in 1927. Most artists put their age back, I believe, unless it serves them to put it up and make themselves older.

I thought deeply about what had happened and looked back at my life. Night-time was the worst: I couldn't sleep a wink. I kept turning things over in my mind, and I had to hold back the spirit of both joy and hate, although I'd learned to forgive James for the years he held his foot on my neck and caused me physical sickness. Whenever anything went wrong I'd always felt it was his fault or had something to do with him. Even to the men in my life and my children. Yeah, even my children. As a child Sherrie was teased by other kids that James Brown was her father. She didn't like him, thought he was ugly. I never thought that: he definitely had something sexual in his aura. But my daughter knew nothing of that – she was young and just went on looks.

As I tried to sleep I thought of my time with James. I was only with his revue for two and a half years, but it felt like a lifetime. I didn't ask to be his woman. Hell, every woman on the show was his: you couldn't be married and work on the show. If you had a husband or boyfriend he'd make sure you wasn't together so he could make his advances. Almost every young woman on the show became his concubine. Only Gertrude Sanders, his hatchet woman, didn't.

In front of everyone I was the queen, Soul Sister Number One, but behind the bright lights I was nothing but a mistreated slave. Thinking about the title James gave me – Soul Sister Number One – hell, I more than earned that title, even though I didn't fully understand it because I always felt that Aretha Franklin was number one. She was my idol for a time – until I met her, but that's another story.

All these thoughts about the past went through my mind. James was at the center of them. Maybe he was a kind of security blanket I held on to even though he tormented me. After all, he'd ruled my life and my thoughts for many years after I'd left him. I'd never really been able to get away from him. Not totally. But now he was gone I felt kind of lost. It was a strange, unreal feeling.

CHAPTER 45

The Funeral

As I said before, I wasn't completely surprised by James's death. When I think about it I don't know how he lasted as long as he did, because his schedule was punishing. Although later he didn't dance as much as he did back in the old days, health problems like a heart condition and diabetes took their toll. But that didn't stop him, and right up to the day he passed I think he really was the hardest-working man in show business.

Despite what I suffered at his hands I couldn't rejoice at his death, although to be honest I wasn't that unhappy either, simply because of the pain he'd inflicted on so many people over the years.

I had some interesting phone conversations with Mr Bobbitt after James's death. He told me what happened. James wasn't well at the toy giveaway, and getting soaked by the rain didn't help. He'd had a bad cough that he hadn't been able to shake off, and Mr Bobbitt arranged for a doctor to be at a dentist's appointment James had, to check him out. The doctor listened to his chest and thought he had a serious chest infection. He advised Mr Bobbitt to take James to the hospital, where they diagnosed him with pneumonia and congestive heart failure. Mr Bobbitt slept in the room with James that night and then the next night – he told me he remembered clearly it was 1.20am – James said to him, 'I'm leavin' tonight.' Mr Bobbitt thought James was talking about getting out of hospital and doing a show, and tried to stop him. James was sitting at the end of the bed and lay back, his robe falling open. Mr Bobbitt bent over James to put a blanket over him and heard him sigh very quietly three times. James briefly opened his eyes and then shut them. He didn't open them again. His life just drifted away.

My sleeplessness continued. I can't explain it, but I kept getting a feeling that James was tired of everything and wanted to be with his mom and dad. That might sound crazy to most folks but I kept picking this feeling up, for the people in the Church of God in Christ are often tuned into the spirit world.

At first I was certain that I wanted to go to the funeral, for I really had to see for myself. Then anger and different moods passed by me. I prayed and I talked with my Pastor, Chief Apostle Nathalia Jones, and I talked to my mom and a couple of friends. Joann Houston, who had called me to give me the news of James's death, said I shouldn't even think about missing the funeral. 'Girl, this is your legacy,' she said. But money was tight – as it always is during the Christmas period. It helped a lot when Joann invited me to stay with her. I wondered if I'd get the cold shoulder from James's people. I still fussed, trying to figure if I shouldn't go even as I packed my suitcase.

Mama said, 'If you don't go they'll talk about you like a dog, so go.' I decided to go. *At least they'll know I'm not dead,* I thought.

On the eighteen-hour Greyhound bus ride to Joann's home in Atlanta I couldn't sleep very much. During the trip I heard someone talking wrong about James and I straightened them out. I began to think how only a few days before, James had been in Kansas City, working at one of the casino river boats. He asked Mr Bobbitt to call and asked me to work with him. I think Mr Bobbitt was surprised when I said I didn't want to do it, that I didn't want to perform in Kansas, which I felt didn't respect me and always ignored my achievements. I told him that I appreciated James asking, but my hair and nails wasn't done (and knowing how James trained us in presentation, I thought he'd accept this). Besides, it seemed like the only time I got to work in my own home town was when he came. I said that if James really wanted to do something for me he should invite me to a part of the country where people hadn't seen me for a long time. I'd been to Vietnam, risked my life and dodged bullets for James, and he never helped me when I really needed him to. So I wasn't going to sing with him in Kansas City: no way. Apparently Mr Bobbitt relayed this message to James and he said, 'Marva's crazy!' But my decision must have made James think. Mr Bobbitt told me later that James felt bad about the way he treated me. I get the feeling I played on James's mind a lot in his later years. In an interview he did in Kansas a few years back he acted strange: he didn't answer the questions, and started to repeat my name like he was in some kind of trance.

I got to Atlanta in the early evening; Joann and her manager picked me up. I'd called Mr Bobbitt and told him I was trying to get there. Me and Joann hadn't seen each other in about thirty-four years, and I had a good time with her and her husband. They took me to dinner and were very gracious hosts: they treated me like a queen.

The previous day, Thursday 28 December, James's body had lain in state at the Apollo Theater in Harlem where thousands of fans had queued to pay their last respects. On Friday James's body had come back to Augusta, Georgia, for his funeral. The Baptist church at Carpentersville was a beautiful building, but it wasn't big enough for all the people wishing to attend. A large crowd was gathering outside. You could feel the love of the people; they just wanted to be in the service. Somehow I got split up from Joann, her family and manager, but God had angels waiting for me. I was blessed when I saw my old friends Alan Leeds and Harry Weinger waiting outside the church. Harry said, 'Marva, see that man over there. That's the man they call Super Frank, James's agent.'

I looked over across the street to where Frank Copsidas was standing. In order to keep together and make our way through the large crowd outside the church, Harry, Alan and me were all holding hands. I said, 'Harry, I can't call that man Frank. He's the biggest booking agent in the land.'

Harry said, 'Go on,' and I went. I felt kind of silly, like a bashful schoolgirl, but I introduced myself and he was so happy to meet me: he took me in like family right away.

We all ended up in the line, hand in hand: Alan Leeds, Harry Weinger, a banker friend of theirs, Super Frank and others of James's family. They said to me, 'Marva don't worry, you'll get in.' We pulled to the left and to the right, then Harry got in and tried to pull me behind him.

One of the security people didn't want me to go in. 'This is Marva

Whitney,' shouted Harry, 'you gotta let her in!' – and finally we were all sitting in the last row of the church.

I'll let Harry take up the story:

Marva wouldn't say who she was. I said, 'Marva, call out your name,' and that's when everybody said you got to let her in. Anyway, we get inside, I go to view the body, go round the side to the aisle and Marva and I are in the last seat in the very last row with Alan Leeds. We sit down and everyone's kind of numb. I mean the whole drama of getting in the church combined with the heat inside and all the events of the day was taking its toll. Then there's the media outside and the family and people are wondering what Tomi Rae's going to do and what's going to happen. We'd been outside for two hours so we were glad to sit down. You just want to be respectful.

I felt so sorry for Mr Bobbitt, who was looking worn out and was working so hard to try and get everyone in. He did a hell of a job, but even so, that church couldn't hold all the family and friends. Even James's doctor couldn't get in.

When I entered the church I went straight to the coffin. It was gold with a white lining. I had to try and hold back the tears. James looked peaceful. In my mind I spoke to him. You gave me a break but for so many years you held me back, preying on my fears. I thought you loved me. You did in your own way, maybe, but you couldn't for very long. You sent no food for my table and that's why I didn't want your baby. I knew how you were by then and there was something else I didn't give you, my soul. I never returned after I left so you couldn't brag that you took me back on my knees, the way you wanted me, the way others did. We were both born under the sign of Taurus. I told you I'd submit to your will but not to beatings and slavery. But yes, I loved you and I love you even now. So rest in peace, James. You can come to me in spirit as long as you are gentle. Maybe I can love another now.

Then I moved on. There were still lots of people behind me. Over to Harry again:

While we're sitting at the back Marva starts sobbing. I looked at Alan Leeds and he looked at me and I said, 'We'll switch seats,' and he said yeah, because he's known her longer. So we switched seats and he put his arm around her. Also Marva dropped her purse in the church, flipped it upside down. When she stood up everything just went flying. She was trying to get to somebody and she was nervous and so that was kind of indicative of her state of mind.

I was glad I was with Harry and Alan. The choir took my mind off things: they were awesome. And the Reverend Al Sharpton gave a beautiful sermon. When the choir sang, the Holy Spirit was high and I couldn't hold my place in my seat; before I knew it I jumped up. See, I'm a holy roller, praising God, and I could feel the power of the Holy Spirit that day. I looked around and everyone, Alan Leeds, Harry Weinger and Frank was jumping up and clapping too. I almost laughed, for it is written that the Holy Spirit is like fire shut up in your bones, and here it was moving down the line to these rich, powerful men. It was hot and just like one of James's old shows. No way could you just sit. You had to let the spirit move you.

When the funeral was over, and a few people were left in the sanctuary, Mr Bobbitt came up to me and said that James had requested I should sing at a concert in his honor. I was so shocked by this that I was almost speechless. I didn't even have a change of clothes; I'd have to wear the dress I'd worn at the funeral. I was glad I'd kept my coat on most of the time. Mr Bobbitt said that James wrote how he wanted the show to proceed and who should sing. He said I could only sing a James Brown song. I really couldn't think of anything fitting, but in the end they let me do 'Kansas City', for that's where it started for James and me. Later in the day, when we rehearsed, I discovered that some people – like my good friend Martha High, who'd worked faithfully for James for many years – were not on the show. Her feelings must have been hurt, but that's the way it was; the way that James always worked. Somebody's feelings would always be trampled on.

'The band's over at the James Brown Auditorium,' Mr Bobbitt said. 'Go over there, Marva.' I went, but I waited almost two hours before I did. I started fretting. Joann had to go back to Atlanta and my money was getting short. The hotel would cost a mint, I thought.

So I told Mr Bobbitt my circumstances. He said, 'No problem. I'll get you a room.' He did too.

After rehearsing, I went to the hotel, put in a request for a wake-up call and went to sleep. The concert, billed as 'A Homecoming Celebration for Augusta's Native Son', was set for a 1pm start the next day at the James Brown Arena (with the Reverend Al Sharpton officiating). I wondered who the other entertainers were. I always felt that the concert was put together quickly, which meant some entertainers who'd have liked to have played couldn't, because they had performances booked elsewhere.

The place was packed to capacity, which is about eight thousand, I believe. Family, friends and other VIPs congregated on the main floor in the middle of the arena while the public sat in the stands at the sides. James's open casket lay in front of the stage.

There wasn't enough seats at first, and Danny Ray got pissed 'cause he thought there should have been chairs for us veteran entertainers. He made a fuss and some chairs got put up for us.

First there was a procession to the strains of 'Georgia On My Mind', followed by a viewing of James's body, which was dressed in black rhinestone-studded suit and red shirt and lay in an open casket. The Reverend Jesse Jackson, Al Sharpton and Dick Gregory – all renowned activists for black rights – as well as James's family and friends were among those who filed past the open coffin.

After this there was a video presentation about James's life on a big overhead screen, showing clips of him performing on stage. Then came a musical tribute, where James's band, the Soul Generals, backed up me, Vicki Anderson, James's wife Tomi Rae Hynie and several other singers. Michael Jackson came into the arena to pay his respects as the Soul Generals went on stage. I heard people trying to hold back the screams. You could see the sadness of the occasion in him. I looked deep into his face – as far away as I was – and my heart began to say, *Lord keep him in your care.*

The Soul Generals broke into a stirring version of 'Soul Power'. Vicki Anderson did 'It's A Man's Man's Man's World' and her husband Bobby led a version of 'I Know You Got Soul', with Bootsy Collins playing bass. Tomi Rae did 'Hold On I'm Comin', while Ali Ollie Woodson from The Temptations also performed a song.

It might have seemed strange to some people seeing James's open coffin lying in front of the stage. But it didn't bother me when I came on and sang 'Kansas City'. I looked down and thought, *You just had to be the boss all the way, even in your grave: you didn't even tell me I was gonna be on the bill – nobody knew who was gonna sing. That's just like you – a control freak to the end.*

The Soul Generals were outstanding and I enjoyed the fellowship with them. Everyone did a wonderful job. The band played like it was their last time together and their lives depended on it. Though I'd never played with them before, they made me feel like I wasn't with strangers. They played for me like they played for James, but they were surprised when I sat down at the piano halfway through my song and played a few licks. I can't explain why, but for some reason something told me to go for it and get into the groove. I heard the Lord saying, 'You've been gone a long time, Marva. Let them know I still want you to maintain your craft.'

When the band burst into '(Get Up I Feel Like Being A) Sex Machine', James's long-time MC, Danny Ray, produced a cape that he draped over James's coffin. It was a dramatic moment that brought cheers of recognition from the crowd. At the same time the former rapper – now a preacher – MC Hammer did a dance. The band gestured to Michael Jackson to join them on stage, but he declined. After the music finished several people made speeches about James, and one of these was Michael, who talked about the impact James and his music had had on him; I remember he said James was his greatest inspiration. Michael's hair was long, big dark glasses concealed his face, and he wore a white shirt with a black tie and matching black leather coat. He stood solemnly in between Jesse Jackson and Al Sharpton. Unfortunately I didn't get a chance to meet him. As for Jesse and Al, people around me was saying it was like an old boys' club and this was their last stand. Even so, they acquitted themselves well.

Backstage I heard people saying negative things. James's young wife, Tomi Rae, was there, and while most people gave her the cold shoulder I talked to her real good. I felt sorry for her. She seemed nice, but she began bitching about how she couldn't get into James's house after he died because the lawyers kept her out. She had no money and they were treating her like trailer trash; she said that even James called her trailer trash. I asked her to calm down and trust that fairness would eventually be done. 'You're gonna be OK,' I said. 'As long as you got that baby you're gonna need half his money to take care of him. Just be cool.' But I don't think she took my advice: it went in one ear and out the other. It was said that her marriage to James wasn't legal, and that's why she was shut out when he died. I told her I didn't think she was a soul singer but had more a chance doing something like Janis Joplin or being a country and western singer.

Another thing that was a talking point was the news that Spike Lee was going to make a movie about James. For the sake of me and others that suffered, I just hope they give the full story. James was no saint, but I expect they'll give him the Hollywood treatment and make him look whiter than white. I hope that if the film gets made that Mr Lee has enough sense to let us that are living do a cameo.

The journey back from Augusta was hell. I had to endure eighteen hours on the bus. There's no baggage help any more on the Greyhound – with each transfer you take your own bags – so I was weary and exhausted when I got back to Kansas City.

James's homecoming was featured in *Jet* magazine, of course, but it kind of pissed me off when I saw that there was no picture of me or Vicki. The only singer pictured was Jesse Jackson's daughter, who sang gospel. *Jet* had interviews with Bootsy, Bobby Byrd and a lot of other heavyweights, including Aretha, but there was no mention of JB's original funky divas. I feel very strongly that there should have been a group picture of all the James Brown Show people together. And my home town didn't even give me a mention in the local newspapers after I was on the show. That's Kansas City for you.

A few days after I got back home a rumor circulated that James hadn't actually been buried. Apparently the family was disputing his place of burial, and until that was settled with the lawyers he'd remain above ground.

When I got back from Augusta my mind was in turmoil. After seeing the thousands of fans standing in line to see his body lying in state, I realized how popular James still was. I was worried that his fans would hate me for some of the things I've written here in my memoirs, or think I was cashing in on his death. I talked it over with my pastor, my mom and friends, and they gave me advice I didn't even ask for. Wait, they said, you've been given favor. Don't put that book out just yet, because James put you up there again. He gave you millions of dollars of publicity over his dead body, but he knew exactly what he was doing: stopping any bad press and, most of all, the book. Gain your momentum, and then put out the book. So I put the project on hold, coming to the conclusion that while the contents of this book are true, I had to let the man get cold before it came out. I didn't want to do this, but I felt that if I published I really would be damned. Of course I wish James was alive to read it, so he'd know what I suffered at his hands.

After a lot of heart-searching and consulting my co-writer, Charles Waring, I eventually decided the time was right to finish the book. Most of it was written before James died, but we still had the final part to do, where my story comes up to date. Some people might condemn me for the portrait I paint of James Brown here, but I stand by it. Everything happened like I say, and things went down just the way I've described. In a way, writing this memoir has been a kind of therapy, and I know that airing my deepest feelings will help me to heal some of the psychological scars I've carried all these years: I'm convinced of that. But I'll never be able to erase James from my life. Even though he's gone all those things he did still live in me; I replay them all in my head. I can never truly escape James Brown. He'll always be a part of me. For several months after James's death he came to me in my dreams and talked to me. 'I'm tired of being with all these dead people,' he said.

Now James is dead all kinds of skeletons are coming out of the closet. I had a phone call in the middle of the night just after James died from a young woman who claimed to be his granddaughter. How the devil she got my number I'll never know. She told me her mother was James's daughter and is the spitting image of him. But her grandmother didn't want it known and they kept it a secret for many years. The grandmother recently died and now they want to tell the world. She don't want no money, she said, just wants the recognition that James Brown was her grandfather. There wasn't much I could tell her, just that her best bet was to go to a tabloid publication like the *National Enquirer*. I'm sure there'll be many, many more people coming out of the woodwork claiming James was their father now that he's dead. Everyone wants a piece of the pie.

A strange thing happened a few weeks after James's passing. A friend sent me a link to YouTube, where a short movie called *Beat The Devil* had been posted. It's a film that James starred in a couple of years before in which he sold his soul to the devil. What was scary for me was that when I was on the James Brown show there were some people who believed James had actually done that. It sounds crazy, but I almost believe it too. There was a time in the late '50s when James didn't get a hit for a long time. 'Please Please Please' had done well in '56, but after that he really struggled and his career looked in the balance for several years. It's said that he went somewhere to take part in rituals that would help his career. Apparently he asked Bobby Byrd to go with him, but he refused. Bobby said that when James got back he was howlin' like a wolf. When he sang he always did this high-pitched howling noise, like a blood-curdling scream. It could have been his mantra. You got to remember James was a geechy – a country person from the South; usually a mixture of black American, native American, African and Jamaican. And geechy people go in for rituals. Geechy culture is big in South Carolina (where James was born) and Georgia. And James never went to sleep to my knowledge or anybody's knowledge until the next day came in – so that too might have been part of the ritual. But James knew God too, so may he rest in peace.

CHAPTER 46

James Brown Reunion

I worry about my mother a lot. She turned eighty-four in October 2011. She has a pacemaker and the baddest back trouble you can have. She's in constant pain from back surgery: the surgeon went too far up her back with the knife (at least that's what he told her). She had a fall in early 2007. She was looking into the freezer to try and get something and she just fell down. When she called me I went over and took her to the hospital. They checked her over and she was OK. The next day we took her to her doctor and he said there was a virus going on that made her dizzy. They tried to give her a walker, a Zimmer frame, but she refused to take it outside; she's got a cane she uses. Mom's not as strong as she was but she's a fighter. She's the glue that binds us all together.

Other than that, all my family are doing well. I don't see my children much, though. My son, Ellis Jr, lives in California. He's forty years old now and has three beautiful children and a good wife. He loves music, and writes and produces it. He can stand flatfoot and really sing. He's always been lovable to me.

Me and Sherrie haven't spoken in over three years, and she doesn't speak to my mother, her grandmother, who helped raise her. This is the third time she's done this.

Sherrie found it hard coping with the death of her first son, my first grandson, who died just before he was ten from an incurable disease and heart trouble. He was called Rah'mon, and we used to call him the little drummer boy because he loved the drums and played them for the children's choir. He also loved the Lord and he was well aware he was going to die. There was nothing at all they could do for him, not even give him another heart. I was at his birth and I noticed that he looked a little grey. They kept him to run some tests. When they finished and called Sherrie to the office she went alone, and I stood outside the door. I heard a scream and she shouted, 'This is not my baby, you got it wrong.' My heart sank; there was nothing I could do. All I could do was ask why, Lord, why? Understandably, this tragedy has taken a toll on Sherrie.

Thankfully, her second son, Stanford, is fine. When Rah'mon was alive, though, it used to make us laugh because he kept Stanford on the straight and narrow. Stanford didn't like to go to church but Rah'mon made him get baptized. This was so funny because his grandfather and some of his uncles were preachers and pastored churches. Rah'mon seemed to have a spiritual gift, and amazed us by just accepting that he was going to die any minute, which was a miracle in itself. They say love conquers all and I believe his mother's love mainly kept him alive as long as it did.

A few years later, Sherrie had a girl, Kimberley. At the age of six to eight months Kimberley had a sickness, which has lasted until now. She had a stroke of some kind with high fever. Sherrie has taken care of Kimberley beautifully and put her in the best schools. Sherrie told me that the doctors said she was a $100,000 baby because of the amount of care she needed. She's still in diapers, can't talk and eats through a drip to her stomach. Sherrie takes care of her, but I believe it's taken a toll on her over the years. I've helped as best I could but not to the extent she might have thought I should, perhaps. Kimberley is twenty-four now, but I don't know if she knows she's in the world. For all her ailments the child is strong, and her mother's the only one who can handle her.

Sherrie's forty-eight now. She's a smart girl: she went back to school, became a beautician and runs a daycare center. She lives in a very beautiful home and can really sing, though she's never pursued it as a career. My daughter has always been a Daddy's baby, though: we have a problem because of that. Sadly I've never been her unconditional cup of tea.

On 5 August 2007 I went to Sete, in France, to perform as part of a James Brown Tribute Reunion. We had what I call a real get-down ball. The hospitality was great and we were treated like royalty. The event made me think how great James Brown's legacy was. The band line-up was awesome: Pee Wee Ellis and Fred Wesley with their fantastic musicians set the funk up. Pee Wee has always had a special place in my heart and his better half, Charlotte, has been right there by his side for many years now, making sure everything was in order (for as Marvin Gaye once sang, it takes two). That is why I'm blessed to have DJ Pari by my side, and Drika, his wife, too: they make sure everything is on the one.

I first heard Pee Wee play way back in 1967 during my very first introduction to the James Brown organization. He could tell you what key you were singing in with an instrument nowhere in sight. It used to tickle me when he would tell Mr. Brown, 'No, sir, you said it like this…' as we all tried to keep a straight face. I thought I had heard the best of Pee Wee, but he has gone on to another level, playing funk, jazz and symphony music that comes back to the one in a rolling kind of way.

Back at the concert, the audience went into a state of hysteria, and as I was getting ready for the show off-stage I started dancing to the music. I couldn't help it, it was so addictive. Then my buddy Fred Wesley blew his trombone and sang, and knocked the show out of the park. I'm so glad we're family. The band left the stage smoking and the people stomping for more. I thought the building was coming down. Then came Ms Martha High and she started burning it up all over again. The audience went crazy. It got real serious then and I was glad that Sweet Charles Sherrell's time was next because I began to think deeply and asked myself: *What the heck is there left to do, Soul Sister Number One?* My mind said nothing. Yeah, nothing. I really believed for a moment that there was no way I could follow or top what had gone before. But I looked up to my heavenly Father and said I needed help from above. Well, I got to the stage floor and the crowd started hollering – that was before I'd even sung a note or said a word. I said, 'Thank you, Father, don't leave me.' I was so grateful. For the show's finale, Sweets (as we called Sweet Charles) was in charge. He worked that stage with us all for at least an hour. I got close to Martha, and said that if he didn't stop someone would have to carry me off. I was moving so much to the music that the strap on my shoe came loose. I was worried I'd fall over.

CHAPTER 47

More Heartache

I visited Belgrade, the capital of Serbia, during September 2007 – the first time I'd been there – to perform at a James Brown tribute show that took place in Parliament Square. About 10,000 people – at least that's what they reckoned – turned up. It was awesome. Serbian TV televised the whole show, which featured some of my old James Brown buddies – Martha High, Fred Wesley and Pee Wee Ellis. Bobby Byrd and Vicki Anderson was supposed to attend, but sadly Bobby passed a few days before the show, and at one point it looked like it would have to be canceled as Bobby's funeral was on the same weekend. In the end, though, we decided to go ahead with the concert – we all agreed that's what he would have wanted – and as a tribute to him Martha and I did a version of his song 'I Know You Got Soul'. What made it special was that Fred Wesley played the same solo he put down on the original record. I'm sure Bobby would've approved.

Bobby was seventy-three. It really tripped me out that he and James had gone within a year of each other. What I remember most about Bobby was his smile. It always agreed with his eyes and that told me that he was a good man – which he always proved to us. His home was our home when we came together to rehearse for a show and sometimes we'd stay several days. He was so warm. We'd always have fun; we'd cook and he'd say, 'Oh my, I can't wait till that's ready, it smells so good!' If he wanted something he'd call out, 'Mama,' (that was Vicki Byrd, you know) and she'd be there in a second saying, 'Yeah, Daddy...' When I had my low moments on tour, Bobby could sense it and would encourage me to hold on. He was one-of-a-kind. He was also blessed when it came to songwriting. He co-wrote '(Get Up I Feel Like Being A) Sex Machine' with James Brown and had several hits under his own name, like 'We're In Love' and of course 'I Know You Got Soul'. Bobby seemed to bubble out tunes. We'll miss our second in command – often, though, we thought of him as the leader, for we could talk to him more easily than to James Brown. He was approachable. We didn't have to address him as 'Mister' like we did with James Brown – he was just Bobby, someone you could be a relaxed person with.

So Bobby's gone but he'll never be forgotten. We got ourselves another angel now, for the spirit never dies. Bobby, I know you're enjoying your mansion in the sky, 'cause I know you got soul!

With James, Bobby and so many of my old friends and colleagues gone to glory now, I get nervous sometimes, wondering when my time will be up – but I've asked the Lord to hold back the night on me and allow me to keep going.

There were some good things in 2007, though. One was meeting the young English soul singer, Joss Stone. She sent me the most beautiful bouquet of flowers. It just about knocked me off my feet. I first met Joss over in Japan in July 2007 when I did a tour with Osaka Monaurail. It was only a short tour – just three dates, one in a place called Sendai and two at the Fuji Rock Festival. Joss and me got talking and Pari, my manager, gave her one of my albums. She said she listened to it all night and was so excited she couldn't wait to call Pari to tell him she loved it. We did a concert together – I had a small stage, of course, while she had the big stage – and I watched her show. In her band she had a couple of James Brown's former musicians – sax player Jeff Watkins, and trumpeter Hollie Farris. Both the guys sat in on my show. Then she came here to Kansas City later in 2007. She's starting up a radio show, something like Oprah, but over the airwaves. This is something she's doing on the side. I think I was one of the first people that she interviewed for the show. She says she wants to do a tune with me and I feel very honored, so hopefully we'll get that done one day soon. I just keep praying. God's good in spite of the tears. He's been so good to me in spite of all the disappointments and sadness I've had.

At the end of 2007 I hooked up with Osaka Monaurail again for a short European tour. They did some concerts on their own but I joined them for three gigs – in Dublin, London and Paris. The reaction from the audience was wonderful. There were so many young people there, which always surprised me. I liked touring with my Japanese buddies – Ryo, their leader, is a perfect gentleman, and would look after me like I was a queen. The band was always on the one and sometimes they made me feel that it was 1969 all over again.

In December 2007 I had some more bad news. My favorite aunt, Aunt Margaret, died. She traveled with me when James Brown let me out to do shows on my own. When he tried to boss her about, she once said to him, 'I don't work for you, James, I work for my niece, Marva.' I still laugh when I think about it. I miss her but I have memories that will never leave.

The day after Christmas 2007 I got news that Annetta Washington, the singer known as Cotton Candy, had died from a stroke. She was seventy-six and regarded as the number one blues singer in Kansas City. I went to the funeral with my close friend Toni Sheffield, who I mentioned earlier in the book.

I had been friends with Toni for about twelve years and was really close. Toni was a radio DJ on a local Kansas City station, KKFI, and hosted a late night show on Sundays called *Blues Overnight*. She was helping me organize a forthcoming trip to LA. I'd been asked to do an interview on camera for a documentary about James Brown's televised concert at the Boston Garden in 1968. That was the time when Martin Luther King Jr had just been assassinated and James helped stop a riot. The TV company wasn't going to pay me but they were happy to cover my travel expenses out to the west coast.

As I prepared to go to California I got news that Harry Whitney, my ex-husband and daughter's father, had passed away. Harry's funeral was going to be on a Saturday and two days before, on Thursday night, I had a long phone conversation with Toni Sheffield. We talked excitedly till late about my forthcoming trip to Los Angeles. When I got a call early the next morning, when I was still in bed, I assumed it was Toni again, though she always knew not to call me too early in the day. I was sleepy and just rolled over and ignored it. The phone rang again. I picked it up and said abruptly, 'Toni, this better be important.'

The person, a woman, on the other end said, 'Ms Marva, this is not Toni – she died last night in her sleep.' Still feeling drowsy, I was a little bit annoyed and snapped that Toni should quit playing. But it was no joke. The woman said, 'Ms Marva, this is not Toni and I'm not playing.' I could tell by the anxiety in her voice that she was deadly serious. *Oh my Lord,* I thought, Toni and me had just talked the night before and she was so happy to go be going with me to LA. She was fulfilling her dream by going there. As my assistant she'd worked hard on the schedule all week long, organizing our flights, the hotel and the time of my interview. A few days before we'd been jiving about how everybody was leaving us. I said, well, I'm getting older and I could leave here but one thing about it, I know whichever of us goes first, we got an angel to look over us. I said that not knowing what time it was for her. We were laughing and she was happy. She went to sleep happy. Oh, mercy, this was her dream for many a year. That's what gets me. And she was only about fifty-two. Her husband said that she went into a kind of seizure a month before. She went back to the doctor and he changed the medicine to a new liquid one. It appears that she had a seizure in her sleep. When she passed over he told people that he wanted an autopsy to find out why she died.

Two days after Toni passed, I went to Harry Whitney's funeral. It was at Mt Vernon Missionary Baptist Church, 39th and Prospect, Kansas City, Missouri. The place used to be a movie theater and me and Harry went there on dates before it became a church. He played there for about forty-three years. They called him Doctor Harry Whitney. If they hadn't told me it was him, I wouldn't have known him when I saw him in his open casket. He really suffered. I hooked up with my daughter Sherrie there. I think she was kind of glad to see me. She'd lost so much weight and she looked just like me. There was a time when she looked more like her father, but now we look like twins and that's scary.

The Sunday after the funeral I went to LA to talk about the Boston concert. Betty Ann, my mud pie buddy from the old days, went with me. The interview went well but the fact that Toni wasn't with me dampened my spirits. To tell the truth, after Toni's death I was in a strange place mentally. Some of the things that Toni said are still on my answering service – and I won't take them off. I didn't know what to do without her. I sat thinking and praying. I said, Lord,

I've lost about five or six girlfriends in the last five years or so. I'm in a space that I don't like. To cap it all, our old neighbor from Armourdale, Miss Ressey, passed away. She was ninety-one. It seems a lot of people I've mentioned in this book are checking out. It's creepy at times.

2008 was mostly a quiet year for me career-wise, but in the fall I joined forces again with Osaka Monaurail for another trip to Europe. We played Dublin, Ireland, and did two shows in England – one in Southampton, on the English south coast, and the other at the Jazz Café (which was like a second home to me) in London.

CHAPTER 48

Back In New York

The first half of 2009 was pretty quiet for me but on 26 September I had a gig booked in New York. Wow, I was excited. I hadn't been there since I'd quit the James Brown show forty years previously: that had been at the Apollo just before Christmas in 1969. Pari booked me to do a show at Southpaw in Brooklyn and hooked me up with a group of musicians who went under the name of the Divine Soul Rhythm Band. Their leader was a guy called J.B. Flatt. His name made me laugh because his initials were J.B. For the first time I had white backing singers – a bunch of girls called the Sweet Divines, who had previously sung backgrounds for the singer Sharon Jones. They were on the one and they were sexy. We did a dynamite show and people that saw it said it was 'The Bomb'. I got some great reviews, so I was really pleased. What was even more pleasing was to see my old buddy, Ron Taylor. He was the young boy who'd witnessed James Brown beating on me all those years ago. Ron helped me choose my outfit for the evening because he's great at mixing and matching.

In the fall of 2009 I returned to Europe. Pari, my manager, had booked me a bigger tour than usual. Again I was backed by Osaka Monaurail. We went to London, but for once we didn't play at the Jazz Café – instead Pari had booked me into a famous London venue called the 100 Club. It was jam-packed that night and we did a great show. We then went on to Birmingham, where I'd never been before. There was a small club there called the Yardbird. Charles Waring, my co-author, met me there and ended up picking me up from my hotel in his car and driving me to the venue with Ryo and his assistant. The place was packed, and afterwards lots of young people came to my dressing room to thank me and asked me to sign records for them. Then we moved on to three more English cities – Bristol, Leeds and Manchester – before crossing the English Channel and heading for France. Paris was our first port of call – I always love going there, I get such a warm response – followed by shows in Bordeaux, Marseille and Montpellier.

CHAPTER 49

Going Down Under

All this was quite tiring, though, and I was glad to get back home – but I didn't have much of a rest as I was preparing to go on tour to Australia. Not only that, but I was also trying to get my new apartment together (I've moved closer to my mother). So I'd had a few restless nights because I didn't want to leave the house in disarray and didn't want to return to a mess. I was waking up two or three times a night and praying, as I've found that praying sometimes puts you to sleep.

I was happy to get on the plane headed for Australia, for I hadn't been there since I sang with Paul Robi and his Platters at the end of the 1970s. My manager had booked me seven shows, which would take me right through the Christmas period until the first few days of 2010.

I flew from Kansas City on 21 December to Los Angeles, where I met up with Pari. I was feeling really tired – I don't think I'd fully recovered from my European trip – but didn't say anything to Pari (though I think he could tell I wasn't quite my normal self). It was an incredibly long journey and we had to change planes several times. We traveled for thirty hours and were on planes for twenty-one of them. We eventually flew into Melbourne about noon two days later, on 23 December. I was exhausted – I slept hardly a wink on the long flight – but there was no time for rest as I had to go straight to a local radio station called PBS to do an interview. That was great, but my body was on Central Standard US time. So when I was working and having a ball I should have been asleep, according to my body.

The following day, Christmas Eve, I met up with the musicians who was going to be my backing band on the tour. They called themselves The Transatlantics. I knew nothing about them but they were really hot in rehearsal. They'd certainly done their homework and studied all my records. I was impressed. I learned later that their leader, Ross McHenry, had been rehearsing them for several months. The same night I performed with them at the Corner Hotel – it wasn't a real hotel but a concert venue – in Melbourne. My shows are geared to uplift the heart, for you would be surprised to know how many people suffer a need for a spiritual lift: it's what you say, and you don't have to be in church all the time to receive it. So many married and single folk have said to me, 'You've helped our relationship.'

A group called Deep Street Soul opened for me. I was impressed with their lead singer, Shirley Davis, and later we became friends. I was still feeling tired from all the traveling we had done. When it was time for me to do my part of the show I was worried that I wouldn't be able to get through it. I did the opening number, 'Unwind Yourself', and then asked Pari to bring me a chair so I could sit down. I could see he was surprised and concerned. I explained to the audience that I felt a little jetlagged after thirty-six hours of traveling, but would still give my all and put on a great show for them. I carried on, and luckily only needed to sit down a couple more times during the show. It went down well with the crowd and I ended up signing autographs till one in the morning, which made me even more tired.

Thankfully I had Christmas Day off. Pari and the Transatlantics was going to celebrate it at a local Vietnamese restaurant, but I wasn't that keen to join them. I was too tired and needed some rest. In the end Pari persuaded me to go with them and I'm glad I did – it was an enjoyable time.

It was back to work the next day, Saturday 26 December. It was a late night show – I think I went on stage at midnight – at the Esplanade Hotel in Melbourne. It was well received, as I recall. I always try and give my all even if I'm not feeling 100 per cent.

We had Sunday off, and on Monday the band, Pari and me made a four-hour journey south of Melbourne to a place called Lorne, on the coast. I really enjoyed the ride and looking at the beautiful sandy beaches we saw on our way down. It's a beautiful place, and I'd live there if I could just bring Mama over with me. It's so clean. The water's extra pure and the sea's so blue. I didn't see any raggedy houses or things like that. It may not have been perfect but it looked like it had some class to it. The buildings were beautiful too and the people were so sweet and friendly and polite. I've never been to a place in my life where you can feel calmness like I did there.

I had a rest when we arrived and later, at about 6pm, we all traveled to the mountains just up from the coast where I was due to perform. I was booked to appear at what was called the Falls Festival, which Pari told me was one of Australia's major music festivals. All the performers was appearing on a stage in a big tent. It was a new experience for me. I wasn't expecting to see a tent, and it kind of shocked me a little.

I wasn't feeling myself. I was feeling very cold backstage, sitting in my light stage gown waiting to go on. People expect Australia to be hot all the time, but it wasn't high in the mountains. I'd taken a coat with me, but not a heavy one, as I expected the weather to be warm. Needless to say, it didn't keep me warm. Someone was kind enough to put their coat on me as well, but I was still asking where the heaters were. There wasn't any. I knew I had to get ready to get into it and get involved, like J.B. taught us, but I was still cold as hell. The strange thing is I'd woken up that morning with a funny feeling. I'd said to Pari earlier, 'I don't feel right, I feel nervous.' It's usual to feel a little bit nervous before a show, especially after working with Soul Brother Number One, but not this nervous. *Something isn't right in my spirit,* I thought.

Some men in the crowd had their shirts off and was dancing, but I was still cold to the bone when it was time for me to go on stage. I remember Deep Street Soul came on before me, followed by my backing band, The Transatlantics, at about 8pm, to play some James Brown instrumentals. After they'd done their set I was to join them for my show. When we started the first tune they blew some dry ice onstage to give a smoky effect. Pari told them to turn it off and said, 'We don't use that.' Something else was wrong. The band sounded out of tune and that really upset me. Being a professional, I soldiered on. Still feeling the cold, I thought to myself that I'd have to move about a bit to keep warm.

We got though three songs, and still I was cold and the band's sound was aggravating me. I was singing in one key and the instruments were playing in another. It was so out of tune that my ears hurt. In between songs I kept saying to them they were out of tune, but they couldn't hear it. It wasn't their fault. I said to Pari, 'How in the hell can everybody be out of tune?'

He said, 'Well, what happened was they had so many groups before us that no one got a soundcheck,' – not even my own band, and I was headlining.

The fourth song was 'He's The One'. It was the last tune of my first set – after that the band would go on to play some of their own numbers, to give me a rest. But something strange happened during that song. I felt kind of faint, and when my head started to spin I knew I had to hold onto the microphone stand. As far as I know, I'd never fainted before in my life. I felt myself falling down and told myself to try and stand up. I heard the Lord say in my mind, 'Don't you hit your head, don't you fall down on your head.' I was confused and didn't know what was going on, but Pari got to me just after I fell. This is his recollection of that time:

Marva waited sitting in a chair in the wings complaining that she was cold. By the time I walked her on stage, about 3,000 fans had gathered in front of the stage, with more people arriving. Marva started with 'Unwind Yourself' followed by 'Things Got To Get Better.' I noticed that she struggled a bit with the sound (as often with festivals, there had been no soundcheck, just a linecheck). But by the time she did the third song, 'Your Love Was Good For Me,' she enjoyed the sound and crowd and she did one of the most heartfelt versions of this song ever. I even texted my wife and told her how beautiful it was. She then did 'He's The One', and about halfway through the song I looked into the crowd (I stood in the wings) and saw them go 'Ooooooooohhhh,' many holding their hands over the faces in shock. I looked at Marva and saw her collapse. She went down like a sack of rice. At first I thought she'd tripped over something, but I noticed that she wasn't getting back up. I ran towards her, and tried to pull her up. I couldn't: she was too heavy, and made no attempt to help me. The band had stopped playing at this point, but I told Ross McHenry of The Transatlantics to continue. A security guard came to help me get Marva back on her feet, but she wasn't standing. Shirley of Deep Street Soul was also with us. I noticed that the left side of Marva's face was hanging down, and so were her left arm and leg. She was confused, talking like a drunken sailor, constantly calling out my name, asking for her microphone back. I tried to calm her down, but she wanted to sing. It took us five minutes and three guys to carry her off stage, and then the festival paramedics came. While this was going on, Marva could hear Tara Lynch, the backing singer of the Transatlantics, sing lead on 'Daddy Don't Know About Sugar Bear', and she got extremely aggravated. 'Why is she singing my song? That's my song!' she cried.

They helped me backstage and sat me down. I remember asking Pari where my left shoe had gone because I'd lost it. They cost a lot of money. I didn't realize that I was paralyzed down one side, my left side. When I heard someone else singing 'Daddy Don't Know About Sugar Bear' I became confused and angry, and Pari had a job to calm me down. I was insisting on going back on stage to finish my show. I didn't even realize I was paralyzed. My speech was slurred, but I didn't realize it at the time: I was just talking out of the right side of my mouth. When the ambulance came, I remember saying to Pari, 'Don't let them take me to a hospital where you go in and you never come out again.' I've seen that several times. I said, 'Call my brother.'

Then I started thinking about Lyn Collins and the way she'd died suddenly. Then I saw the face of death a little bit. That's when I started to pray in my mind. I knew because of my faith that my soul was ready, but it dawned on me that I wasn't ready to go. I thought, *Death, take your hands off me.*

Over to Pari again, because my own recollections are hazy:

The paramedics took Marva to the medical tent and measured her blood pressure. It was over 200. By that time we suspected she'd had a stroke, because she had no feeling in her left leg and she couldn't move her left hand. The ambulance arrived minutes later, and the paramedic immediately diagnosed a stroke. She wanted to get a helicopter as the nearest hospital was in Geelong, a city about 200km away. But there was no helicopter available. While all this was going on Marva was very uncooperative. She yelled at the paramedics, physically tried to fight them. She constantly asked for her meds, which were in her hotel room, and she refused to go to the hospital. She was moved into the ambulance, and I got in with her. The ambulance sped at 150kmh to the hospital. During the 90-minute drive Marva constantly babbled, and she threatened me. 'Don't let them do this, Pari', 'Stop them, Pari', 'You're in trouble, Pari', 'I'm gonna kick your ass, Pari'. I told her that if she kicked my ass tomorrow I'd be very happy about the progress she was making. The cussing and yelling continued in the emergency unit at Barwon Health Geelong Hospital. The neurosurgeon on duty was Dr Thomas Kraemer. They moved Marva into the CT scan and found a blood clot in her brain. They told me they'd try to dissolve it with medication, but the problem was that her blood pressure was too high. By that time Shirley Davis and her friend Chantal Mein had arrived. We all tried to calm Marva down, as time was running out. Marva got the drugs and they told me to come back in the morning. It was about 1.30am. We were somewhere between Lorne and Melbourne, no money, no ID, no luggage, nothing. I didn't know if Marva was going to live. I thought she'd at least be paralyzed. If the drugs didn't work they'd have to operate. The situation was really bad.

Pari was on the one. He stuck with me, and I'll always be grateful for that. They said I never lost consciousness and I vaguely remember being put in this room where they was doing every test possible. They gave me lots of shots – even though I am scared of needles, I didn't even holler. That's a biggy for me. I just told the nurses and doctors that I had little veins and would need little needles. I said to them, 'Don't give me no penicillin: I don't want no penicillin.' My father and brother was allergic to it and I didn't want to take no chances in case I was too. Apart from that, I think I was a good patient. I had a headache for a day or so, but they said that was a side-effect of the medicines they were giving me. I guess people were expecting the worst given that I'd had a stroke – but I'm a fighter, and the next day I surprised them all, especially the doctors and nurses. They said they'd never seen anybody get up on the second day after having a stroke. My memory is affected by what happened to me, but I'm told it will get better in time.

They didn't want me to see myself so I must have looked pretty bad. Pari came in to see me and looked at me so pitiful, but I said I was feeling all right. In fact, the paralysis on my left side seemed to have gone. The doctor said, 'How in the devil did you recover so quickly? What did you do?' I said I'd taken my medicine. He said, 'Ma'am, that's what saved you.' I'm a stickler for taking my medicine on time: I've been taking blood pressure tablets since 1980. I'm a stickler because almost everyone in the Manning family has died from high blood pressure, so I don't play with it at all.

I was still feeling weak but they said I was stable. My confusion and fear had mostly gone. I accepted that I'd been seriously ill and had to rest. I told Pari that the band should continue the tour without me, and even suggested that he should go out and do some DJing to make some money. He laughed. I knew he was loyal and would stay and keep an eye on me.

Hour by hour, my condition seemed to improve over the next couple of days. The care I received was first class: the doctors and nurses were very attentive and went above and beyond the call of duty. They never asked if I had health care insurance (even though Pari had taken a policy out for the tour). The hospital food wasn't very good, though: that was my only complaint. Too much mashed potato. The medical care I received made me think of my president, Mr Obama, who's trying to introduce free health care in my home country. To my amazement, nothing was said about medical insurance till I was well and ready to go. They told me not to worry about it; it would be taken care of.

Pari told me he'd put it on Facebook about my illness because there'd been rumors circulating that I'd died. To my surprise he got hundreds of messages from fans and well-wishers, including emails from Fred Wesley, Pee Wee Ellis, Martha High, Clyde Stubblefield, Jabo Starks, Sharon Jones, the entire Daptone family, Bobbi Humphrey, Lady Miss Kier from Dee-Lite, Deep Street Soul, The Bamboos, Speedometer and many others. I had so many wonderful cards and messages from well-wishers and fans. I didn't know so many people thought that much of me, and that made me cry. I was so surprised. My fans are all different ages – from teenagers to people in their forties and fifties – which is unusual. I'm blessed. I want to thank all my fans, friends and family for the cards: I'll never forget the love and the flowers and cards. My Master hasn't told me to stop but I'll rest for a while. Thankfully there have been no after-effects from the stroke.

On the Thursday I was told I could leave hospital. That was great news, but we was short of money and had no place to stay. The tour was supposed to last until 11 January and I'd been booked for shows in Perth, Adelaide, Byron Bay and Sydney. The promoter had lost a lot of money because of my illness and wasn't able to help us. We couldn't even get money from the Falls Festival, because I'd only done half my show. Mercifully we had some newly made friends who helped. Shirley Davis had a friend called Chantal who offered me the guest room at her flat (it wasn't far from Shirley's place, where Pari was staying). They were my angels. They wanted to make me feel like I was at home and their hospitality was awesome. The two ladies were sweet and really classy, and you could tell that they had raised their children very well.

After picking me up from the hospital – and I want thank all the Geelong staff for taking care of me, especially a nurse called Marg – Shirley took me to the beach. 'She just needs to feel the breeze, look at the waves and sun, and life will come back,' she said to Pari. She was right. I started to feel my old self again. We had ice cream and I had a great time. While I was enjoying myself, Pari was trying to sort out our travel arrangements to go home. It was a headache for him. The chance of an earlier flight back to the States looked bleak, because almost all the seats was taken. We also found out that even if a flight was available it would cost us about $2,500 to exchange our tickets and get home. When Pari told me this I was sick to my stomach. I knew I couldn't find that much money, being on Social Security. So I got devilish. I thought, *I'm going to see who my friends really are.* Pari called one and he said, 'I don't have the money.' I could understand that. So I called another, Ryo – the leader of Osaka Monaurail – and he said he didn't have that kind of money either. But he said that every day I had to stay in a hotel I could charge to his credit card. You find out who your friends really are when you're down on your butt.

At first we was talking about leaving on 11 January. I told them that there was no way that I could stay there until then. If I wasn't working, it would be very boring. I was ready to go home because I didn't have nothing to do. I didn't want to sit around and wait. I said to Pari, 'I guess I'm going to have to do what I've already made my mind up to do – call my mother.' I didn't really want to do it – it was a last resort because I thought I'd catch hell from her. But I thought I had to tell her what had happened and be prepared for the worst. I told my brother Gee Gee, 'Don't you tell Mama nothing.' I told Pari, 'Don't you all laugh if you see me crying, 'cause she'll get on my ass and I don't want to hear it.' But you know what? Mama was sweet as cake. She was so nice.

She said, 'Yeah, baby, you come on home. What do you need? Don't get upset. You're gonna be all right. OK, well tell me how to do it and I'll send the money.' I passed the phone over to Pari for him to explain. I was so surprised. I thought she was going to give me a good telling off – but I've always had support from my family, from my mother and my father, if I've ever got in trouble. One thing they knew about their children was that we never came to them unless we couldn't get help anywhere else. If something is important and we have to have it then they've never said no.

While we waited to get a new flight Shirley took me and Pari to Melbourne Zoo. I loved it, seeing all the animals. I felt well enough to do a radio interview and went back to PBS, where I talked about what happened at the festival, and made sure I thanked all the folks who helped me and made me feel welcome in Australia.

On New Year's Day 2010 Pari – with Mama's money – changed our flights, and we left Australia on 3 January. Shirley took us to the airport. I was glad to leave after what happened, but I'd like to go back there one day when my strength has returned. It's a beautiful place with beautiful people.

I received more good news when I got home. Pari had started talking to the New York record company Daptone (home to the singer Sharon Jones and her band the Dap-Kings) and they seemed keen for me to record for them. So although 2010 had started off badly, it looked like the year was going to get much better.

Or that's what I thought. To tell you the truth, health-wise I've never been quite right after my stroke. Of course I'm no spring chicken, but I still have a lot of life left in me. The doctor told me that when you have a stroke of any kind – whether small or large – it can take up to about three years for you to know that you're completely out of the woods. In the summer of 2010 my breathing started to become labored. I thought it was my sinuses and I went into my doctor's office. When I got there I felt weak. I was barely in the door before my legs started to give way. I just made it to a chair in the lobby, where I gasped for air. I called the nurse and they took the oxygen level in my blood. It was low. When I got my breath back they walked me around the office. I was scared. Really scared. I thought I was going to fall over and faint. When my doctor sent me home he put an oxygen tank in my room. I was on two liters, which is very low, and that worked for a while: I'd inhale it when I was short of breath. They diagnosed me with pulmonary hypertension, a heart condition where high blood pressure in the pulmonary artery causes dizziness and shortness of breath.

Not long after that I got so weak when I was at home that I had to call 911. That happened about two or three times and they patched me up, but I don't believe they were very thorough. After about the third time my daughter Sherrie and my cousin came over to the house as they knew I wasn't feeling well. I got up from the bed to go to the bathroom and down I went on the floor. Thank God they were there: they called the ambulance for me. My spirit told me not to go back to the same hospital but to go out to KU instead, Kansas University Hospital. So I went to KU, which is a school of doctors in every field of medicine. When they got me there they put me into an intensive care unit. I'd contracted pneumonia and ended up staying there for several months. My family, and my daughter in particular, were very attentive, but it was a frustrating time.

They let me out on 24 December. I was glad to be out of hospital but I couldn't be left alone: my daughter came to look after me. Although it was Christmas I didn't feel in a festive mood: my mind was on other things. I'd got a concert scheduled in New York City at the Bell House in Brooklyn for New Year's Eve. I didn't tell my doctors. Pari had arranged me a flight with Delta Airlines to New York. My brother Gee Gee took me there and I carried two small oxygen canisters with me, one in my suitcase and the other on my person, intending to take it with me on the plane. At the check-in desk I showed them my permission slip from my doctor, which said I should always be allowed to use my oxygen and take my oxygen tank with me. When the woman at the check-in desk read this, she said she wouldn't let me on the flight.

I said, 'But my doctors insist I have to have it.'

'We stopped that two years ago,' she said. 'We can't let you on with it.'

I got angry. I guess I used a few choice words because of my frustration. They wasn't aimed at her, but it was how I felt about the situation. What angered her, I think, was when I said, 'I guess I'm going to have to call Channel 9, the TV people, and get them out here.' What did I say that for? She immediately called the police and the security on me and got me taken out of there. I caused quite a scene and was upset by all the commotion. They escorted me away from the desk and I sat down. I decided to call my brother; I thought he might still be in the airport somewhere and could easily double back and collect the canisters. He came back, took them away and I thought everything would be fine. So then I went back to the Delta check-in desk and told them the oxygen had gone so could I get on the flight. They were adamant I couldn't go. There was another commotion and the police came again. I was angry and frustrated. The police was very calm and nice and told me that if I went back up to the desk I would be arrested. I'd been banned from flying with Delta.

I sat down in the airport and considered my situation. I decided to call Pari, and also Richard Lewis, the promoter of the Dig Deeper soul night in Brooklyn that had booked me there the year before. It was a big problem finding a flight at short notice, because it was the week after the biggest snow storms the city had seen in the past 100 years. Thousands of passengers was stranded across the US waiting on available flights, and bus or train travel wasn't an option to get me to New York on time. But Pari and Richard got on their phones, and within two hours managed to book me on the only available seat on the only flight left for New York that weekend. When I walked up to Frontier's check-in desk I was apprehensive. I didn't dare open up my mouth, and didn't mention about needing oxygen. I just went on through the gate. So when I got on the plane I opened the overhead vents to the max. Just a little extra air improved my breathing.

When I eventually got to New York – around midnight – I discovered that my old friend Ron Taylor, who'd been working at a hospital since he left James Brown's employment, had put two oxygen tanks in my hotel room. Bless his heart: he was always good at taking care of me.

The Lord fixed it that we didn't even have a rehearsal before the show. I'd worked with the band (the Divine Soul Rhythm Band) and the background singers before, the last time I was in New York City, so they knew my stuff. Pari always made sure that the music was right and everyone knew what they were doing. I could see that he was worried about me. He knew I'd been ill, but I don't think he realized what bad shape I was in. I couldn't walk from the cab to the dressing room without having to sit down after walking ten steps. I told him I'd have to do the show sitting down, something I'd never done before. I was a little apprehensive about it, but it was the only way I could do the show. And if Solomon Burke could do it, I could do it. I got exhausted standing for just a few seconds. Pari, Ron and I put our heads together about finding a suitable chair for me. Ron started looking in some things that were stacked up behind the stage, and lo and behold there was a chair. It looked like a golden throne, so Pari played on the idea of me being the Queen of Soul.

I was able to walk onto the stage, but then sat down. We had a ball. In my set I performed a duet of James Brown's 'It's A Man's Man's Man's World' with Billy Prince from a group called the Precisions (Pari told me they had a big Northern Soul hit with 'If This Is Love' on Drew Records). I was also impressed with a young white singer Eli 'Paperboy' Reed, who opened my show. As for me, I was in good spirits. The Lord favored me – my voice didn't seem affected by my breathing problems. The place was packed and the crowd was really appreciative. I was very happy. It was a great show.

The next day I had to get straight back to Kansas City. I guess I was about an hour into the two-hour flight when my breathing deteriorated. I walked up to the front and told the hostess I had a problem breathing. She sat me in a chair, and they opened up a closet and out came oxygen. Thank God. They kept me on this until I reached Kansas City, where they had a wheelchair for me. But a couple of days later – on 3 January 2011 – the same things started happening again, and I had to go back into ICU. I told my doctors that I went to New York City to do a show. They said, 'You did what?' They've since become fans of mine. The word got around, and God gave me favor with all of the doctors.

From that point until the middle of April 2011 I stayed in hospital. When I came out my daughter Sherrie cared for me and attended to my needs. She's been a Godsend and, thankfully, some of the issues we've had over the years have been put aside. After all, blood's thicker than water. I've been put on steroids, and my face is swollen and I have a double chin. I laugh about it but I hate the shape that I'm in. My kidneys ain't working at the level they should be but I'm able to function. I'm still working on getting better. I have therapy which consists of exercises to help me breathe properly. The doctors are satisfied with my progress. They say I look well. And don't forget, I'm a fighter. Just like my mother. She's a fighter too. We never give up. Not ever.

CHAPTER 50

Final Thoughts

James Brown's death was the end of an era. But everything changes. Take Kansas City – it's almost unrecognizable from the city of my youth. I still live there today but the town of my younger days has gone. Almost everything has changed. White people and other races now own 18th Street, which was once a thriving line of bars and clubs owned and run by blacks. It's empty early and the white folk here act like they invented jazz – they also get the best jobs and the most pay. Hell, they've just taken over, so we black folk don't bother to pack it out anymore.

We still have the Black Federation, where we can hang out, where Charlie 'Bird' Parker, the late Jay 'Hootie' McShann – who died while I was writing this book – Pearl Thurston and many others used to gather. That's the place where I studied under Willie Rice. The Blue Room, a jazz club that later became a museum, has been moved from the corner where it originally stood to a spot next door. All the other old clubs have been torn down. Some of us here thought this would be our New Orleans Basin Street, but to me it just don't come close – blacks don't like it, and they have little spirit for 18th Street and Vine. The big hotel on 19th where Paul Robeson and blues singers from way back used to go was vacant when I last passed it. When I was in my teens it was the YMCA. I hope they renovate it, for it was the only place blacks – called Negros at the time – could stay.

Looking back at my career, I'm amazed how things have turned out. Sometimes I feel I'm living in a twilight dream world. It's difficult to believe that my career is really taking off again after all these years. Never in my wildest dreams did I think that my music would last like it has. I'm not a fan of rap or hip-hop, but the fact that they've sampled my records has given my old songs like 'It's My Thing' and 'Unwind Yourself' a new lease of life and helped revive my career. It's also given me a great sense of joy to know that young people love my music. Even so, I'm still struggling to make ends meet here in Kansas City – and I'm still owed a lot of royalties from way back that were sent to James Brown instead of me: I wasn't paid my residuals even though I was signed up with King as a solo artist. I started to get royalties coming though in 1988 when Universal took over the King catalogue, but over the years I've lost a lot of money and it's probably too late to put a claim in. Because of that situation I'm struggling for pennies, and have been on Assisted Living for a few years now.

Although my career has gotten a second wind, I'm not looking to be in a race with the youngsters. I remember watching the Grammy Awards recently on TV, and I'm so happy that I don't have to be in that rat race. Oh God, them girls have got to starve themselves to the point where they're so bony; and people are looking at them like they're things or objects instead of artists. I thank God that for some of us it don't matter no more. That I survived in some kind of way with my right mind is a blessing. If I can just work a little bit now and then and somebody gives me a little TLC I'll be fine. If I could be like anyone it would be a singer in the mold of Diana Ross or Gladys Knight. From their past merits those ladies are able to make a respectable living, and that's all I want. I don't have to work every week: I don't think I have the stamina for that anymore, and I also need my freedom and the opportunity not to be locked in a box. I have to keep my options open. If anybody had me lock, stock and barrel – like James Brown once had – I think I'd go out of my mind.

Today I remain a lady who's been through hard times and wants to survive. Miss Tina Turner is an inspiration to me. I take my hat off to her. She shows all of us if we hold on – for she went through the same thing as me, suffering abuse – that good things can happen. That's why me and Lyn Collins just believed that if we held onto our dream we'd see the light and it would come true.

As little as it may seem to some people, because I didn't really make it into the big time, I was blessed to go as far as I did. I was always taught by my family that humble is the way, and I want to stay humble because as long as a person stays humble then the Master can use you. I'm a common person and just like everybody else: I eat, I sleep, I go to the bathroom and I'm going to die. But God anointed me, and my task in life was to sing. Other than that, I'm no better than nobody else. My family always believed that your gift will make room for you, and if you do the right thing within your heart then something good is going to happen. I still believe that.

And that's what is happening right now. I believe that, I really do. I also believe that Ms Lady, Lyn and my other friends gone on to glory know of my struggles from the heavens. Before they went to glory the system seemed to be against me. I feel they've tried to make things right for me up there, and that's why my career is picking up again.

I've always wanted to do a one-woman show where you use songs to tell a story, like a musical. Me and Martha High have talked about that because we have plays here in Kansas City and, boy, they're very good. I imagined we could have a stage set using coffee tables and chairs like we're in the front room, and we get up and sing songs and things. That's something I'd like to do in the future.

I'm happy that my God has put me in a position where there's a roof over my head and food to eat. What more do I want? God has blessed me to live in a pretty decent neighborhood. My children are grown and I don't want to go through the hustle and bustle of the showbiz life anymore – but I do miss my audience, my fans. A few gigs here and there is fine. I'm glad that I don't have to do what I did with James Brown and go on the road and sing night after night. We were lucky if we got three weeks off in a year. James was a workaholic, so everyone who worked for him had to be as well. I can go at my own pace now, and I can pick and choose. Some places offer me gigs, and they think that because I haven't had a hit in forty years I'll take anything; but I'm not prepared to sell myself cheaply. I sometimes ask myself if I should keep going now I'm over sixty. Does the end justify the means? Do I really want to put myself into the rat race just to get a little further up the ladder? I just have to trust God to lead me and guide me, and whatever He wants me to have that's what I'll have. As long as you do the positive thing that's right for you it'll bring you closer to your maker, because He's the one who keeps you sane. You know, people are looking for other things and I just want to throw out a word of encouragement to people who've been working on things for a long time. Sometimes, as I've found out, your last years are your best years.

My gift has helped me to see the world. I've been all over the place: to Europe, Africa and the Far East. There are still lots of places I'd love to go, like Spain. It's a sad fact – and I hate to say it – but my home country, the United States of America, has not been good to me. People in places like Europe and Japan treat me with love and respect. Over here in the United States, though, they couldn't care less. America isn't interested in nostalgia and the past; all Americans are concerned with is the here and now. They rarely look back. Because of that, they're ignorant of their country's great musical heritage. I find it both strange and sad that I'm treated better overseas than I am in my mother country.

I want to thank Mr Brown for all the hits that he gave us. I've learned to forgive, but forget, no, I can't do that. What I suffered was a lesson for me. Whatever comes before me now I'll hopefully understand better and know how to handle. And I want to thank God for bringing me back into the light because I've been through hell and high water. I want to follow my course and finish this dream that Lyn, Martha and me started a couple of years ago. I don't want this dream to stop. Not ever. I'm still walking down the Yellow Brick Road.

Afterword

It is with a feeling of profound sadness that I write this addendum to Marva Whitney's life story. I learned of her passing on Friday 22nd December 2012 via Facebook and it shocked me to the core.

I knew that Marva had been ill – in fact, she was never the same after the stroke she experienced in Australia three years earlier – but I had spoken with her on the phone in November 2012 and had enjoyed a good conversation. Although, through illness, her voice was reduced to a breathless hoarse rasp she still seemed like the Marva of old – warm, full of life and passionate in the expression of her opinions. Perhaps as if sensing her time was near, she was also growing increasingly frustrated with the delay to her autobiography, a pet project that she regarded as the fulfilment of a long-treasured dream.

As it transpired, she never lived to hold this book in her hands – a fact that burdens me with an inconsolable sadness. But knowing Marva as I did and given her unshakable belief in life after death – in a place, she once told me, where she hoped to meet up with departed family members, dear friends, music biz colleagues and even a certain Mr Brown – it's possible to find a small degree of solace. She was not afraid of death and viewed it as a necessary and natural stage of our existence that led to a new life for the human soul in a world beyond this one.

Even though Marva's not here anymore her music still is: vintage raw funk grooves and bittersweet soul serenades that are still in demand with connoisseurs and collectors all over the world. Those records together with this book – the main text of which has not been revised or altered since her passing – will ensure that the memory of Marva Whitney cannot be easily forgotten.

Charles Waring
Evesham,
February, 2013

Marva's Acknowledgements

This is my first book and it's a dream come true. There are so many special people that my Heavenly Father ordained to help me put it together and rally behind me. Firstly I want to thank my God, which art in heaven. I'd also like to thank Mom and Dad (Mr and Mrs Ray Manning) and my whole family (the Mannings and the Collinses).

Other people helped along the way to make me realize my dream: my fellow funky divas Lyn Collins and Martha High; my manager, Markus Schmidt (aka DJ Pari) of Soulpower Management and his wife, Drika. I want to thank Charles Waring for hearing the call, and Ron Roelofsen for preserving my video archives; also the Godfather of Soul, Mr James Brown, who will forever be Soul Brother Number One.

I'd also like to extend my gratitude to: King and Polygram Records; Mr Laurence and Malcolm Prangell at Soul Brother Records; the Jazz Café in London, England for inviting me to open up my first solo show since 1969; Ace Records; Baba (Soulpower); Harry Weinger, Alan Leeds and Cliff White; my Kansas City comrades Toni Sheffield, Eugene Smiley, Dwayne Gilley and Donald Cox as well as all my Kansas City musician brothers in the Kansas City Musicians Union (including my mentor, Ms Pearl Thurston); my pastor, Chief Apostle Nathalia A. Jones; Hal Neely (of King Records) and Ms Jeanne Bennett of Personality Productions; my friends Shirley Parks, Shirley Kidd and Bettyan Turner McConnell; Tommy Gadson and The Derbys; Marvin Augustus; Mr Clarence Cooper; Charles Spurling, Pee Wee Ellis, Fred Wesley, and Bootsy Collins; Ron Taylor; Toby Walker; also my physician, Dr Vinaya Koduri.

Thanks, too, to the DJs, magazines and especially all my fans who've supported me and kept faith in me all these years.

Marva Whitney
July, 2012

Charles's Acknowledgements

First of all, I'd like to thank Marva Whitney for giving me the opportunity of a lifetime. I never thought a dusty old 45 I bought back in 1988 would lead to our eventual friendship and this book collaboration. Thanks also to the invaluable contributions from DJ Pari, Pee Wee Ellis, Fred Wesley, Bootsy Collins, Charles Spurling, Alan Leeds, and Harry Weinger.

I'd also like to say a big thank you to my wife, Kate, and stepchildren Holly and Kurtis; and my parents, Michael and Ceretha Ann Waring, for all their love and support over the years; my brothers Jeremy and Marcus Waring; and especially my maternal grandmother, Ceretha Randle, who was instrumental in nurturing my passion for music.

Charles Waring
January, 2020

Marva Whitney Discography

45rpm Singles:

'Your Love Was Good To Me'/'Saving My Love For My Baby' Federal F12545, 1967.

'If You Love Me'/'Your Love Was Good For Me' King K6124 1967

'Unwind Yourself'/'If You Love Me' King K6146, 1968.

'Your Love Was Good For Me'/'What Kind Of Man' King 6158, 1968.

'Things Got To Get Better (Get Together)'/'What Kind Of Man' King K6168, 1968.

'I'll Work It Out'/'All My Love Belongs To You' King 6181, 1968.

'I'm Tired, I'm Tired, I'm Tired'/'If You Love Me' King 6193, 1968.

'What Do I Have To Do To Prove My Love To You'/'Your Love Was Good For Me' King K6202, 1968.

'Tit For Tat (Ain't No Taking Back)'/'In The Middle' (Part 2) King K6206, 1968.

'You've Got To Have A Job' (w/James Brown)/'I'm Tired, I'm Tired, I'm Tired' King K6218, 1969.

'It's My Thing'/'Ball Of Fire' King K6229, 1969.

'Things Got To Get Better (Get Together)'/'Get Out Of My Life' King K6249, 1969.

'I Made A Mistake Because It's Only You' Part 1/'I Made A Mistake Because It's Only You' Part 2 King K6268, 1969.

'This Girl's In Love With You'/'He's The One' King K6283, 1970.

'Just Won't Do Right'/'I'll Work It Out' King 6327 Unissued, 1970 (test pressing only).

'This Is My Quest'/'Giving Up On Love' T-Neck TN922, 1970.

'Daddy Don't Know About Sugar Bear'/'We Need More (But Somebody Gotta Sacrifice)' Excello 2321 (also released as Forte 1114), 1972.

'Live And Let Live'/'Don't Let Our Love Fade Away' Excello 2328, 1972.

'Unwind Yourself' and 'It's My Thing' on 12-inch UK-only single (Vicki Anderson's 'Super Bad' and 'Message From The Soul Sisters' on the B-side) Urban BX35, 1988.

'I Am What I Am' (Part 1)/'I Am What I Am' (Part 2) Monaurail & Empowerment OBV-025-A, 2006.

'Soulsisters (Of The World Unite)'/'It's Her Thing' Shout 1001, 2006.

Reissue of 'Unwind Yourself' and 'It's My Thing' on 12-inch UK-only single (Vicki Anderson's 'Super Bad' and 'Message From The Soul Sisters' on the B-side) Urban 9838894, 2007.

As Marva Whitney-Taylor:

'(Hey You & You & You) I've Lived The Life'/'Nothing I'd Rather Be (Than Your Weakness)' Forte 1115, 1974.

As Marva and Melvin:

'All Alone I've Loved You'/'(Get Ready For) The Changes' Forte 1117, 1974.

As MWT Express feat. Marva Taylor:

'I've Lived The Life'/'Nothing I'd Rather Be (Than Your Weakness)' Forte 6045, 1974.

ALBUMS:

I Sing Soul With James Brown (unreleased album) King K1053 1969
It's My Thing King K1062,1969.
Live And Lowdown At The Apollo King K1079, 1969.
I Am What I Am (with Osaka Monaurail) Soul Power/Shout-201, 2006 (Released in the UK by Freestyle Records FSRCD025 2007).
Live in Japan (with Osaka Monaurail) Soul Power/Shout-202, 2006.

JAMES BROWN ALBUMS FEATURING MARVA WHITNEY:

James Brown Presents His Show Of Tomorrow, King K1024, 1968.
Two tracks by Marva featured: 'If You Love Me' and 'What Kind Of Man'.

Live At The Apollo Volume II, King K1022, 1968
Deluxe Edition Polydor/Universal CD 314 549 884-2 2001
Marva features on 'Think', a duet with James Brown.

Gettin' Down To It, King 1051, 1969.
Marva features on 'Sunny', a duet with James Brown.

Duets, Polydor CD 841 516-2, 1989
'Think' and 'You've Got To Have A Job (If You Don't Work You Can't Eat)'

Say It Live And Loud – Live In Dallas 08.26.68,
Polydor/Universal CD 314 557 668-2, 1998
Marva sings backing vocals on 'Try Me'.

James Brown - The Singles Vol. 5: 1967-1969,
Hip-O Select, B0010411-02, 2008
'You Got To Have A Job (If You Don't Work You Can't Eat)'

Live At Home With His Bad Self The After Show
Universal Republic LP B0030985-01, 2019
Marva sings 'Respect' and 'You Got To Have A Job'

Cutting from Jet showing me playing the piano aged five with the triplets

Manning Gospel Singers 1950s - that's me at the back

A PR photo from the late 1960s

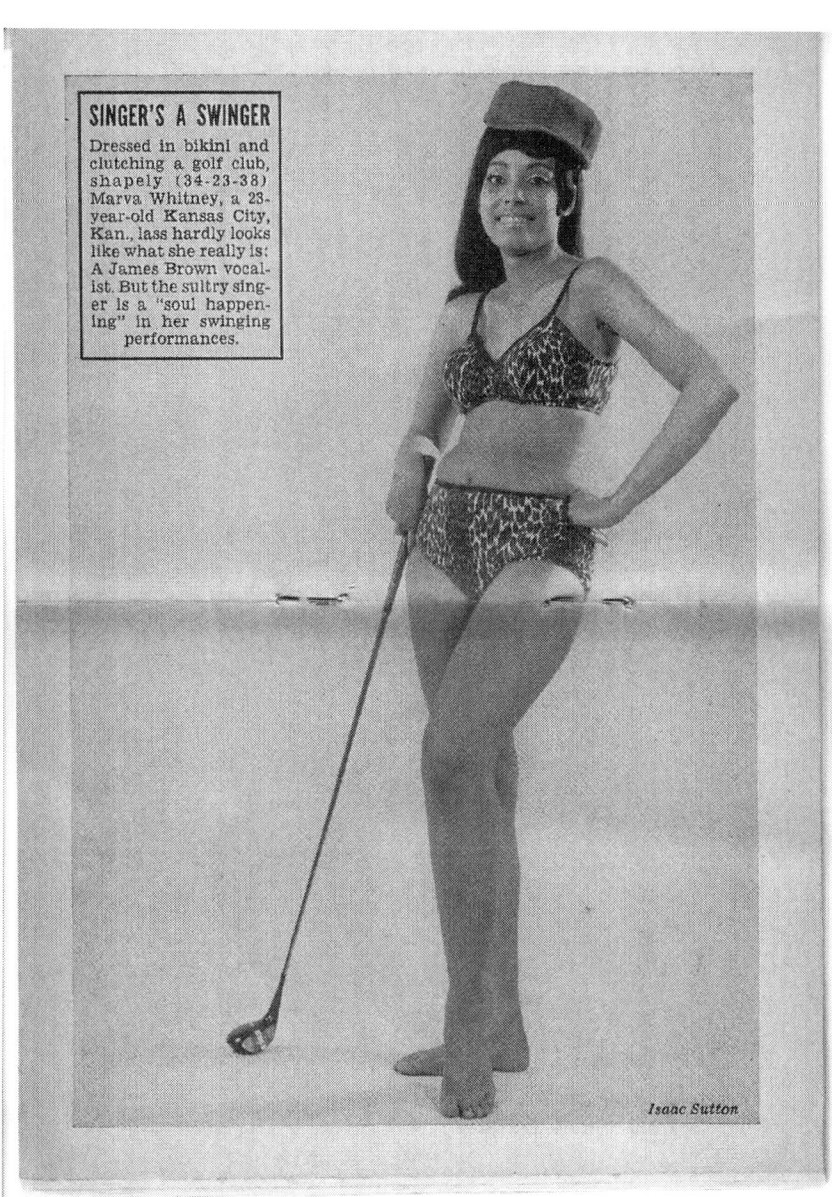

Isaac Sutton

My Jet magazine Centrefold in March, 1968

Me with short hair in the late 60s

In the late 60s

Marva poster

Me with TV show host Dick Clark

Me on stage 60s

Me on stage in the late 60s

On the cover of Jet magazine August 1969

On the cover of The Scene magazine, 1969

Me in concert during the late 60s

With JB in a magazine advert

Me on the Joey Bishop Show

With James Brown and the Dee Felice group on TV 1969

Dave Green

▶ Newest Discovery: Making her debut at Harlem's Apollo Theatre singing *Your Love Was Good For Me*, Marvelous Marva gets vocal assist from James Brown, who discovered her singing talents in Kansas City. The newest "Soul Sister" will tour with "Soul Brother Number 1."

Magazine cutting - me and JB on stage

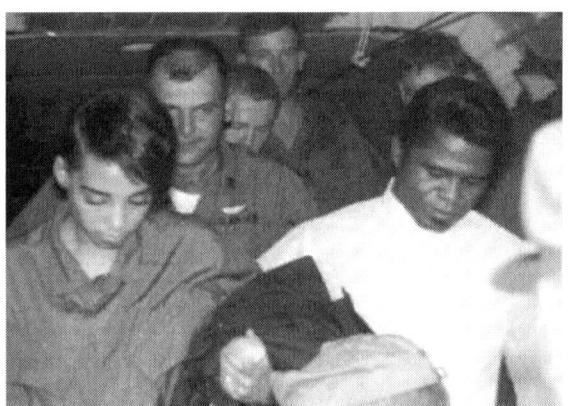

With James Brown in Vietnam 1968

Department of Defense

United States Military Assistance Command, Vietnam

Certificate of Appreciation

is awarded to

MARVA ANN WHITNEY

FOR YOUR OUTSTANDING CONTRIBUTION TO THE MORALE AND WELFARE OF THE
UNITED STATES AND OTHER FREE WORLD MILITARY ASSISTANCE FORCES IN
THE REPUBLIC OF VIETNAM WHILE TOURING THE COMMAND, ENTERTAINING
PERSONNEL OF ALL SERVICES. THE SIGNIFICANT AND LASTING IMPRESSION
YOU MADE ENHANCED THE MORALE OF THE FIGHTING FORCES AND REFLECTS
GREAT CREDIT UPON YOURSELF AND YOUR PROFESSION.

SAIGON, VIETNAM

Date 15 June 1968

CREIGHTON W. ABRAMS
General, United States Army
Commanding

The certificate I got for going to Vietnam

Me with the Warren Durrett Orchestra early 70s

On stage with Paul Robi's Platters Japan 79

MARVA WHITNEY

Marva PR photo 1980s

The Alma Whitney singers 1987

My mother, 1981

Mom and Pop - Ray and Willa Manning in the early 70s

My brother, Marvin Manning

Marvin's twin, Melvin Manning

Our youngest brother, Winfred Manning

Me withThe Platters

Marva Whitney

A 90s promo pic

The Funky Divas looking like they mean business 1998

Coffee, Cream & Sugar

Coffee, Cream & Sugar

Pictured with James Brown 1994

With Pico Payne

Looking cool in NYC 98

Me on stage 2000s

Live in Japan

Live on stage 2005

Pictured with Osaka Monaurail and my manager DJ Pari (squatting, front right)

On stage with Osaka Monaurail

Backstage at London's Jazz Cafe 2005

In 2006

With some fans in Japan 2006 (DJ Pari on far right)

ABOUT THE AUTHORS

Marva Whitney:

Hailed as 'The First Lady of Funk,' Marva Whitney (1944-2012) was a Kansas City-born American R&B singer who began her music career in her family gospel group as a child. She later rose to fame in the late 1960s as part of soul music icon James Brown's famous touring revue. She released nineteen singles (scoring three US R&B hits in 1969) and two albums during a career that saw her appear on US TV many times and perform all over the world. Her travels even took her to war-torn Vietnam in 1968 when she performed with James Brown in front of American troops. After her acrimonious departure from the James Brown show in 1970, she was unable to emulate her earlier achievements and spent the next thirty years struggling to make a living. Her solo career blossomed again in 2006 when she recorded what became her final studio album, *'I Am What I Am.'* Though triumphant, her comeback proved short-lived and after several spells of illness, she died in 2012 at the age of 68.

Charles Waring:

A well-respected authority on jazz, soul, and funk, Charles Waring began writing about music for *Blues & Soul* magazine in the late 90s and shortly afterwards joined *Crime Time* where he was the TV/music editor for 11 years. In 2002 he began contributing regularly to the UK's premiere rock/pop music magazine, *MOJO*, and in 2004 he joined *Record Collector* as their monthly jazz columnist. As a freelance record company consultant Waring has put together countless compilations while his liner notes (over 300 to date) have graced myriad CD reissues, including the critically-acclaimed Donny Hathaway box set, *'Never My Love: The Anthology'*, in 2013. He was also a consultant on the 2014 BBC documentary, *Killing Me Softly: The Roberta Flack Story* and contributed to the award-winning 2008 reference book, *British Crime Writing: An Encyclopaedia.*

INDEX

Printed in Great Britain
by Amazon

40608823R00203